THE POLITICAL QUARTERLY

IN THE THIRTIES

EDITED BY

WILLIAM A. ROBSON

ALLEN LANE THE PENGUIN PRESS

First published in 1971

Allen Lane The Penguin Press
Vigo Street, London W1

ISBN 0 7139 0201 9

Printed in Great Britain by
Latimer Trend & Co. Ltd, Plymouth
Set in Monotype Plantin

To J. L. R.

CONTENTS

THE POLITICAL QUARTERLY
IN THE THIRTIES

William A. Robson

THE period between the two world wars was in many ways a momentous one both for this country and the world. There occurred several events which have had a considerable influence on our thought and attitudes towards contemporary problems. The prolonged and severe unemployment was a traumatic experience which has left a deep mark on every post-war government, on the political parties and on trade unions. The abortive Suez affair was partly due to Mr Eden's belief that he was dealing with a situation similar to that which Chamberlain had faced in his dealings with Hitler, and Eden's desire to avoid the weakness and gullibility which Chamberlain had shown. One could give other examples. They all point to the need to have more than a nodding acquaintance with the inter-war years if we are to understand the events of the present time and our own reactions to them. This is particularly true of the generation which was born within the past twenty-five years and whose members are now adult citizens.

The essays presented in this volume show how some of the most acute and well-informed minds of the 1930s approached a wide range of contemporary questions which claimed their attention. But first it will be of interest to say something about *The Political Quarterly* in which the essays first appeared.

I conceived the idea in 1927 of a serious political review in which progressive ideas could be discussed at adequate length, and shortly afterwards I found that Kingsley Martin had arrived at a similar idea. We felt the need for a forum where a philosophy, a policy and a programme could be hammered out for the socialist movement, which was growing in strength but was lacking a coherent body of ideas. The existing quarterly and monthly

9

reviews were either quite general in their interests, or conservative or right-wing liberal in outlook, or moribund. Some of our elders and betters whose support we sought were of the opinion that the day of the quarterly had passed. This view seemed to be confirmed by the demise of the *Edinburgh Review*, once the most famous and politically influential of periodicals, in 1929, a few months before *The Political Quarterly* began publication. The *Westminster Review* had come to an end in 1914.

Kingsley Martin and I took the lead in bringing the idea to fruition. We were then junior members of the teaching staff of the London School of Economics and Political Science. We were both convinced of the need for a political review and were prepared to devote a great deal of time and energy to getting it established. We worked closely together despite the fact that in the autumn of 1927 Martin went north to join the *Manchester Guardian* as a leader writer.

The Political Quarterly was conceived as a device to provide a bridge between the world of thought and the world of action, between the writer, the thinker and the teacher on the one hand and the statesman, the politician and the official on the other.

Our drive to launch this review was largely motivated by a desire to improve the condition of Britain by injecting new ideas, new proposals, new ways of looking at the problems confronting the nation, the Empire and the world. The conduct of affairs since 1918 had been highly unsatisfactory. The post-war governments of Lloyd George and his 'hard-faced businessmen', Bonar Law (1922), Baldwin (1923 and 1924) and Ramsay MacDonald (1924), had been uninspiring and unconstructive. At home, the General Strike of 1926 was a reflection on the attitudes of the coal owners, the trade unions and the Government; unemployment was rife; little progress had been made in education, public health, social security, the position of women, or better opportunities for the underprivileged. Abroad, Lloyd George had almost got us involved in another war with Kemal Ataturk; our Government had backed the anti-Bolshevik forces of Kolchak and Dennikin, thereby poisoning our relations with the U.S.S.R. for years; we had demanded very heavy reparations from Germany regardless of the consequences against which Keynes had warned us; and there had been no serious attempt to disarm Germany or to adopt a genuine disarmament policy ourselves.

In these circumstances there was a clear and urgent need for a great deal of new and vigorous thinking in every aspect of public affairs, and this demanded new channels of communication, a focusing point for vigorous and progressive minds. The new political review was intended to respond to this need.

In launching *The Political Quarterly* we were guided by a theory about the structure of public opinion in Britain. This theory rests on the belief that all or nearly all new ideas or progressive policies begin with discussions or writing among a very restricted circle of persons of exceptional ability and concentrated interests. This applies not only to bodies interested in political reform like the Fabian Society or P.E.P., but also to those interested in particular spheres of public policy, such as the Howard League for Penal Reform or the Town and Country Planning Association. The membership of these élites and the circulation of their publications is very restricted, and perhaps numbers only two or three thousand persons. After intensive discussion in these narrow circles, ideas or proposals which survive and win acceptance are presented to a wider audience through the weekly papers. By means of such journals as the *New Statesman*, the *Spectator*, the *Economist*, *Time and Tide*, the *Statist* and *New Society*, and now through some of the more sophisticated radio and television broadcasts, new ideas reach a larger section of the public, including that elusive and ill-defined person the general intelligent reader. The number of this wider circle is probably between 250,000 and 350,000 persons. After this second level of discussion, ideas or proposals which survive criticism and offer promise of desirable change then break through to the mass audience in the national daily and Sunday newspapers.

Leonard Woolf, who served as joint editor for many years, has expressed his own views on the subject in the fourth volume of his great autobiography: 'Practically all journalists, from the great Press Lords down to the humblest reporter, suffer from the grossest delusions about the "influence" of the newspaper which they own, edit or write for. The megalomania probably increases as you go up from the humble reporter through the pompous editor to the paranoic owner. I am not sure that the evidence, such as it is, does not point to the fact that the larger the circulation of a paper, the less influence it has upon the opinions of its readers, or even that the influence of every paper is in inverse proportion to the number of copies sold or to the number of people who buy or read it. Certainly the millions who read the popular press seem to be singularly impervious to its propaganda, for vast numbers must vote Labour who habitually read anti-Labour Dailies. I do not know whether this should be a subject for rejoicing among the angels in heaven or the Left-Wing intellectuals on earth. . . .

'I feel some encouragement too when I contemplate the other end of the scale where are journals of small circulation like *The Political Quarterly*. There is no doubt that, if their standards, both journalistic and intellectual, are high, they can have considerable influence. The reason is that they are . . . written by experts for experts. . . . *The Political Quarterly* is partly a technical paper in which the professional politician, the administrator, or the civil servant can find information and ideas of the greatest importance to his work and unobtainable elsewhere. . . .'[1]

Before a new quarterly could be started it was necessary to obtain the support of a wider circle of persons of much greater reputation and influence than Kingsley Martin or I possessed. We accordingly enlisted the interest of about forty or fifty leading intellectuals whom we invited to a private meeting at the London School of Economics to discuss the project. It was very favourably received. Soon afterwards we were able to issue the following printed prospectus. The signatories included adherents of both the Labour and Liberal parties, and some were not known to belong to any party. All were persons of intellectual distinction with a keen interest in public affairs.

The prospectus read as follows:

[1] *Downhill all the Way*, pp. 207–8.

Introduction

A POLITICAL QUARTERLY

It is proposed to establish a Quarterly Review, which will have as its special object the discussion of social policy, public administration and questions of industrial and political organisation, primarily in Great Britain, but also, from time to time, in other countries. Its aim should be to do for these matters what the *Round Table* has attempted to do for imperial politics. While treating them in a scientific spirit, it would have as its subject current political and social problems, not political science in the abstract. It would differ from the existing reviews, partly because the space at its command would enable it to aim at a standard of thoroughness impossible in a short article, and partly because it would be planned by a group of writers holding certain general political ideas in common.

While its intellectual basis would be an acceptance of the view of the necessity of industrial and social reconstruction it will not be mortgaged to any one political party, nor be committed in advance to any particular programme. To discover truth and promote social well-being will be its only definite loyalties: and as a journal it will know no other allegiance. Thus it would welcome contributions from persons of different political connections, provided that they were of the necessary quality. It should be realistic and critical in spirit, and should attempt to handle its subject with sufficient authority to attract the attention of all persons seriously interested in political and social questions, whatever their political views. While it would naturally be mainly concerned with questions of topical interest, it should endeavour to treat them in a broad and philosophical manner, and should aim at diffusing knowledge and stimulating thought, rather than at presenting a case. It should draw on the experience of the Continent, the U.S.A., and the British Dominions, as freely as on that of this country, and should appeal not only to English readers but to all serious students of political, economic and social questions.

The reasons for thinking that such a journal would meet a demand are as follows:

1. There is no journal in England today which attempts to deal authoritatively with questions of social policy and political organisation. The whole tenor of political discussion in England is at the present time in a profoundly unsatisfactory condition. The national daily newspapers, with scarcely more than one exception, are either controlled by a handful of millionaires who definitely prevent the effective expression of opinions from which they differ, or else are harnessed to the yoke of a particular political party. The weekly sixpenny journals,

excellent though they are as commentaries on current events, are unable to devote the necessary space required for the adequate discussion of the larger political and social questions; while the monthly reviews, attempting, as they do, to cover every field of human activity, necessarily do so in a superficial manner. It is a serious matter at the present juncture, obviously a critical period in English history, that there should be no recognised avenue through which new ideas on social and political affairs can emerge for intelligent printed discussion.

2. Political and social questions are occupying an ever-increasing amount of public attention and will continue to do so more and more in the future. Apart from pamphlets and books, the great development of experience and thought in these fields, both in Great Britain and in other countries, has never been made accessible to the man in the street. He will not read a Quarterly Journal, but he will read the daily Press, and the Journal would influence him by supplying the materials upon which the more reputable newspapers could draw.

3. The discussion of all political and economic questions suffers because there is no organ in which they are treated thoroughly, with reasoned arguments and a candid presentation of the available evidence. The result is that the general public is at the mercy of catch-words. There is also a growing number of persons who are not committed to any programme but who are nevertheless interested in a serious discussion of social and economic policy. Consider, in the light of these demands, the almost entire absence of any serious discussion in the Press of the real nature of the coal problem, or of unemployment, or of the problems of combinations and monopolies, or of trade unionism, or of the experience of our own and other countries regarding the possible methods of organising industries under public ownership and of their advantages and defects. There has probably never been a period in which so many political and economic experiments have been made in Europe as in the last ten years. Yet hardly any serious attempt has been made to estimate their significance and value.

Whatever views may be held as to questions of policy, in the sphere of political or economic organisation, it will be agreed that the first condition of a sane treatment of difficult questions is that the relevant facts should be known and should be discussed with candour and impartiality. A Quarterly, such as is suggested, would do valuable work in helping to spread an understanding of the real nature of the problems with which the country is confronted. The probability that within five or ten years a Government will be returned which is pledged to large measures of economic and social reconstruction makes the diffusion of such an understanding all the more important.

Introduction

The size and format of the proposed Journal would be so arranged as to include, among other regular features, reviews of current English and foreign literature and relevant official publications, and a digest of judicial and administrative decisions of public significance. But the main value of its contents will lie in its special articles.

We believe that it will be possible to form a group of contributors sufficient to ensure a continuous supply of matter of adequate quality, and it is believed that the Editor contemplated is one who will command general and cordial approval.

The main difficulty to be overcome is the question of finance. It is estimated that an initial guaranteed sum of £2,000 will secure the Journal for a period of at least two years. It is hoped that afterwards it may become self-supporting.

The signatories to the prospectus were:

P. J. Noel Baker	F. Lavington
Ernest Barker	A. D. Lindsay
C. Delisle Burns	C. M. Lloyd
A. M. Carr-Saunders	J. J. Mallon
Henry Clay	T. H. Marshall
G. D. H. Cole	Kingsley Martin
G. Lowes Dickinson	C. S. Myers
P. Sargant Florence	Percy Nunn
Margery Fry	Olivier
T. E. Gregory	W. A. Robson
Lynda Grier	C. P. Scott
Freda Hawtrey	R. H. Tawney
L. T. Hobhouse	Beatrice Webb
J. A. Hobson	Sidney Webb
Eva Hubback	Leonard Woolf
H. J. Laski	Barbara Wootton

The next step was to raise money. The minimum amount considered necessary to ensure a trial run of three years was £2,000, allowing for substantial deficits during this period. This proved to be an arduous, time-consuming and exhausting task. Few of the signatories were able to contribute anything substantial. Eventually we persuaded a number of our friends and acquaintances to contribute sums varying from £5 to £150, but the total came to less than half the amount needed. I have related elsewhere in some detail how I succeeded in inducing Bernard Shaw to give me £1,000 for *The Political Quarterly*, and it is certain that without his help we should never have got the review started.[1] I had known G.B.S. well for several years and he had shown me much kindness and encouragement. But it took me eighteen months to overcome his reluctance and scepticism, though some of it was possibly assumed in order to test our keenness and persistence. He insisted on his donation being kept a secret, and that the finances should be handled in the most businesslike manner. This was very typical of G.B.S., who perfectly understood that the quarterly was not intended to be a commercial enterprise – he was, of course, quite right. Then with the help of a colleague in the Law Department of L.S.E. I formed a small company called The Political Quarterly Publishing Company Limited. The cost of doing so must have been the lowest since joint-stock companies were invented!

Meanwhile, we had set up a small committee to take responsibility for launching the quarterly. This consisted of Leonard Woolf, A. M. Carr-Saunders,[2] Harold Laski, J. M. Keynes, T. E. Gregory,[3] Kingsley Martin and myself. The Committee decided to appoint Kingsley Martin and me as joint editors.

In the autumn of 1930 Martin was sacked by the *Manchester Guardian* as a leader writer and came south to London. Soon afterwards he was appointed editor of the *New Statesman and Nation* to which he devoted the next thirty years of his life. It was obvious to both of us that no one could edit a weekly review and a quarterly periodical simultaneously; one or the other would suffer, and in this instance the *New Statesman* had a much greater claim on Kingsley's time and attention. So in the summer of 1931 he retired as joint editor and was succeeded by Leonard Woolf. Martin remained a member of the Editorial Board until his death in 1969

[1] See my article 'Bernard Shaw and The Political Quarterly', in *The Political Quarterly* for July–September 1951. This was reprinted in my book of essays entitled *Politics and Government at Home and Abroad*, (Allen & Unwin, 1967). A fuller account is given in my article, 'The Founding of *The Political Quarterly*' contained in the Fortieth Birthday Number, Vol. 41, January–March 1970.

[2] Then Professor of Social Science at Liverpool University.

[3] Then Professor of Banking at L.S.E.

and he took a continuing interest in the paper he helped to found. For many years he regularly contributed both articles and surveys.

Leonard Woolf and I were joint editors from 1931 to 1958, except during the years 1941 to 1945 when he was in sole charge. I was then engaged on war work in the Civil Service and had no time or energy to spare for anything else, quite apart from the propriety of even a temporary Civil Servant editing a periodical such as this. After he withdrew from the post of Joint Editor in 1958, Leonard Woolf acted as Literary Editor until 1962 when he was succeeded by Richard Greaves. He continued to be an active member of the Editorial Board until his death in August 1969.

The prospectus for *The Political Quarterly* printed above put forward strong arguments on the need for a new review which would discuss social, economic and political questions at adequate length, but gave very little idea of the subjects which would be dealt with. This was partly due to the fact that editorial content would be a matter for the editor to decide, and no one had then been appointed; and partly because although the signatories were mainly people of Labour or socialist sympathies, they also included Liberals of various hues, and it was safer at that stage to keep to generalities on which everyone could agree. The only questions mentioned in the prospectus as needing discussion were social policy, public administration, industrial and political organization, unemployment, combinations and monopolies, public ownership, trade unionism, and the coal industry. We promised to include reviews of English and foreign literature, official publications, and digests of judicial and administrative decisions.

The first number contained articles on 'Democracy and the Expert' by Alfred Zimmern, on 'The Problem of the Mines' by G. D. H. Cole, on 'The Question of High Wages' by J. M. Keynes, on 'The Future of Trade Union Law' by W. A. Robson, on 'How Far can a Labour Budget Go?' by Josiah Wedgwood,[1] and on 'The Disappearance of the Governing Class' by 'A Political Correspondent' who was none other than Beatrice Webb. G. Lowes Dickinson contributed one of his remarkable political dialogues.

---

[1] The son of Colonel (later Lord) Wedgwood, the Labour M.P. He subsequently became the head of the family pottery firm.

The book reviews included a long review of Lord Hewart's polemical book *The New Despotism* by Harold Laski, who also preserved his anonymity under the signature 'XYZ', and two reviews by J. A. Hobson of books on inheritance and unemployment. The first number also contained some of the surveys which became a regular feature. Kingsley Martin began his public opinion survey, which continued for many years, with an analysis of the attitude of the Press to the Government during the preceding nine months. A survey of Current Social Statistics was another original feature which A. M. Carr-Saunders contributed regularly. It began with an inquiry into population movements into and out of Britain and Northern Ireland. The first number dealt in a knowledgeable manner with a group of problems of unquestionable importance at the time. Several of them are still of importance today.

In examining the questions which were of chief concern to the editors during the years preceding the Second World War I shall not look at the contents of each issue but group together articles published between 1930 and 1939 under a number of major headings.

The articles dealing with industrial questions reflect the deepening anxiety caused by the severe and prolonged unemployment and the failure of successive governments to take effective action to prevent or remedy the terrible suffering and demoralization which it caused to millions of men and their families. A fifth of the employed population in the U.K. was out of work in 1930–31. The great depression had begun; and the existing government in almost every Western country had been or was soon to be ejected from office. We find Sir William Beveridge (as he then was) returning once again to the theme he had so powerfully argued in his book (published twenty-one years earlier) that unemployment was a perfectly curable disease if we were prepared to pay the price by changing our habits and ideas.[1]

The political consequences of unemployment were discussed by Professor John Hilton in a long article on the report of the Royal Commission on Unemployment Insurance.[2] 'The devotion of immense and highly competent labours to the devices by which an

[1] July–September 1930, p. 326.
[2] January–March 1933.

insurance scheme which is not an insurance scheme can be made and kept solvent and self-supporting at a time like the present is a spectacle before which the mind aches,' he wrote. A little later Sir Ronald Davison was analysing critically the new scheme of unemployment assistance introduced by the Government for able-bodied unemployed whose rights to unemployment insurance were exhausted. In 1936 A. M. Carr-Saunders was pungently exposing the operations of the Unemployment Assistance Board which had led to 'the greatest fiasco in the whole history of social administration in this country'.[1] The following year saw an article on the 'drab tragedy of the distressed areas'.[2] About the same time Colin Clark was showing that unemployment was an international problem,[3] but this was of little or no help in enabling us to overcome it in this country. Two articles on the coal industry emphasized the exceptionally depressed condition of what had been Britain's major industry, the foundation of our prosperity at home and our chief export.[4] These articles help to explain the demand for nationalization by the N.U.M. and its realization in 1946.

The only other articles dealing with specific industries were two by C. S. Orwin on the agricultural problem. But numerous contributions showed our interest in economic, financial and fiscal policies of general application to the economy. Thus, the traditional belief in the virtues of free trade in a period of deep depression and high unemployment was questioned by Sir Ernest Simon (then an M.P.),[5] and reasserted in an unequivocal manner by Ramsay Muir, the most influential spokesman of the Liberal Party.[6] Theodore Gregory explored the case for Empire Free Trade, for which Lord Beaverbrook was campaigning vigorously.[7] E. F. Wise, one of the more thoughtful Labour M.P.s, put forward an elaborate scheme for Import Boards to purchase and handle imports, with reciprocal

[1] October–December 1936.
[2] July–September 1937.
[3] January–March 1936.
[4] 'The Next Step in the Coal Industry' by G. D. H. Cole, January–March 1937; 'Coal in the Commons' by Ivor Thomas, April–June 1938.
[5] 'Some Questions about Free Trade', October–December 1930.
[6] 'A Reply to E. D. Simon, M.P.', January–March 1931.
[7] April–June 1930.

agreements for the development of exports, as a superior alternative to tariffs.[1] This was condemned by Professor Robbins not because it was a socialistic proposal but because State-regulated trading is directly opposed to internationalism of all kinds and leads to the most dangerous and illiberal forms of nationalism.[2]

There were many other indications of the growing belief that capitalism was in such a parlous condition all over the world that drastic remedies would have to be sought in place of the allegedly self-regulating mechanisms which had broken down. George Schwartz, not yet a professional journalist, contributed a biting article pillorying 'Capitalism on the Dole';[3] Colin Clark, then an eager young Fabian Socialist, demonstrated the need for State planning in regard both to the economy and physical development.[4] Wise wrote an article advocating the socialization of banking;[5] Cole on the essentials of socialization.[6]

In the 1930s, as in the 1960s, the bad state of the economy was a continual worry for serious observers of public affairs and for practical politicians. But there were several differences between the two periods. In those days Keynesian remedies had only begun to be formulated, were widely disputed by many economists, and were not accepted by the Government or the City. The emphasis was on unemployment, the depressed industries and the depressed areas. No one talked about economic growth. The balance of payments was little discussed until we were forced off gold in 1931 and even that seemed to make little difference to everyday life. Above all, in the 1930s our distress was shared by all the leading capitalist countries, including the United States; whereas in the 1960s Britain's economic maladies have been contrasted with the exuberant economic performance of Germany, Japan, Australia, France and many other countries.

[1] April–June 1931.
[2] 'The Economics of Import Boards', April–June 1931. Wise replied at length in a subsequent issue; see 'A Reply to Professor Robbins', July–September 1931.
[3] January–March 1936.
[4] October–December 1931.
[5] April–June 1933.
[6] July–September 1931.

Introduction

The issues from 1932 onwards reveal the increasing preoccupation of *The Political Quarterly* with the threat to world peace posed by the Japanese invasion of Manchuria, the rise of Hitler to power in Germany, the failure of the Disarmament Conference, the progressive decline of the League of Nations, the Italian invasion of Abyssinia, the Spanish Civil War and the weakness of British and French diplomacy. It is difficult for those who have not lived through those years to share the feeling of impending doom and the conviction that the preservation of peace was the supreme issue beside which everything else paled to insignificance; and the growing belief that those in control in France, Britain and the U.S.A. were unable or unwilling to take the steps which might have averted the disaster.

In January 1932 Alfred Zimmern explained the origin of the Manchurian question and declared that the Japanese occupation 'unless retrieved by subsequent action' was inconsistent not only with the League Covenant and the Kellogg Pact, but with the older system of the Concert of the Great Powers which was the basis of nineteenth-century diplomacy. He sounded a note of extreme alarm at the behaviour of the Great Powers in face of this act of aggression.[1] This was followed by a scholarly article by a Japanese socialist living in England, the late Sobei Mogi, who concluded that the Manchurian problem was not easy to solve because Japan was an imperialist country, while the Chinese Government was a feudalistic dictatorship.[2] Further articles on the same question appeared in the next issue by two eminent international lawyers, Sir John Fischer Williams, K.C., and Herman Lauterpacht, later a judge of the International Court.[3]

In 1933 Leonard Woolf contributed one of his profoundly disturbing articles on foreign policy, utterly realistic and merciless in its analysis of the inevitable consequences of the failure of the League in the Sino–Japanese dispute, in the Disarmament Conference, in the World Economic Conference, and above all in retain-

[1] January–March 1932.
[2] ibid.
[3] 'Shanghai and Manchuria'; and 'Japan and the Covenant', April–June 1932.

ing the confidence of the peoples, the loyalty of governments or even the lip-service of politicians.[1] Earlier in the same year he wrote an article with the prophetic title 'From Geneva to the Next War' which explained the deadly futility of expecting a world of unregulated armaments such as had developed despite the League to provide either peace or security. The choice lay between armed nationalism and disarmed internationalism.[2]

Other contributors shared his mounting anxiety and deepening pessimism about the international jungle. Among them was Quincy Wright (then Professor of International Law at Chicago University) urging preservation of the League and the adoption of measures to universalize its membership. The U.S.A. and the Soviet Union must be persuaded to join, Brazil to rejoin, and Japan and Germany to withdraw their notices to resign. It must enlarge its support in world public opinion, and subordinate all its activity to the supreme end of preserving peace.[3] Sir Alfred Zimmern was calling on all governments genuinely desiring peace to organize what he called the peace world.[4] Hugh Dalton was pinpointing the ways in which Britain's foreign policy in the hands of Sir John Simon had contributed to the darkened outlook, and made proposals for a more constructive approach to peace even at that late hour.[5] Norman Angell described how Britain had for the first time in her history as a World Power acquiesced in an immense weakening of her strategic position in the Far East and in the Mediterranean by remaining passive in the face of Japanese aggression towards China and the assault of Mussolini on Abyssinia. The erstwhile British imperialists had indeed supported the Japanese action and applauded the Italian contempt for the League. How, he asked, could the supine conduct of the capitalist and Conservative order in Britain in the face of the Japanese, German and Italian challenge be explained? Why was Conservative distrust and dislike of the League so much stronger than fears for Imperial security with a

[1] 'Labour's Foreign Policy', October–December 1933.
[2] January–March 1933.
[3] 'Is the League of Nations the Road to Peace?', January–March 1934.
[4] 'Organise the Peace World', April–June 1934.
[5] 'The Present International Situation', July 1935.

hostile imperialism straddling the route to India? Angell drew his own conclusions about what he called 'The New John Bull' which are still worth revealing today.[1] In the same year Sir Arthur Salter argued the need for reform of the League of Nations.[2]

Several further articles reveal Leonard Woolf at the height of his powers. One was entitled 'Meditation on Abyssinia', reprinted in this volume;[3] another 'The Ideal of the League Remains'. In the latter he pinpointed with deadly accuracy the responsibility of the British and French Governments in destroying any hope of effective action either in the Abyssinian invasion or in any future conflict, and was analysing the utter futility of Mr Eden's (the Foreign Secretary's) endorsement of the Archbishop of Canterbury's statement that 'we could not abandon or even whittle down the ideal for which the League of Nations stood'.[4] It is painful to read the prophetic vision which Woolf brought to his study of the situation in which the Foreign Secretary seemed to indicate 'the actual course which the Government is inclined to select as the best for wobbling along into the abyss'.[5] Subsequent articles from the same pen were 'Arms and Peace' (January 1937), 'The Resurrection of the League' (July 1937) and 'De Profundis', published in October 1939 and included in the present volume.

We gave relatively little space in *The Political Quarterly* to the Spanish Civil War. This was mainly due to the huge, incessant coverage given to it by the national daily and Sunday newspapers and the weeklies. I think we felt that everyone was being saturated with news, views and assertions on the subject. We did, however, give serious attention to the analysis and interpretation of Spanish politics. In 1932 we printed an optimistic account of the revolution which had set aside the monarchy and established a left-wing republic in the peninsula in 1931. This was by H. R. G. Greaves. In July–September 1936 we published another article by H. R. G. Greaves entitled 'A Soviet Spain?' which emphasized the remarkable rise of the more extreme left wing at the recent elections, but this was before the outbreak of hostilities. In the following

[1] July–September 1936.   [2] October–December 1936.
[3] January–March 1936.   [4] July–September 1936.
[5] July–September 1936.

number Kingsley Martin did a survey on Spain and British public opinion. This was an extremely penetrating analysis of the dilemmas and embarrassments and conflicts within the political parties; the sympathies, hopes and fears of people of different parties; and the resultant neutrality or paralysis of the British Government. It was followed by a similar survey in April–June 1937 by Charles Fenby. He concluded that both the right and the left were divided: Tories between the conflicting loyalties of class and of Empire, Labourites and Liberals between anti-Fascism and pacifism. The desire to combat Fascism was nullified in some quarters by a horror of war, while in others an abstract sympathy with the lawful Spanish government was nullified by a fear of Communism. Thus, while it was impossible to be non-partisan, the mass of British opinion was negative so far as any positive action was concerned.

From its earliest days *The Political Quarterly* was fully alive to the parliamentary and constitutional problems arising within the British political system. In 1930 an article by Harold Laski showed how the maintenance of constitutional government in democratic states depends on the avoidance of race divisions, national conflicts, or economic divisions so acute as to lead to a conflagration. Peace abroad and social justice at home can alone protect the precious constitutional heritage.[1] Two years later, following the defection of Ramsay MacDonald, Snowden, J. H. Thomas and Lord Sankey from the Labour Party and the formation of the so-called National Government, Ivor Jennings wrote a notable article entitled 'The Constitution under Strain' which, while not alleging any improper action by the King, nevertheless showed that the developments following the break-up of the Labour Government led towards Fascism.[2] Sidney Webb, who had held Cabinet office in the second Labour Government, published his famous record of 'What Happened in 1931' in our pages.[3]

We were much concerned about improving the effectiveness of Parliament. We published articles on the inefficiency of Parliament by H. Sidebotham who, as 'Scrutator' of the *Sunday Times*, was one

[1] 'The Prospects of Constitutional Government', July–September 1930.
[2] April–June 1933.
[3] January–March 1932.

of the best-known members of the Press Gallery, and by Major
Walter Elliott, M.P., who contradicted his contentions.[1] In 1931
Sir Herbert Samuel, M.P., wrote for us inquiring whether Parliament was properly fulfilling the tasks it ought to fulfil, and if not
what changes were desirable and practicable.[2] In the same number
John Strachey, M.P., and C. E. M. Joad expounded the proposals
of Sir Oswald Mosley's New Party relating to parliamentary reform.
In 1931 Beatrice Webb presented the Webb's scheme for 'A Reform
Bill for 1932' involving a functional devolution, to a new subordinate elected National Assembly and its Executive, of the social
services, public health and education, pure water and clean air,
town planning and open spaces, insurance and industrial regulation,
leaving Parliament more free to deal with overseas relations,
defence, law and justice, sovereignty, etc. This ingenious scheme
gave separate Assemblies and Executives to Scotland, Wales and
England. The Webb's plan aimed to sweep away at one stroke 'the
three-fold evil of an over-taxed Cabinet, an hypertrophied bureaucracy and a paralysed House of Commons'.[3]

Parliamentary procedure was discussed at length by Hugh Dalton
in 1934 when he explained the Labour Party's proposals on the
subject.[4] In his article he declared 'The House of Lords must
go'. It should be treated as 'an antiquated traffic obstruction on the
democratic highway' and be removed. A. L. Rowse had in a previous issue given an account of its past misdeeds which attacked the
idea that the House of Lords is a harmless or even useful piece of
constitutional machinery whose power for evil had been removed
by the Parliament Act of 1911.[5]

A particular measure which raised serious objections from the
constitutional point of view was the Incitement to Disaffection Bill
of 1934, which aroused strong criticism from people of all parties.
We published a knowledgeable article on the Bill by James E.
MacColl and W. T. Wells, Q.C., M.P. Ammunition provided by the

---

[1] July–September 1930.
[2] 'Defects and Reforms of Parliament', July–September 1931.
[3] January–March 1931, p. 21.
[4] October–December 1934.
[5] 'The House of Lords and Legislation', July–September 1933.

Haldane Club, the New Fabian Research Bureau, and the recently formed Council for Civil Liberties induced the Government to remove the worst provisions of the Bill menacing public liberty, despite no breach in the ranks of its huge majority in the Commons. This achievement was commented on by Ivor Jennings in an article on 'The Technique of Opposition'.[1]

The practice of delegating subordinate legislative powers to Ministers and of conferring judicial functions on administrative tribunals had been strongly denounced in sensational terms by Lord Hewart, the Lord Chief Justice. This led to the appointment of the Committee on Ministers' Powers in 1932. I gave evidence before the Committee and wrote a highly critical article on its report,[2] which is included in the present collection. In January 1933 *The Political Quarterly* published an article by me entitled 'The Central Domination of Local Government'. The immediate occasion was the extraordinary events which had occurred the previous year as a result of the financial crisis and the fall of the Labour Government; but I pointed out that it had long been evident that central control over local authorities had been increasing rapidly in terms both of power and of influence. This article evoked a long letter of protest from Sir Arthur Robinson, permanent secretary of the Ministry of Health, then the responsible department.

The abdication of Edward VIII led Sir Ivor Jennings to discuss some constitutional aspects of the affair in an article which appeared early in 1937.[3]

In 1939, a few months before the outbreak of the Second World War, we published Herbert Morrison's reflections on 'Social Change – Peaceful or Violent', reprinted in the present collection. This was partly an inquiry into the condition of political democracy in Britain and partly an attempt to answer the doubts posed in two books by Harold Laski and H. R. G. Greaves whether British democracy would stand the strain of the transformation from capitalism to socialism. Laski had assumed that a Labour Government returned to power with an effective majority would carry out decisive changes which would transform the economic and social

[1] April–June 1935.   [2] July–September 1932.
[3] April–June 1937.

structure of Britain; and he had grave doubts whether parliamentary government would survive such an onslaught on established interests. He believed that in such circumstances it was possible, and in his not infrequent moments of pessimism probable, that the privileged classes would resort to Fascism or some form of unconstitutional action. Morrison refused to accept the view that there was little or no possibility of peaceful, fundamental social change, although he conceded that one must be prepared for anything. But to expect a breakdown in democracy was, he argued, to create an insoluble dilemma.

Another article worth mentioning was a penetrating analysis by Tom Wilson of the causes of division between Ulster and Eire, and the possibility of overcoming them. This article makes interesting reading today and is included in this volume.

Although preoccupied with contemporary problems in the world of public affairs, we were always eager to probe and understand the philosophy or the psychology of political thought. We were as ready to publish a translation of Mussolini's own presentation of 'The Political and Social Doctrines of Fascism'[1] as a scholarly piece on 'The Place of Hitlerism in the History of Political Thought', based on a number of books on Nazi theories.[2] Professor Harold Lasswell contributed an analysis of the psychology of Hitlerism.[3] We also explored the nature of Fascism and the Corporate State. The essay by Trotsky entitled 'Is Stalin Weakening or the Soviets?', which is included in this book, appeared in our issue for July 1932.

A more wide-ranging analysis of the contemporary trend was made by Bertrand Russell in an article on the revolt against reason and its causes.[4] Equally broad in its outlook was an essay by J. A. Hobson entitled 'Thoughts on Our Present Discontents'.[5] We even entered occasionally into the realm of relations between Church and State and published two articles on Disestablishment.[6] Three of these contributions are included in this volume.

---

[1] July–September 1933. [2] April–June 1934. [3] July–September 1933.
[4] January–March 1935. [5] January–March 1938.
[6] 'Ought the Establishment to be Maintained?' by Hensley Henson, Bishop of Durham, September–December 1930; 'The Dilemma of Church and State', by A. L. Rowse, July–September 1936.

Introduction

Our interest in social questions extended to many spheres which had been little explored in those days and whose importance is now recognized. Patrick Abercrombie, our greatest town planner, wrote on methods of defending the English countryside;[1] Dr C. P. Blacker on the question of sterilization of mental defectives;[2] F. J. Osborn on the problem of great cities (the Barlow Commission was sitting at the time); S. K. Ruck on the increase of crime and its causes.[3] Ruck's article was quoted with approval by Sir Herbert Samuel, the Home Secretary, in Parliament. Ivor Jennings discussed public order at a time when the meetings organized by Oswald Mosley had led to violence and caused much disquiet both inside and outside Parliament and the passing of the Public Order Act.[4] I wrote on the need to bring our factory legislation up to date,[5] and on the deplorable system of workmen's compensation which existed before 1946.[6] C. P. Scott, the great editor of the *Manchester Guardian*, wrote for us what I believe is the only signed article which ever appeared under his name – a short but eloquent piece entitled 'The Function of the Press'.[7] The essays by Abercrombie, Jennings and Scott are all included in the present book.

Some of the best work in the 1930s was contained in the surveys which were a feature of the *Quarterly* from the beginning. These provided a great deal of statistical information and expert knowledge on topics of current interest, and they sometimes supplemented articles on the same subject. I have already referred to Kingsley Martin's surveys of public opinion as reflected in the Press, and these continued until the Second World War. They were a unique feature which no one else has attempted. Carr-Saunders wrote many of the surveys of current social statistics, dealing with such subjects as emigration and immigration,[8] crime

[1] April 1930.
[2] 'The Problem of Mental Deficiency', July–September 1930.
[3] April–June 1932.
[4] January–March 1937.
[5] 'The Factory Acts 1833–1933', January–March 1934.
[6] 'Industrial Relations and the State', September 1930.
[7] January–March 1931.
[8] January 1930 and July–September 1933.

and punishment,[1] the universities,[2] agriculture,[3] population trends,[4] the educational ladder,[5] divorce and separation,[6] housing,[7] etc., but others also contributed to these surveys. We also commissioned surveys on 'Recent Developments in Laws, Constitutions and Administration' in foreign countries by Professor B. Mirkine-Guetzevitch, General Secretary of the International Institute of Public Law in Paris.

It was through the surveys that we tried to make *The Political Quarterly* a source of reliable information as well as a forum of ideas. In a letter which I had sent to Kingsley Martin in 1930 I wrote: 'I feel most anxious to get some real *knowledge* into the paper, as well as opinions.'

In the 1930s the future of India was one of the great and inescapable problems. We published numerous articles on the subject by British and Indian writers. The first one appeared in April 1930 and explained why the negotiations between Mahatma Gandhi and the Indian Government had broken down, and it stressed the unbridgeable gulf which separated them. It was by a young English Quaker named Reginald Reynolds who had been chosen by Gandhi to carry his final message to the Viceroy concerning the inauguration of civil disobedience. We published two further articles later that year. One was a criticism of the Simon Report for failing to see the need for full Dominion status for India. It was signed 'X' and was written by John Coatman, a former member of the Indian Police Service and subsequently a Regional Controller of the B.B.C. The Rt Hon. V. S. Srinivasa Sastri, a delegate to the Round Table Conference, criticized the Simon Report for its failure to grapple with the immediate need to incorporate the three hundred separate Indian States into an integrated federation. H. N. Brailsford wrote a more hopeful piece urging the need for speed in implementing the report and strengthening its weak features.[8] The Labour Party was committed to granting India full Dominion status and to promoting the work of constitution-making on a

[1] April 1930.   [2] September–December 1930.
[3] January–March 1931.   [4] April–June 1931.
[5] January–March 1933.   [6] April–June 1934.
[7] July–September 1935.   [8] October–December 1931.

basis of equality with all sections of the Indian people. The Tory Party's policy was very different, and after the fall of the second Labour Government the whole situation changed, though an attempt was made to conceal this behind a façade of words. The Rt Hon. Wedgwood Benn (senior) explained the real position and its serious consequences in an article published in the summer of 1935.[1] Major Graham Pole, writing on 'Indian Federation Problems' in 1939, again emphasized the lack in the Government of India Act of any mention of Dominion status as the ultimate goal or the possibility of a progressive advance to fully responsible government, in direct contradiction to the explicit principles laid down by the Simon Commission. He foresaw that unless the Indian Princes gave way on the twin questions of introducing responsible government in their states and of accepting election instead of nomination of their members to the Federal Parliament, a revolutionary agitation might erupt all over the sub-continent with unforeseeable effects.[2]

The emancipation of African colonies occupied us to a much lesser degree than India, but Britain's attitude towards the native African populations and their political future were problems which attracted our interest. Even progressive opinion had hardly moved beyond the concept of an enlightened trusteeship so far as the immediate future was concerned. In 1932 we printed an article by Dr Drummond Shiels on the report of the Lords and Commons Joint Committee on East Africa. He concluded that the recommendations gave 'abundant evidence of the determination to make our trusteeship in East Africa a reality'.[3] Yet the Committee had made no positive proposals for the political future of the African population. Later in the same year Margaret Hodgson wrote a trenchant article declaring that despite the British claim to accept the policy of trusteeship, which implied the right, 'if not necessarily the ability, of the inferior race to advancement towards the position of the superior' and the obligation of government to put it on that path, it was doubtful whether the practice had led to a result very

[1] 'The Outlook on the Indian Reforms', July–September 1935.
[2] April–June 1939.
[3] January–March 1932, p. 86.

Introduction

different from exploitation in the protectorates of Bechuanaland, Swaziland and Basutoland.[1] Another expert contributor, Professor W. M. Macmillan, returned from a visit to Rhodesia, explained that already in that colony the vision of Cecil Rhodes of a country to be made or marred by and for the white race alone stood unimpaired.[2] We also carried articles by Mrs Ballinger[3] and Norman Bentwich[4] describing, analysing and criticizing the racial policies of South Africa.

The claim of Nazi Germany to a return of the former German colonies produced an ambitious scheme by Sir John Maynard, a former member of the I.C.S., for the universal application of the principle of self-government to all colonies. The principle could be applied in the immediate future to our Asiatic dominions and to the West Indies. Elsewhere there would have to be an international commission appointed by the League to assist and direct the advance of the native peoples towards self-government. This internationalization of colonies and the process of emancipation was to be the answer to German claims on the eve of the outbreak of the Second World War.[5]

Our most comprehensive effort on this and wider problems was the production of a special number on the Empire in October 1938. This included, *inter alia*, articles on the 'Dominions and Foreign Policy' by Hugh Dalton; on 'The Empire As a Sacred Trust: the Problem of Africa' by Leonard Barnes; on the development of self-government in the Crown colonies by Charles Roden Buxton; on the Colonial Civil Service by Harold Laski; on the Empire as an economic unit by Lord Marley; and on the Empire seen respectively through Canadian, Australian, New Zealand, South African and Indian eyes.

Our desire to keep abreast of public opinion and political events in other countries during the 1930s stemmed mainly from the supreme importance of the attitudes and foreign policies of those countries towards the threat of war. We published many informative articles on France, Germany, the United States, Spain, Italy,

---

[1] July–September 1932.   [2] October–December 1932, p. 554.
[3] July–September 1936.   [4] July–September 1939.
[5] July–September 1939.

31

Japan, the Soviet Union and also lesser countries such as Greece, Hungary and Turkey.

The United States and the Soviet Union commanded our special interest, though not because we regarded them at that time as great military powers. Indeed, the U.S.S.R. had experienced a series of terrible purges in which many of their military leaders were executed on charges of treason, and this had thrown grave doubts on the military capacity of the U.S.S.R., which in any event was untested before the Second World War. Our interest in the U.S.S.R. centred on its economic and political regime, which was far less known than it is today. We published several articles by Sidney Webb and others explaining the system as they saw it.

Our interest in the U.S.A. began with the Roosevelt victory in the Presidential election of 1932. Oswald Garrison Villard, then editor of the New York *Nation*, wrote several pieces for us on the importance of that and the 1934 election, on the prospects of America's national recovery and on American lawlessness. But as the decade advanced, the American role in world affairs became an insistent question, and in 1935 we published an authoritative article by Raymond Leslie Buell, then President of the Foreign Policy Association, on the U.S.A. and the Pacific. This dealt with possible ways of arresting the headlong course of events on which Japan had embarked and on the need for Anglo–American cooperation in the Orient.[1] In 1939 Lindsay Rogers contributed an analysis of American reaction to the Munich disaster. He explained that nothing could have increased the isolationism of the U.S.A. so much as the appeasement of Hitler and Mussolini by Neville Chamberlain.

*

There were many other interesting subjects which were explored in our pages during the 1930s but space does not permit me to go beyond the limits of a broad outline. In sketching this I have tried to show what were the main problems which occupied us during the years preceding the outbreak of the Second World War, and the manner in which we tried to tackle them. In the course of doing

[1] July–September 1935.

so we introduced some journalistic innovations but these were incidental to our main purpose, which was to provide a forum for the enlightened discussion of the most serious problems of our time. We were fortunate in attracting contributions from a great number of the best intellects of the day although we avoided any attempt at dressing the window with well-known names.

In choosing the essays to be included in this volume I have been guided mainly by the relevance of the subject to present-day problems and by the significance of what the author had to say. Looking at the list of contents, one is struck by the way in which the problems of the 1930s have persisted into the 1970s; or to put it another way, how the problems of the 1970s were already matters of concern four decades ago. Thus, the dilemma between economically sound and unsound policies which Keynes saw was facing the Labour Party in 1932 still faces the Party today whether in power or in opposition. The revolt against reason which Bertrand Russell analysed with his penetrating intellect is today on view throughout the world in the never-ending displays of violence, intolerance, racialism and armed conflict. The maintenance of public order discussed by Sir Ivor Jennings is a problem of much greater dimensions both at home and abroad than it was even in the heyday of Nazi and Fascist rule. The relations of Ulster and Eire have become a very sore spot in the public affairs of the United Kingdom, and are likely to remain so for an indefinite time. G. D. H. Cole's analysis of the essentials of socialization is highly pertinent to much current discussion and writing on public enterprise, including the recent report of the Select Committee on Nationalized Industry on Ministerial Control and proposals of the Conservative Party to dilute public ownership in the steel industry. The threat to the English countryside, and what should be done to prevent or minimize it, has become far more urgent in 1970 than it was in 1930 when Sir Patrick Abercrombie wrote his percipient article. Tawney's devastating indictment of the Labour Government's failure of conviction, of purpose, of principle and of nerve can all be applied to certain policies and numerous events of the Wilson Government with at least as much force as it could to the MacDonald Administration of 1929–31. Leonard Woolf's diagnosis of the causes which had led to

B 33

the breakdown, or rather the non-fulfilment of the purposes of the League of Nations, can, *mutatis mutandis*, be used to diagnose the failure of the United Nations to prevent or end war in the Middle East, in Vietnam and Cambodia, between India and Pakistan, or the Soviet military invasions of Hungary and Czecho-Slovakia. Trotsky's fearless indictment of Stalin's autocratic and bureaucratic rule is as pertinent to the revival of Stalinism as it was in the days when Stalin was alive. My own criticism of the Donoughmore Committee's fumbling and confused attitude to administrative justice and the nature of the judicial process leads straight through the Franks Report to the recent statement of the Law Commission on Administrative Law and their recommendation for a Royal Commission on the subject. Mrs Stocks's contribution on London Government shows that in the 1930s some of us were working out reforms which were reflected in the London Government reorganization in 1963, the Maud Commission's proposals for Metropolitan Areas, and the recent White Paper *Reform of Local Government in England*.[1] Richard Crossman's allegation of a contradiction between the Labour Party's foreign policy and its attitude towards defence and military power is still applicable to the left-wing dissidents of the Parliamentary Labour Party who believe that there are no limits to the reductions which can and should be made on defence expenditure in order to improve the social services.

After reading this brief account of *The Political Quarterly* in the 1930s the reader may ask: 'What were you trying to do?' I will attempt to answer that question in general terms. We were trying to give a wider and deeper understanding of contemporary problems, some of which were being reported in the daily Press or debated in Parliament at a superficial level. We were also trying to direct attention to questions which were not being discussed at all and which we felt were important or likely to become so. We were trying to formulate and advocate public policies which were appropriate to the needs of the time. We were trying whenever possible to base those policies on philosophic principles or theories, and also on a firm foundation of expert or specialized knowledge. We were trying to show that many social, economic and political

[1] Cmnd 4276/1970, H.M.S.O.

reforms were required in a Britain which had not had a government willing and able to introduce reforms since the Liberal administration of 1906–14. We were trying to show the way to a more just, prosperous and civilized society and to a more peaceful and secure world. And we are still trying.

THE ENGLISH COUNTRYSIDE

Patrick Abercrombie

I · A TWOFOLD PROBLEM

IT must always be remembered that the rapidity of the change that
has come over the English Countryside is due to the impetus coming from two directions simultaneously, an external invasion and a
disintegration on the spot. The towns have spilled over their
boundaries in all directions, their inhabitants rifling the deepest
recesses of the country, and the rural landowners have been forced
to break up their estates, quitting country houses which were built
for a more spacious age than ours. Before attempting to suggest any
remedies for the damage to rural beauty that has resulted, it may be
well to analyse a little more deeply the causes of this twofold destruction and to catalogue some of the disfigurements that have
occurred. These causes have frequently been commented on, but
generally somewhat superficially, the advent of motor traffic being
given an undue prominence and the financial receptiveness of the
countryside towards change being underrated or neglected.

II · THE URBAN ATTAQUE

It is quite true that the sudden invasion of the country by motor
traffic has opened it up continuously along the main roads instead
of at wide intervals at railway stations. The latter favoured a sort of
spot development, the former a linear: but, of course, the railways
notoriously neglected the stopping traffic, the slowness of steam
engines in getting under way being accentuated by the dilatory
methods of the country station. The motor bus actually covers the
ground quicker and will stop practically wherever it is wanted. It
has thus become the normal country passenger carrier, threading
its way to pick up traffic off the main roads and giving greatly
increased convenience to rural life. There follows naturally the
motor van, feeding the village shops and linking up the multiple

branches in the small towns with their headquarter stores, without the interminable delay and double-handling of railway delivery. Added to this greater facility of access, there has been a widespread dissatisfaction with our dirty, ugly English towns. This was strongly felt by the younger people who returned from a life of open-air hardship endured during the war, and who were determined not to be cribbed in the respectable rows of suburban houses built under the sanitary by-laws. Hence, egged on by housing shortage, that sudden springing up of congeries of shacks, bungalows and caravans-grown-stationary, which soon became insanitary and have had a certain reputation for lawlessness of life. Many a Medical Officer and, indeed, officials from the Ministry of Health have been puzzled how to deal with them and they still remain today, a travesty of the hut in the wilderness. Closely allied, though the owners might not relish the connexion, was the simultaneous desire for a country cottage planted in a beautiful spot and visited at week-ends during summer and for the longer holidays. These buildings, of impeccable sanitariness, are often as ugly as the shack, owing to the unfortunate but understandable fact that all these people had an urban mentality nourished upon the example of the towns of the least artistic town-builders of Europe.

The Dean of Manchester has well pointed out that you cannot expect a good use to be made of the country by however ardent an enthusiast for open spaces if he has had his sense of fitness dulled by inhabiting Ancoats or Salford. Though the Dean did not exactly say so, his admirable generalization might be expressed in the variation of an old saying, 'What Lancashire thinks today, England does tomorrow,' which is being translated into, 'What Manchester looks like today, the English Countryside will look like tomorrow.' Unless of course, while we are taking steps to stop the destruction of the country we are at the same time cleansing the foyers from which this destruction proceeds, namely, our aesthetically degrading towns. Much of this destruction in this light is seen to be quite involuntary; it is due to those who desire to use and enjoy the country having lost the sense of how to do it. The familiar example would be the little boy from the slums who pulls up all the flowers he can see and leaves his banana skins lying about; but equally apt is the case of the wealthy motorist who is used to his spotless and highly scavenged suburb and who throws down the carton plates on which he has eaten his aspic lunch, subconsciously expecting that unseen hands will clean up the mess.

This increased use of the roads, as well for casual rides as for the more serious business of getting from house to town and for industrial transport, has naturally led to the creation of new and the widening of old routes, a change upon the face of the country nearly as marked as that caused by the railway cuttings and embankments so deplored by Ruskin. Fortunately, though there has been some tendency for the engineering worship of gradients to give to roads a railway harshness of attitude to the contours of our largely undulating land (the use of unemployed labour in embanking and cutting has perhaps encouraged this), the new roads are less unsympathetic to local conditions than were the Roman streets. Indeed, the idea of a national system of roads, similar to that planned by the Romans (something more than a piece-meal joining up of existing roads and by-passing of towns) has been gaining ground; it cannot, however, be said that anything approaching the Autostrada of Italy have as yet been constructed here.

The deposit of new houses lineally along the roads – old and new – was naturally to have been anticipated. Ribbon building is, of course, the natural formation of all communities; but whereas in the past they have usually been in short lengths knotted or bowed together into bunches for purposes of safety or proximity to wells, the ribbons are now untied and unrolled in interminable lengths; this happens more particularly, of course, as an extension of existing towns. The practical and social disadvantages of the ribbon have been frequently stated: houses facing main and noisy traffic routes, and thus dangerous for children; the impeding of through traffic, by a unit of slow and stopping vehicles on each side (unless this is specially provided for, which so far has not been done); the greater depth and cost of drainage with a continuous 'fall' as compared with a series of short lengths; the general unsociability of the arrangement and difficulty of convenient shopping centres (except through access to the main centres by bus); the distance of children from school (with the likelihood of the education authority having to convey them by bus). But compared with these real and permanent disadvantages there are two immediate advantages: in the first place the method follows the line of least resistance – there is no thought required in the placing of the house, it is on the bus route. In the second place there is the singular anomaly in English law that if you would make a new road and build houses upon it, you are mulcted on behalf of the public by having to make up a road; if you make it up to a certain specification, the public will reward you by annexing it for its use and paying for the upkeep; and you may be sure that you are made to spend as much upon the initial road as possible in order to minimize the amount of upkeep. If, however, you build upon an existing road, whether it be a main road or a country lane, you get off free, however much the public may have to pay for remodelling the road to make it suitable for a built-up area or street. The Public Health Act of 1925 had a clause which appeared to many eminent lawyers to remedy this anomaly; but it has been stated to mean something entirely different and no one has yet brought a test case to the High Court to see what the clause does mean. So the man who builds upon an existing road escapes perhaps £50 of roadmaking and he is willing to put up with other inconveniences. Indeed, the case is loaded against the builder on a new road who attempts to place a little group of houses adjacent to the high road (which is so frequent a situation of the old villages): though the roads of the group will not be traffic routes but merely approaches to houses and though the model clauses issued by the Ministry of Health expressly advise inexpensive road works and narrow carriageways, the Highway Committee of the local authority, which is frequently in opposition to the local Town Planning Committee, insists upon a quite stupidly costly road. On the outskirts of a Lancashire town, a reinforced concrete carriageway was asked for a cul-de-sac on which a dozen houses faced; when the developer protested, he was told that he was lucky to get off without granite setts; the present state of Lancashire prosperity is apparently able to afford these luxuries.

But there is a more sinister agency than the antiquated Highways Committee which is confirming this practice of building along the roads; syndicates have been formed to buy up the actual road frontages in the country surrounding our towns, exploiting a natural tendency for their material gain. The practice becomes much more difficult to eradicate, or the stream of building to be diverted into the sounder channel of grouped building, when money has been sunk in the old methods: vested interests are there ready to defend themselves against any reform.

Finally the electricity grid scheme is acting as another factor of change not only in the actual routes of the grid or trunk lines but in the more detailed electrification of the countryside for light and power, with the possibility of industrial development springing up where transformer stations are located. The indiscriminate scattering of industries on the country will probably be curtailed by the cost of the transformer station and the absence of labour. And it must be remembered that the Local Government Act of 1929 has considerably altered the attitude of the rural local authorities towards industries invading their areas. Formerly they were welcomed for the increased rateable value they brought; that is no longer so much the case, and the increased number of workingmen's houses is an incubus rather than an advantage, as their rates do not pay for the services which they entail. It would seem, therefore, that the electricity scheme will not encourage industrial growth except at certain spots which should be carefully chosen for suitable position and active stimulation by additional as well as electric means. We are here rather anticipating than recording a change.

III · THE RURAL DISINTEGRATION

The conquest of the country by the attacking town would not have been so easy if there had not been rural disorganization. If the country had remained in the hands of the same families who have done so much to create its typical English beauty of park, farm, village, lane, copse and hedgerow tree, there would have been an unchanged landscape, except for a few new roads and the electric pylons of the main grid. The greater use of the country demanded by this generation might have been directed into certain more defined areas in the form of regional and national parks or public open spaces, the bulk of normal country remaining unchanged.

As in the case of the urban attaque there is one dominant and obvious cause of rural disintegration, namely the change of the hands that hold the wealth of the country: but there are several side issues. In the first place in the case of least anticipated alteration of conditions, where a newly rich family has acquired land from an old country family for the purpose of succeeding as resident owners, there is usually a tightening up or curtailment of the privileges which the public has enjoyed. A slight but subtle change tending to alter the sense of obligation on the part of the local public for what remains or is of unquestioned right. Thus when the outside public arrives by car the local inhabitants are no longer the guardians of the local beauties. The next change, and of more obvious importance, was the sale during and after the war of the farms to their tenants. Here at once the incentive which a large landowner has to the preservation of the amenities of the whole disappears. Nor can anyone blame the farmer, who has bought his land during a period of prosperity, for trying to realize money during agricultural depression. It is he, rather than the big land-owner, who is anxious to sell off his road frontages to pay the interest upon his mortgaged farm: and no one can blame him. If farming had remained prosperous he might have been badgered into selling off a plot here and there, but he would probably have refused to cut himself off from road access and to curtail his area by fringing his roads with houses. In hard times, too, it must be remembered these householders are a ready market for his milk and eggs.

But it must be confessed, too, that there is apparent today a certain vein of callousness on the part of owners who sell out for one reason or another. There is a tendency to take the best price and impose no restriction on what becomes of the estate. This is perhaps natural, but it is new, except in the desperate cases of sudden poverty: the cases under consideration are not of this extreme urgency and the excuse given that the local authorities have the power to prepare a town planning scheme reveals the fact that the responsibility for England's loveliness is handed over to the Rural District Council, a body for which the penny rate produces perhaps

£70 per annum. And here again a sinister element has crept in: if the old landowner had to sell off his estate piecemeal himself, he could never have brought himself to extreme measures – his family traditions would have prevented it. But a new trade has risen up – the land butcher – a personage entirely ruthless and untrammelled by traditions. He is in a big enough way to pay a lump sum to the landowner, who retires to his other estate or to London; and then he is free to butcher the land and break up the house. This latter is, perhaps, the less blameworthy, as it is difficult to find a use for large country mansions; but it is deplorable when the house is a noble piece of architecture and should be a national possession. But the technique of estate breaking has been carefully worked out and is regularly applied. A sale is announced at short notice: well advertised and garnished with grisly details: the most beautiful parts cut up into small building lots: features that should belong to the National Trust are to be sold or divided between several villas' back gardens: glorious trees are offered in parcels to the timber merchants; the public sees them in its mind's eye cut down and carted. At once there is an appeal in the Press for public money to avert this outrage: the butcher has anticipated or rather played for this – the date of the sale cannot be postponed – a mysterious haste is necessary – and a huge sum is raised often by local people who are much less well off than the original vendor. If the principal feature of the estate is thus saved, the land butcher probably sells little else at the auction and proceeds to develop the remainder in the most brutal manner, encouraging any form of building and no form of layout, daring a feeble authority to control his efforts. He has been known to chop down copses whose shrubs and saplings are only useful to furnish forth bonfires. Thus the country is rendered defenceless to the town invasion.

It is to be feared that there are reputable firms of auctioneers who practice, at any rate in its earlier stages, this programme of the forced sale. A retired businessman, for example, has bought more land than he actually requires for the view from his drawing-room window and he wishes to sell off the surplus. The auctioneer points out that instead of getting his money back, the businessman can make 100 per cent on his outlay if he will leave it in his hands; the businessman, though nominally retired, cannot resist this chance of a deal. This means, perhaps, stripping the country of trees – in one case 12,000 of the most beautiful beeches in England were scheduled for destruction. Again the public is called in to pay and perhaps the businessman will contribute something to avert the disaster which his ignorance has produced; or, as has happened more than once, he has had his eyes opened to the enormity of the offence and has boldly withdrawn the lots from sale.

In another case a wealthy owner of some of the most famous mountain land in the world is selling off odd farms, or parcels of land facing on to roads that lead through the passes without any restrictions whatever. There is nothing forced or hurried about this, but a gradual unloading of outlying property and probably an entire lack of imagination as to the result of the peddling of these frontages in lots for shacks and stock pattern bungalows.

Probably the greatest extent of change of ownership is being continuously caused through the payment of death duties which fall most heavily upon those whose estate consists in unremunerative acres; there is no question of choice here and the country, in return for a comparatively small sum gathered by this form of taxation, sees its chief beauties exposed for sale and usually, though of course not always (for there are shining examples to the contrary), the worse off for the change. It would be interesting to see upon a map of England the amount of land that has thus changed hands since the war; probably upon the whole country it would not appear very large but looked at in the opposite sense, as centres of change for the worse, it is quite enough to provide ample opportunities of plague-spotting.

IV · CONTROL OF GROWTH

Rural England cannot undergo the inevitable change of modern usage and continue beautiful by the negative method of avoiding disfigurement. The change, the attaque from the towns, needs to be converted into a new process of colonization. There is, of course, a legal and aesthetic aspect involved in carrying this out.

Professor George Trevelyan in his manifesto, *Shall England's*

Beauty Perish?, has said that the only safe way to prevent this is to buy up our countryside and hand it over to the National Trust to administer. And he has courageously made a start in this gigantic enterprise by himself purchasing and presenting farms in the Langdale valley. Certainly if this policy were realized for England, complete control, artistic and legal, would be obtained. But it is a counsel of despair; to purchase the whole of England's acreage would be beyond most governments' resources; or if, alternatively, the land were nationalized we have no guarantee that it would be much safer in the hands of government departments.

In order to attempt some more practical method of dealing with the control of the developing part of the country and the retention of the unchanging areas, the Council for the Preservation of Rural England was formed in 1927. It is a federation of some thirty national bodies, all of whom (in addition to other functions) deal at some point or other with the country: in addition there are affiliated a large number of local preservation societies which, in time, will cover the whole country either by counties or other suitable areas. An organization so constituted may be somewhat cumbersome but it carries great weight when it does move. The general conclusion arrived[1] at is that the sole alternative to purchase of the developing areas is to apply country planning in the same way that town planning is applicable to areas under direct urban influence. But just as this change (originating from the mobility of urban populations) is to be formulated into planning schemes, so the static condition of other parts of the country is to be safeguarded from disintegration: some suggestions for securing this will be considered in section V.

For the moment we are concerned with *the direction of change*. There is, of course, a large body of legal powers in existence, under various acts, e.g. town planning, advertisement control, scheduling of ancient monuments, regulation of petrol pumps, prevention of litter, etc. So large, in fact, and complicated are these existing powers (the same results being frequently obtainable under different Acts[2]) that the C.P.R.E. has for months been preparing a

[1] Commander Hilton Young's Rural Amenities Bill, clause 2.

[2] E.g. Advertisement control under the Advt. Regulation Acts or under the

vade mecum for use by the general public. The contents of this pamphlet, therefore, will not be anticipated here.

But the following general aspects of change may be noted. In the first place the Minister of Health in his annual report for 1928–9 has pointed out that under present powers there is a limit to the amount and type of land which may be included for rural or county planning. There is, however, no limit to the places where change may at any moment occur; it follows that the powers must be extended. This extension, to include wide areas in which only a small amount of building will occur, at once introduces a new element in planning. The Town Planning Act contemplates (as its name suggests) primarily land 'likely to be used for building purposes' and consequently reasonable limitation of density of buildings upon that land is not subject to compensation: *per contra*, if it is desirable to keep some of this land open for farming or recreational purposes, compensation may be payable to owners who are prevented from putting this land (also presumably likely to be used for building purposes) to its fullest use. The first type of area is called a Zone, the second a Reservation, and this distinction, that no compensation is payable for a Zone, but is claimable upon a Reservation, is fundamental.

But when we come to deal with wide rural areas, it is manifestly ridiculous to be liable for a claim for compensation over thousands of acres which are scheduled as an agricultural reservation; and yet there is always some chance that, under no system of control of grouping, building might occur either in ribbons or spots. To zone it all at an average of five or six houses per acre would give virtually no control over placing. It is agreed that, for practical as well as aesthetic reasons, what building is likely to occur should be grouped, either round existing villages or forming new centres, called satellites when they appear to be offshoots of some parent mass (as in the case of Welwyn and London). The Minister of Health has rightly pointed out that much may be done to stimulate this natural grouping by giving facilities at certain points, e.g. providing public

---

Town Planning Acts, the recent road widening powers and the Public Health Act, 1925, or the Road Improvement Act, 1925.

services, water, electric light, drainage, etc.: this has been called *persuasive* planning and it is certainly an essential feature of the scheme. But it is not enough.

The simplest method of effecting this control would be to amend the Act so that (at any rate in rural planning) neither Reservation nor Zone were subject to compensation. If the land in any given scheme were in one ownership, there would be no hardship in this; and, indeed, the landlord has done this instinctively on his estate in the past, dividing it up into house and garden, home park, farm lands, village centres, etc., and keeping a tight hold upon this segregation of his land. And, indeed, it is a commonplace that town and country planning would be a comparatively simple matter if it were a question of dealing with a few large ownerships.

But as soon as the small ownership is introduced such a simple amendment of the Act would introduce hardship: one man being possibly allocated all building land and another all farm land, to take an extreme case. But the single ownership establishes the principle that there is no loss whatever in values through grouping, merely a transference: a concentration of higher value on one part and an elimination from another. Indeed, there should be a net gain owing to economy of working. There is, in other words, a readjustment of values which should be harmonized with the hazards of ownership. It has been, therefore, suggested[1] that some cooperative pooling arrangement between landowners should be devised in order that the increment may be shared equitably 'on the basis of each owner's legitimate and recognized interest, or by the promotion of suitable exchanges of land so as to give each owner his proper proportion of building or other land'.

This is confessedly not an easy matter and is foreign to our invincible individuality where business matters are concerned. But it appears to be the most practicable solution, and it would automatically put a stop to ribbon development.

It has also been thought desirable to supplement the powers of Authorities when constructing new roads. The Ministry of Transport (and the Middlesex County Council) have the right when

[1] First put forward by the C.P.R.E., Memorandum No. 5 and forming clause 4 in Commander Hilton Young's Rural Amenities Bill.

buying land for a new road to purchase an extra strip on either side up to a maximum of 220 yards from the centre. This should be extended to all County Councils:[1] the purchase of this extra land should not be for the purposes of resale for building but in order to keep building off the main traffic routes by means of an open strip which until development behind occurs could be left in the riparian fields and later treated as a parkway. The strip would vary up to the maximum in width, but if it were always purchased (to a minimum say of 20 or 30 yards) it would give valuable control over the placing and spacing of the entrances of side roads. These greatly impede through traffic if they are closer than a quarter of a mile apart. The admirable effect of this strip, both as securing through, unimpeded traffic on the main roads and a pleasant quiet situation for the villages can be seen in many old parts of the country, for example, the road from Abingdon to Faringdon and on the Oxford to Banbury Road (with good contrast of the opposite effect at Kidlington).

In the preparation of rural or country planning schemes, three stages, or rather, processes would appear to be necessary. In the first place a preliminary survey is essential,[2] in order that all the factors affecting change or stability can be fully realized. A survey of this type has recently been published[3] for the Thames Valley from Lechlade to Staines: with a similar document before them, there should be no danger of planning schemes being inadequate or arbitrary. If artificial control is to take the place of natural solution it must be based upon a close study of conditions.

Regional planning schemes for rural areas must then be undertaken. Plans have already been prepared for the majority of areas in England which are under urban or quasi-urban influence. The large remaining areas may conveniently be grouped upon a county basis for general regional reports, and then subdivided, if necessary, into rural planning schemes; the rural, urban and county councils are enabled to cooperate in this work under the 1929 Local Government Act.

[1] Commander Hilton Young's Bill, clause 5.
[2] Commander Hilton Young's Bill, clause 6.
[3] By the London Univ. Press for the Thames Valley Branch of the C.P.R.E.

But it is necessary to go even further than these three processes of preliminary survey, regional report and rural planning scheme, if the whole country is to come under some form of control. National Planning is also essential: the nation nearly stumbled upon this when Mr Lloyd George set up a Development Committee after the War, consisting of representatives of the Ministries of Agriculture, Health, Trade and Transport; but it was axed in its early infancy by Sir Eric Geddes, its original chairman, who had not apparently grasped its economic object. At present we have Departmental national planning in watertight compartments for roads, electricity, afforestation and, tentatively, housing and railways and water supply: but there is no adequate coordination between them and no relation to a scheme of planning in which certain areas are stimulated and others are preserved. Some form of State Development Department should be set up in order to direct the broad lines of this national planning. This would provide the only satisfactory body to consider such a question as to whether Brighton, the capital of south coast amenities, was the best place to set up a super-electrical power and distributing station, having no local coal and not being a port. The Local Authorities concerned in the case could only protest against six radiating lines of gigantic pylons across the Downs, and clamour for the cables to be buried. But the real error in national planning consisted in selecting Brighton instead of the coalfield of East Kent or some port on the London estuary.

Not much has been said so far about the aesthetic aspect of rural development. The existing English landscape is, of course, with the exception of a few wild areas, a highly sophisticated piece of work, the result of human action extended over nearly 2,000 years, instinctively perhaps at first but later, and notably in the seventeenth and eighteenth centuries, on a theory of landscape enhancement. We owe a great part of the typical beauty of the English scene to the landowners who have planted and laid out their estates and to the country craftsmen who built the houses, farms and churches.

A more thorough study of these components of the landscape is necessary in order that our additions may be in harmony with it

both as to scale, design and colour. It is, for example, idle to compare the effect of pylons upon the Swiss landscape with their probable effect here. Every feature of rural planning has its aesthetic
aspect which must never be neglected; but, of course, the most
obvious need for care is in the design and materials of buildings.

The machinery for this is available, but it is not compulsory and
quite inadequately made use of. The Bath Act and subsequently
the Model Clause under the Town Planning Act definitely established the fact that a bad elevation can be condemned without any
claim to compensation by reference to a tribunal consisting of an
architect, surveyor and a Justice of the Peace. Guidance to the
Local Authority as to when it is necessary to submit designs to this
Tribunal can be had from the Panels of Architects set up by the
C.P.R.E. in conjunction with the Royal Institute of British Architects and approved by the Minister of Health.[1] Where these Panels
are already working the improvement is marked, as informal constructive advice is given to intending builders at an early stage, in
addition to the local authorities; it has been urged that the exercise
of this control should be made compulsory.[2]

V · THE CONTINUANCE OF EXISTING CONDITIONS

So much for the changing face of England: but, after all, the
amount of land required for normal growth is singularly small: it is
estimated that within a periphery of a twenty-five-mile radius from
Charing Cross the total population of the British Isles could be
housed at the comparatively low density of twelve houses per acre.
It is not, therefore, the amount of change, but the flagrancy of its
manner that makes it bulk so large. There are enormous tracts
which would be unaffected, except for the normal additions to the
villages, were it not for the disintegrating influences already mentioned. It is necessary, therefore, to seek some means of stabilizing
large parts of the countryside where, in the interests of national

---

[1] See Minister of Health Circular 940.

[2] Though the control of elevations is not mentioned in Commander Hilton
Young's Bill the power to do so would be inherent in the Rural Planning
schemes which are to be practically universal.

economy, it is not desirable that a violent, nor necessary that even an orderly change should take place.

For limited areas there is already in existence a method under the Town Planning Act known as dedication as a Private Open Space. This has the desired effect of giving security to an owner for an area such as his private park, but it is only really applicable given two conditions, firstly, that he intends himself or his family to go on living there (or to keep the park intact for other reasons), and secondly, that the surrounding land has advanced in value above the normal agricultural or other value of the park. For by dedicating as a Private Open Space the owner is precluded from selling as building land; he, therefore, does not pay death duties upon this building value. What happens in many cases where this method is not taken advantage of, is that after one or two deaths in the family, particularly if they come in close succession, the latest owner has to sell in order to realize a building value, *not* for his own profit, but to satisfy the demands of the Chancellor. The land is forced into the market.

On a wider scale, but still for definite areas, is the National Park according to one definition of the term. Here, in an area of exceptional beauty, such as the Lakes or Snowdonia, it may be possible to obtain what is wanted, not by purchase (although a considerable area may well be bought), but by a more stringent limitation than would suffice for normal agricultural districts. Here then, though there might be a considerable possibility of building exploitation, the give and take under a pooling scheme would not take place if the building were actually excluded. Compensation or a buying out of building values (and possibly mining, quarrying and sporting rights) might be necessary for which national funds would be available. A condition of stability would be brought about by this means.

A third suggestion would apply to less defined areas than National Parks. Country having a national value through its beauty, which is outside the working of the pooling method, should be exempted from death duties (without any tying-up as a Private Open Space), on the analogy of works of art. It is argued that there is some illogicality that death duties need not be paid upon a Turner 'Landscape', but they must be upon the scene which he painted. As is well known, if the picture is subsequently sold, the present owner pays death duties as they were assessed at the time of his inheritance. There are, of course, several differences between land and pictures, the most obvious being that a considerable part of the former is revenue-producing in the form of agriculture, though the Chancellor of the Exchequer would not lose much if he gave total exemption to certain estates. If the death duties were to be paid upon the agricultural value but not upon any building value, this would have the effect of limiting the operation of the scheme to those estates which were in the neighbourhood of developing areas (or in other words, to estates which would have been paid compensation for an enforced agricultural reservation). For an estate which possessed *no* building value would, *ipso facto*, normally pay no death duties beyond agricultural ones. By eliminating the building prospects from large areas the Chancellor of the Exchequer is losing nothing, as the value is transferred elsewhere. Part of the estate could be converted into building land whenever the owner wished; but upon what basis of value the retrospective 'building' death duties should be paid, would require careful consideration.

Mr Maynard Keynes has made a suggestion that goes even further: he would free such estates from Schedule A Income Tax (exclusive of assessments in respect of buildings). He would have a Commission set up for the purpose of scheduling areas for these exemptions which should further be given an annual sum from the Treasury, out of which they would have the right to purchase scheduled areas, and, in the case of land which had a capital value more than double its income value (e.g. potential building land let for agricultural purposes) to pay the owners a percentage on this excess.

The Duke of Montrose has made a further proposal, which is complementary to the relief of death duties; he wishes to make it a normal procedure for a landowner who has to part with some of his estate to meet death duties to pay in land instead of cash. As he points out, this would be a gradual form of nationalization on an equitable basis and it would again prevent the worst danger to rural preservation, the enforced sale.

The code of rural change is embodied in the Bill which Commander Hilton Young has introduced into the House and which has passed its second reading without a division. From the allusions to its clauses which have been made it will be seen that it covers a considerable area of the ground, though perhaps one could wish that the obligation to prepare universal rural planning had been somewhat more stringent.[1]

April 1930

[1] See clause 9.

OUGHT THE ESTABLISHMENT
TO BE MAINTAINED?

The Rt Rev. Herbert Hensley Henson,
Bishop of Durham

I

THE relations of Church and State in England, conveniently
described as 'the Establishment', have now become so unsatisfactory that 'all sorts and conditions of men' are at one in thinking
that they cannot rightly or wisely be suffered to remain unchanged.
There is difference of opinion among English Churchmen as to the
measure and character of the changes that are requisite, but none
as to the necessity of changes that are so considerable and far-
extending that they may well seem to be incompatible with the continuance of the Establishment itself. The two Archbishops are
understood to be engaged in constituting a Commission which shall
review the existing relations of Church and State with the express
object of making suggestions for 'mending or ending' them. For,
indeed, it is apparent that the Establishment has in part ceased to
function, and that even in the limited area in which it still functions, it does so with increasing friction and difficulty. Nor is the
reason obscure or disputed. The system is plainly obsolete, as well
because the assumptions on which it rests have for the most part
lost validity, as because the new factors, social, political and ecclesiastical, which dominate the present situation, can by no possibility
be brought into harmony with its provision. The Establishment
assumes the identity of Church and State. The one is truly national
because the other is confessedly Christian. But this identity has
notoriously come to be fictional. The Nation has so outgrown the
National Church that but a fraction of its citizens now acknow-
ledges membership therein. All lesser dissidences are gathered up
in that broad and vital difference.

Establishment was the logical consequence of Conversion: and since, before the triumph of modern democracy, the Nation was identified with its Ruler, the Ruler's conversion determined the Nation's religion. Of course this national religion based on the Ruler's will was at all times embarrassed by a vast amount of individual repudiation: and certainly it has never at any time been more than a very rough approximation to the actual beliefs of the people. Still, so long as the identification of Sovereign and People could be assumed, there was sufficient truth in the old legal doctrine which prevailed in the Middle Ages, and survived the Reformation, *cujus regio ejus religio*, as to provide a sufficient basis for the organization of the Church. The Nation was legally Christian; the Church was legally National, because both Nation and Church acknowledged the supreme authority of the same Monarch, and he was professedly Christian, 'the Lord's Anointed'. So long as the effective unity of Western Christendom continued, Christianity was one and the same everywhere, and the Monarchs not less than their subjects were members of the one Catholic Church whose ruler was the Roman Pope, but with the Reformation came the disruption of Christendom, and the door was opened for monarchical individualism in the religious sphere. The triumph of nationalism expressed itself in many directions, and in none more notably than in the organization of independent national churches. Medieval territorialism was perpetuated in the new systems, and religious persecution, which was its logical consequence, acquired a new and more monstrous character. In England, where the Reformation was effected by the national authorities, the process is most easily traced. The type of national Christianity varied with the preference of the Monarch. Henry VIII was Catholic: Edward VI was Protestant: Mary was Papal: and, finally, Elizabeth, garnering the lessons of her predecessors' experiments, was Anglican. When the great Queen succeeded in 'establishing' the Reformed Church, she built her 'settlement' on the old assumption, and suffered no variation from the *via media* which she approved. Church and State were frankly identified. In the well-known words of Hooker, the supreme apologist of the Tudor Establishment;

In a word, our estate is according to the pattern of God's own ancient elect people, which people was not part of them the commonwealth, and part of them the Church of God, but the self-same people whole and entire were both under one chief Governor, on whose supreme authority they did all depend.

This doctrine underlies the existing Establishment. The Prayer Book expresses it. The Canons of 1604, which still bind the Clergy, formulate it at length. It has been frankly rejected everywhere else. Religious uniformity is no longer the policy of the State. Nonconformity is not only tolerated, but even legally privileged. Only in the legal system of the Established Church does it persist. Obsoleteness has overtaken the Canon which requires the Clergy 'four times every year at the least' to preach on the Royal Supremacy, and no civil penalties any longer attach to the excommunication *ipso facto* which is pronounced upon everyone who

shall hereafter affirm that the King's Majesty hath not the same authority in causes Ecclesiastical that the godly Kings had amongst the Jews, and Christian Emperors in the Primitive Church, or impeach in any part his regal supremacy in the said causes restored to the Crown, and by the Laws of this realm therein established.

It is too often forgotten that the Establishment, which rested on this conception of Kingship, imposed obligations on the Sovereign as well as subjection on the Church. The first duty of the Christian Monarch was – to use the words of the Oath still tendered to the British Sovereign at his Coronation – 'to maintain the laws of God, the true profession of the Gospel, and the Protestant Reformed Religion established by Law': and the faithful performance of that duty implied, not merely the legal recognition of the existing ecclesiastical system, but also the expansion of that system to meet the ever-expanding needs of the nation. In idea the Establishment was, not static or rigid, but dynamic and elastic. Like the Monarch's civil authority, it was properly co-extensive with the Nation itself. As the nation increased, and its needs multiplied, the ecclesiastical provision inherited from the Middle Ages became apparently inadequate. Accordingly, the State, embodied in the Christian Monarch, was morally responsible for increasing the ecclesiastical provision until it answered to the nation's needs. Such effective assistance by the State was really the consideration on which the Church conceded to the State such large powers of control. Only so could the State secure the benefit of the Church's distinctive service, and only so could the Church receive the assistance in its spiritual task which the State alone could give. In short, the Establishment means essentially the Union of Church and State in securing the effective Christianization of the Nation. Such was the implicit theory of the Establishment, but the practice was never congruous, and soon became actually contradictory. The State's obligations were first neglected, and then repudiated, though the Church's subjection was maintained and even emphasized. Save for the benefaction connected with the name of Queen Anne, and some petty expenditures for Church building, the State, since the Reformation, has added nothing to the Church's resources, with the result that the system of religious provision which the Establishment provides for the modern nation is (save for the additions made by voluntary effort) no greater than that which served the subjects of Elizabeth. Neglect has silently passed into something like unconfessed dislike. This is curiously illustrated in the case of the episcopate. Of all the incidents of the Establishment, the presence of the Archbishops and Bishops in the Upper House of Parliament is, perhaps, the most significant. It brings the Church directly into the process of national government, and shows how it garners by increased opportunity of spiritual influence the reward of its complaisance to the secular power. As the nation multiplied, so, it might have been supposed, would this provision for its spiritual needs have been extended. The Spiritual Estate in Parliament would have kept pace with the population. The secular peers have multiplied sevenfold, thus matching the nation's growth. What is the explanation of the difference? The answer can only be that the State no longer attaches any value to spiritual peers. It tolerates their presence as a bequest from the past, but has no use for their distinctive service. When in the course of the nineteenth century new bishoprics were created, the State, so far from welcoming the Church's effort, accompanied its grudging consent to an increase of the episcopate with a proviso that in no circumstances should the number of spiritual peers be increased. What is true of the episcopate is true also of the parochial system. Such extension as has been made has been the achievement of the Church alone, for the large funds administered by the Ecclesiastical Commissioners, and applied by them to the creation of new parishes, are drawn wholly from the ancient endowments of the Church supplemented by the voluntary contributions of Churchmen. In fact, the State, while for reasons of its own content to perpetuate the ancient Establishment, has been careful to make clear that it does not accept the theory which that Establishment embodies. The Spiritual Estate has been suffered to remain an integral part of the national system but its influence on the process of national government, which was the *raison d'être* of its constitutional position, has been reduced to the shadow of a shade. Yet the State has retained the powers which the Establishment conferred, while repudiating the obligations which it entailed. The Church has even been required to shoulder the State's duty while gaining in return no lightening of the State's control. Thus, in 1868, when Church rates were abolished, and the cost of maintaining churches and churchyards was thrown on the voluntary contributions of churchmen, the parishioners, who were not churchmen and contributed nothing, were none the less allowed to retain undiminished their rights in both. Here also the same twofold process is exhibited. Powers are retained while the obligations which alone could give moral title to their possession are repudiated. Even the Enabling Act of 1919, which for ecclesiastical purposes substituted Parochial Church Councils elected by Churchmen for the ancient Vestries composed of ratepayers, left unaltered the immemorial rights of parishioners. In the sphere of politics the same process is apparent. The parliamentary franchise, which has been extended to all adults of both sexes, has been severed from all connexion with Churchmanship and even with Christianity. It is reasonably estimated that, at the present time, not more than one in fifteen of the Parliamentary electors is a communicant member of the Church of England. Nevertheless, Parliament retains all its old ecclesiastical authority. The spiritual supremacy of Parliament which was intelligible when all its members were communicants, and when all had been elected by communicants, became paradoxical and religiously offensive when it inhered in an assembly which acknowledged no religious profession either in members or in constituents. So with the Crown. The responsible personal action of the Lord's Anointed has been replaced by that of a Prime Minister who may be of any religious persuasion or of none, and who is responsible to a Parliament which is as free from religious connexions as himself. None the less the ecclesiastical prerogatives of the Crown, which include the nomination of the Archbishops, Bishops, Deans, and many of the clergy, remain undiminished. In the judicial sphere the transference of the Sovereign's powers to constitutional officials, over whom he has no control, has told disastrously on ecclesiastical discipline.

The royal Supremacy is now exercised by a frankly secular court – the Judicial Committee of the Privy Council – and the whole action of the ecclesiastical courts, provincial and diocesan, which is subject to its appellant jurisdiction, is thereby tainted with 'Erastianism', and, in the conscientious belief of large numbers of religious Anglicans, as well laymen as clergymen, is robbed of moral authority. Thus the Establishment in every part is seen to exhibit the same paralysing characteristic. Powers have survived the conditions which justified them, and are now exercised, if exercised at all, without any such moral claim as may secure and facilitate the obedience of English Churchmen. The bilateral Covenant between Church and State has been altered to the disadvantage of one of the Parties, and without its consent. The Church is held fast to an Establishment of which both the legal assumptions and the moral justification have ceased. The Establishment ties the State to ecclesiastical responsibilities which it is no longer able to carry; and binds on the Church a system which it is no longer able self-respectingly to accept. Accordingly, the continuance of the Establishment implies discontent, disaffection, and developing disorder.

II

While thus the State has stultified the Establishment by repudiating its own religious obligations, the Church has forfeited its original title to national recognition by losing harmony with the general mind of the Nation. When Puritanism finally elected to exchange Nonconformity for Dissent, it withdrew from the Church of

England precisely that element which was most resolutely Protestant, and thus disturbed irreparably the balance of the Elizabethan Settlement. Anglicanism would in the future develop only from those elements in the established system which were least Protestant. The movement away from the thorough-going Protestantism of the original Reformation, which is already apparent in Hooker, was, so to say, confessed and organized. It advanced until, in the course of time, it has not only destroyed the religious unity of the English people, but has completely transformed the English Church. This process of transformation was, indeed, long obscured by the political risks involved in the anti-Protestant policy of the later Stuarts. The Established Church and the Nonconformists found mutual understanding and common ground in the enthusiasm of patriotic feeling which the imminent danger of the country evoked. Had the policy of comprehension, which the statesmen of the Revolution attempted, been crowned with success, it is possible that the temporary union might have been permanent, and the Protestant character of the Establishment recovered, but the defeat of that policy, and the substitution of the policy of toleration ensured the final severance of the Church of England from specifically Protestant Christianity. Evangelicalism, the progeny of the Methodist Movement, lay apart from the normal course of ecclesiastical development, and has never, even in its most prosperous days, been at home in the Church of England. Its true affinity is with the Dissenters. It looks naturally to 'the pit from which it was digged'. Accordingly, when, after the long domination of Whig Erastianism, there was a spiritual revival within the Established Church, it drew its inspiration, not from the sixteenth century but from the seventeenth. The Non-jurors, not the Elizabethan divines, were the spiritual ancestors of the Tractarians. The *via media* of Anglicanism, which had originally signified a moderate version of Protestantism, now came to indicate a moderate version of Catholicism. This evolution, however, was ecclesiastical, not national. The prevailing sentiment of the English people as a whole remained unalterably Protestant, for that sentiment had its roots as much in political history as in religious tradition. It was a blend of religious conservatism and patriotic instinct.

It is important to emphasize the influence of the secular history of the nation on its religious development. Politics have entered deeply into English religion, and nowhere so deeply as in the continuing controversy with Rome. For the two centuries which part the accession of Elizabeth from that of George III, English patriotism had been bound up with opposition to the policies and pretensions of the popes. The two English sovereigns who were personally devoted papists were also the two who cared least for English independence. Mary I would have bound England to the policy of Spain, and James II to that of France. In both cases the Monarch's religion was seen to conflict with the nation's liberty. Thus the association of protestantism with patriotism became an English tradition. That tradition survives still in the intense, unarguing antipathy to the Roman Church which, from time to time, flares out in 'No Popery' agitations. This inbred hereditary hatred for everything Roman survives in many English minds every other element of ancestral religion.

The Church of England has ever been, and is still, strongly anti-Roman, but it is consciously and proudly Catholic. On the distinction between Roman and Catholic the validity of the specifically Anglican version of Christianity may be said to turn. That vital distinction, however, is quite unintelligible to the average Englishman. The popular identification of whatever claims to be Catholic with whatever is believed to be Roman, which since the time of Hooker has confused English minds, has tended to create a very difficult situation for English Churchmen. As the Church of England has recovered the authentic aspect and language of pre-Roman Catholicism, it has provoked against itself the formidable resentment of popular Protestantism. It would, indeed, be uncandid to deny that the popular error has been strengthened by the procedures of a small section of Romanizing Anglicans, who shared the popular identification of Roman and Catholic, and for that reason sought to conform the English Church to the Roman model. The influence of these 'Anglo-Roman' clergy within the Church of England is out of all proportion to the public scandal which they occasion. For many years the absence of effective discipline caused by the obsoleteness of the rubricks and the 'Erastianism' of the Law-courts, has given practical impunity to clerical lawlessness. The Report of the Royal Commission of 1906 emphasized this fact. It was, indeed, the primary object of Prayer Book Revision to bring this discreditable state of things to an end. That was designed as the first step in the process by which Discipline should be restored. Inasmuch as that Revision was carried through by the Church itself, it could not but express the non-Roman Catholicism which marks the Church's system, and for that very reason it could not fail to arouse the suspicion and hostility of the Protestant multitude.

III

So long as the obsolete Establishment was generally regarded as little more than a picturesque anachronism, it was possible to defend it as a working anomaly, and as such it might long have been suffered to continue. Under the excitement of a popular agitation the older character of a working legal system was suddenly recovered, and it was seen that the Church of England is even in spiritual matters frankly subordinate to the modern secularized State. This complete subordination had not lacked plausible, if insufficient excuse when, as was the case when the Establishment was fashioned, the facts of national religion harmonized with the assumptions of the Law, but in the actual circumstances of the twentieth century it was seen to be intolerable. The full extent of the failure of the legal Establishment was dramatically disclosed, when a frankly secularized House of Commons rejected contemptuously a measure dealing with the most intimate concerns of a Christian Church which had been presented to it with every recommendation which such a measure could possess. Mr Saklatvala, the Parsee Communist who, as the Member for Battersea, voted against the Revised Prayer Book, will in the retrospect of history be seen to have played in the record of the Establishment the role played by another Oriental, 'the little Mortara', in that of the Pope's temporal power. He illustrated the enormity of the paradox implicit in the existing relation of Church and State, and thereby made the ending of that relation morally indispensable. The issue raised by the rejection of the Prayer Book measure was as clear as it was crucial.

Parliament, a single House of Parliament, and that, moreover, one in which the Spiritual Estate is not represented, claimed and exercised spiritual supremacy over the Church of England. Powers which had been reluctantly conceded to a Christian autocrat, himself a member of the English Church, and as such professing the Catholic faith and owning subjection to the Moral Law, and which had been for this very reason justified by Scripture and the precedents of Christian History, were now seen to be vested in a popular assembly, of which the members possessed no religious character, and were elected by constituents who, for the most part, made no profession of Christianity. The merits or demerits of the Revised Prayer Book ceased to be important. A greater question had been raised. Is the Church of England a spiritual society at all? Or, is it but a department of the civil government, essentially identical with the Board of Education? Does its legal Establishment properly imply the loss of the inherent franchises of a Christian Church? Can it not even determine the Form of its Liturgy and the Manner of its Ministration of the Blessed Sacrament to its sick and dying members? Here was no conflict between Church and State of the familiar medieval type. The unending controversies which have distracted Christendom as to the measure of ecclesiastical power which may rightly be conceded to secular authority, have no real bearing on the situation in modern England. As Professor Ernest Barker has pointed out, this conflict between the Christian Society itself, not an Order within it, and the Modern State has no precedent in the Middle Ages. It is the Church as a whole that has been overriden by the House of Commons on a specifically spiritual issue. The action of the House of Commons was met by a solemn protest. In July 1928 the Church Assembly adopted unanimously, and with a remarkable display of enthusiasm, the following resolution:

It is a fundamental principle that the Church – that is the Bishops together with the clergy and the laity – must in the last resort, when its mind has been fully ascertained, retain its inalienable right, in loyalty to our Lord and Saviour Jesus Christ, to formulate its Faith in Him, and to arrange the expression of that Holy Faith in its forms of worship.

In this resolution, which was drafted by Archbishop Davidson himself, the governing principle of the legal Establishment is clearly and categorically repudiated. The Church of England rejects the assumption that the Nation has the last word in spiritual matters. Its 'fundamental principle' is that, not the Nation, but the Church, is supreme in the spiritual sphere. The Church of England, moreover, is an integral part of the Anglican Communion, that is, of a fellowship of Churches which (to adopt the words of the Committee of the Lambeth Conference) 'are independent in their self-government, and are growing up freely on their own soil and in their own environment as integral parts of the Church Universal'.

It is obviously impossible to limit the application of this 'fundamental principle' to the specific matters directly raised by Prayer Book Revision. The franchise of the Divine Society must have its frank expression over the entire area of the corporate spiritual life. Appointments to spiritual office and the enforcement of spiritual discipline come clearly within the range of its exercise. Inevitably, therefore, the entire fabric of the national Establishment of the Church comes into condemnation, for all rests on the same false assumption. When, swayed by ignorant rhetoric and blinded by its fanatical fears, the House of Commons rejected the Prayer Book measure, it decreed, unwittingly so far as most of its members were concerned, the abolition of the Establishment. The formal consummation of its work may be delayed by many circumstances – the reluctance of the general body of English Churchmen to accept the abhorred necessity of Disestablishment, the selfish fears of all whom Disendowment threatens with material loss, the obsession of the public mind with economic problems of the utmost gravity, the play of party politics, the cynical calculations of disloyal minorities within the Church whose evident interest is served by the paralysis of discipline which the Establishment compels, and the like. But be the delay protracted or not, the final result is certain. There can be no going back on the path which the Church of England has deliberately chosen. Disestablishment is only a matter of time, of a short time.

IV

Who gains by maintaining the Establishment? Not the State, which is plainly unable to make good the authority which in theory it possesses. Not the Church, which is compromised in its credit, and disordered in its life, deprived of indispensable disciplinary power, and restrained from the most needed reforms. Not the Nation, which receives from the clergy, instead of that wholesome influence of law-abiding example, which they, beyond all other citizens, should be able to contribute to its life, a woeful spectacle of ill faith and disobedience, which tells balefully on the whole community. Not Religion, which is necessarily discredited and enfeebled by continuing confusion and undiscipline within the Church.

In the best interest of the English people not less than of the English Church, the archaic structure, which perpetuates in the twentieth century the political and social features of the sixteenth, should be taken away, and the Church of England released from the humiliation and practical weakness of an Establishment which is both obsolete in idea, and ineffective in practice.

It may be urged that theoretical difficulties weigh little against practical conveniences, and that Englishmen have a well-grounded reputation for preferring utility to logic. Even principles are easily sacrificed to interest or sentiment. It is not, therefore, surprising that many men, who are neither irreligious nor irrational, hesitate to approve a policy which yet they cannot deny to be just, reasonable, and on many grounds requisite. Disestablishment, however, does not lack recommendations of a utilitarian character. The work of the Church of England is gravely hindered by the costly, cumbrous, and complicated organization which the Establishment necessitates. Even the material loss involved in Disendowment might be no excessive price to pay for freedom to recast the ecclesiastical system, and thus to use such resources of men and money as the Church possesses with greater economy, intelligence, and effectiveness. The cause of spiritual efficiency is certainly not served by the wasteful and even senseless distribution of clergy which the parochial system, as it now exists, requires. The disestablished Church would be genuinely autonomous, and, as such, able to exercise that authority over its own members which, as an Established Church, it is plainly unable to secure. Such recovery of discipline would remove the internal disorder which has long weighed so heavily on the reputation of the Church of England. Above all, Disestablishment would do much to put the clergy right with the general conscience, which is offended both by the light view which many clergymen apparently take of breaking their own solemn undertakings, and by the easy acquiescence of Churchmen in the Erastian subordination of the Church to the State.

Disestablishment ought not to be the subject of political controversy, for it lies properly outside the area of normal party conflict. No party at present includes it in its programme. Not less plainly than Unemployment and the Indian Problem, it calls for the combined action of all parties. Disestablishment by consent ought not to be beyond the capacity of English statesmanship. It is, as we have shown, urgently required in the interest both of the Church and of the State.

September 1930

THE FUNCTION OF THE PRESS

C. P. Scott

THE Press in these days is a tremendous affair and shows signs, here and there, of aspiring to be even much more tremendous. My own direct concern with it has been limited to that branch which dies daily. When I became a journalist – unfortunately a long time ago – the daily newspaper had only recently come into existence. Parliament, not without some reason, had been afraid of the newspaper. The particular newspaper with which I have all my life been connected first saw the light rather more than a century ago and Parliament greeted it with a tax of fourpence a copy duly levied by a red stamp on each sheet and a tax of threepence a pound on the paper on which it was printed. Such was the prudence of Parliament in face of this new competitor for power, and its entire disregard for the tenderness of an infant industry. Since then the infant has developed to a robust maturity and interesting questions arise as to its schooling and its place in the world.

The first function of a newspaper is indicated plainly in its name; it is an instrument for the collection and dissemination of news. But what news? That is a material question. All sorts of things happen in the world every day and every hour of the day. It is all a question of selection, whether of the serious or the frivolous, of the clean or the unclean, of fact or of fiction. Some people like one sort and some another and the newspaper can usually be found to respond to each demand. Here, in the favourite phrase of President Wilson, is the acid test of quality. It is a wonderful function and, with the progress of invention, has been carried far. It ministers to knowledge, to curiosity, to education; in a real sense it makes the whole world one. To know is not always to value, and intimacy may breed repulsion, even hate. But on the whole it is not so, and knowledge not only opens the way to sympathy but mitigates instinctive dislike. For men are extraordinarily interesting and every society has its own character and its own attraction. Perhaps we do not sufficiently realize this. We study with ardour and minuteness the dead civilizations of Greece and Rome and we forget that India and China may have just as much to teach us which is a good deal nearer to hand. The newspaper cannot throw its net too wide. Its folly is to affect omniscience, but its function is to supply all the material needful for those that know.

It may go further; it may and it ought, so far as it is able, to supply some guidance in the maze of things, to act in some degree, not merely as purveyor, but also as interpreter. That no doubt is a delicate operation and lends itself all too easily to abuse. But there are cases in which nothing is so misleading as the bald fact. To be understood it must be seen in its whole connexion, as part of a process, not merely as an incident. That is a work of interpretation and makes all sorts of demands not only on knowledge, but on the impartial temper. Nor does impartiality imply indifference; indifference is an atrophy of the sympathies, impartiality a poise of the mind. The first condition of a real understanding is perhaps a sympathetic approach. And how vital this is all history shows. The worst crimes which it records are perhaps the crimes of ignorance. War, modern war at least, is its child. We are past the stage of sheer aggression; we know too well that in war both sides lose; that there is no such thing as victor and vanquished, but that war is a defeat for both. In this sense all war is madness; its beginning and its end. To each side the other is the aggressor and, in fact, that is the truth. For to be the first to attack is a clear advantage, and when trouble is brewing, each side, knowing this, imputes the intention to the other and in that belief itself determines to be first. How easily this may happen was seen in a crucial and terrible instance that none can forget, yet the spirit of aggression for its own sake was, perhaps, equally absent from both sides. If only each had known, and in its heart believed, that this was so, how easy would understanding have been, how sure the road to safety. Here, surely, is the precious opportunity of all who can form, or influence, opinion. And yet how rarely is it fully used? How often do not newspapers in their assumed vocation of watch-dogs for the nation, ready to bark at every footstep as though it must needs be that of an enemy, serve rather to scent danger where none is and to howl denunciation where, if they but knew, there is not the slightest need for alarm. Not that the error need be intentional. Nothing is easier than to persuade oneself that danger is in the air. Both sides may be equally to blame and sheer ignorance is usually the vice of each. The mischief is easily done. There may be no actual perversion of the facts; a judicious selection may equally suffice, and this apart from any real malice. That is why the sources of information are so important and the responsibility of the purveyors of news is so great. That of those who handle and display it is, perhaps, no less. For the important may be shown as unimportant, and the unimportant as important, by devices so simple and innocent as type, head-lines, or position on the page. It is all a matter of discretion and good faith.

Not that the task is easy. What, in fact, can be more difficult than really to enter into the mind of a man of another nation, still more to grasp the conditions which go to make him what he is – his education, the atmosphere of his home, the traditions of his people. Yet it is all these things which, when the test comes, go to determine his outlook and his action. It is for the Press, so far as it may, to act as interpreter, and one of its first duties is to qualify for the task.

But, after all, men are not necessarily enemies because they are strangers to each other, though that is apt to be the assumption among primitive peoples, and nothing can be more foolish than to regard a neighbour primarily as a possible enemy. Every nation has something in race, in temperament, in history and development which marks it off from other nations and makes it rich in interest and instruction. And the further off nations may be from each other in these respects the more interesting they become and the more worth knowing. Sometimes where a very long development has taken place in complete, or almost complete isolation, a real understanding, a spiritual intimacy, becomes very difficult, or actually impossible. And this is a misfortune. It is the price we pay for the emergence of a type. And the type may be so strong that it must for ever remain apart, self-sufficient, impenetrable. Such types exist. They have their special gifts for the world. But we do not love them. They do not invite love. Such differences may cut very deep, or they may be quite subtle. What is it that divides us from our own past, from the builders, say, of the Middle Ages? What is it they had which we have lost? And why, and at what point, did we lose it? It is in art and above all in architecture that the difference tells. Perhaps it is because beauty is so subtle a thing. Yet these men were bone of our bone and flesh of our flesh as we are of theirs. Differences in time, differences in space, each of these has gone to make up that wonderful complex which we call humanity. The newspaper has at times to adjust itself to both. It must overleap all barriers. It cannot possess omniscience and need not pretend to it. But its interests should be as wide as the field that invites them, and it need not be without allies, or scorn the expert, though it may be wise to observe him carefully.

The newspaper is a vast machine. What matters is the spirit that lies behind it. The world is its province, but that is an empty boast, unless it implies a real fellowship. Europe already begins to think and speak of itself as a unity. America was born one. India, but yesterday an aggregate of disparate peoples, today is finding its soul. The world does move and every day it moves faster. The newspaper stands by to interpret, and, where it can, to help. What a spectacle! What an opportunity!

April 1931

THE ESSENTIALS OF
SOCIALIZATION

G. D. H. Cole

THERE was a time when the contrast between Socialism and private enterprise seemed plain and striking. Under private enterprise, the means of production were owned by individuals who, by reason of their recognized ownership, were able to levy toll of rent, interest and profits upon the community as a whole. Under Socialism, the means of production would be collectively owned and administered; and the toll of rent, interest and profits would cease, the entire product of labour being appropriated to the uses of the entire community. It was all beautifully simple; and in the propaganda of Socialism it was only necessary to point the contrast in order to make out a magnificent ethical case.

Of course, nothing has happened to impair the fundamental justice of the familiar picture. It remains true that, under Socialism, the means of production (or at least all that matter from the general standpoint) will be collectively owned, and that the levy of tribute by a possessing class will have ceased. But, valid though the contrast is, it does not help Socialists greatly when we are facing the day-to-day problems of a gradual transition from Capitalism to Socialism, or trying to insinuate wedges of Socialism into the prevailing Capitalist system. Some Socialists say that the difficulty arises only because we are attempting the impossible, and Capitalism and Socialism (on the instalment plan) cannot live together. Gradualist Socialism, they tell us, is impossible; it must be all or nothing. For such Socialists, the *constructive* work of Socialism can begin only after a revolution which has thoroughly and once and for all dispossessed the capitalist class. They may be right, in the sense that Socialism will never be fully achieved by gradualist means alone. Indeed, I think they are. But it does not follow that Socialists are exempt, in the present, from the need to insinuate bits of Socialism into the economic system; for he who whistles today for the English Revolution is assuredly wasting his breath. For the time being, it is the business of Socialists to get as far on towards Socialism as we can by gradualist methods.

As soon, however, as this limitation on immediate policy is accepted the difficulties begin to appear. They were not serious, when Socialists were merely agitating, without hope of immediate success. But now that we are getting used to the idea of Socialistic, if not Socialist Governments, believers in Socialism have to work out a positive policy for these Governments to apply; and almost the first problem that confronts them is the preparation of plans for the socialization of some at least of the vital industries and services of the country.

The old idea of socialization, on which most of the earlier propaganda of Collectivism in this country was based, had at least the merit of simplicity. An industry – say, railway transport – was to be acquired for the community by buying out the shareholders, who were to receive some form of compensation assessed on an equitable basis, and were thereupon to cease all connexion with the industry. The State, owning the railways, was then to provide for their future management by putting a Minister of the Crown at their head, and conducting them, as the Post Office is now conducted, under Civil Service control. There were, it is true, disputes even in those days about compensation. Some people wished to buy the shareholders out for cash, raising the necessary funds by an addition to the National Debt. Some wished to give Government debt in exchange for the shares, without any cash passing. Others preferred a system of terminable annuities, charged upon the national revenue; while yet others repudiated the principle of compensation altogether. It is curious to remember that in those days the Fabian Society was still ranged, according to its Basis, against compensation, and proposed to expropriate the shareholders subject only to 'compassionate allowances' designed to meet cases of hardship.

There was, in those earlier days of Socialist propaganda, far more talk about the basis of compensation than about the forms and methods of future management and control. This latter question, indeed, was hardly discussed at all in Great Britain until the two or three years before the war when the doctrines of Syndicalism, Industrial Unionism, and Guild Socialism were beginning to make headway. But then this problem came rapidly to the front. Syndicalists and Industrial Unionists, hostile to State action in all its forms, attacked alike State ownership and State control, urging that both ought to be vested in working-class bodies. The railwaymen or the miners were to manage their industries as trustees for the community. There was to be no State ownership, because under the new conditions there would be no such thing as ownership at all, in relation to the means of production. The Guild Socialists for their part wanted public ownership; but they agreed with the Syndicalists in repudiating State control. They wanted the management of each industry to be entrusted to a self-governing National Guild, so organized as to represent the various grades of workers by hand and brain who were necessary to its conduct. A number of Trade Unions, including the miners, the railwaymen, and the Post Office workers, worked out for themselves schemes of socialization which were clearly Guild Socialist in tendency.

I have no space in this article to describe either these schemes or the numerous projects of socialization and workers' control which have been brought forward in recent years. I must come at once to the most recent of all these schemes – Mr Herbert Morrison's Bill for the unification of London Passenger Transport. At once we find ourselves in a different world from that of pre-war nationalization with direct State management, and hardly less far away from the Guild Socialistic plans of the 'reconstruction' period after the war. We are far nearer to the conception which underlay the Conservative Electricity Act of 1926, with some admixture of ideas from the Coalition Railways Act of 1921. Indeed, it is not easy to say, on the face of the matter, whether Mr Morrison is proposing to socialize London transport or to reconstruct it, as the railways were reconstructed in 1921, under private ownership and control.

For Mr Morrison's Bill does not propose that the State should buy out the existing shareholders of the combine. Instead, a new inclusive Corporation is to be created; and the shareholders are to be given stock in this body in place of their present holdings. Power is taken to buy out the smaller privately-owned companies either for cash or for stock; and the properties of the municipal bodies concerned are to be acquired for a consideration payable, not in cash down, but either in annual instalments, or by an issue of stock. Moreover, the dividends payable by the new undertaking are not to be fixed, in the form of an annual interest charge, but are left at the discretion of the Board, subject to Treasury sanction, and are apparently to depend on profits, and to vary between five and six per cent according to the profits earned by the combined undertaking. The earning of five per cent profit is apparently to be a first charge, in the sense that fares, which will be subject to public control, will be fixed at a level designed to yield this rate; but the variable dividend is further to give the shareholders a return if the undertaking is so managed as to increase efficiency and bring down costs. These provisions recall certain sections of the Railways Act of 1921.

An anomalous provision, not included in the Bill, but apparently forming part of the agreement between the Ministry and the combine, gives the stock holders power to appoint a receiver if their five per cent dividend is not paid. It is not clear what the powers of such a receiver would be, or how the provision is justified by the Ministry.

The directorate of the new body, as the Bill now stands, is to be appointed by the Minister of Transport, without provision for the representation of any interest or group. This proposal has already raised protests from three distinct quarters. The London County Council is demanding direct representation of municipal interests; the Trade Unions are demanding representation of the workers; and certain shareholding interests are demanding continued representation of the shareholders.

Now, Mr Morrison's Bill at once raises, in decisive form, the question which this paper set out to discuss. Is the Government proposing to socialize London transport, or to hand it over to monopolistic private enterprise? Both views have been advanced with some show of reason; and it is none too easy to decide between them.

Let us, then, set out, as clearly as we can, the main questions that arise.

If we can answer these questions, we shall be in a fair way both to defining the essentials of socialization, and to deciding in what light to regard Mr Morrison's Bill.

I

Is socialization compatible with the continued existence of a body of share or stock holders, with claims to interest or dividend upon the undertaking?

In any scheme of socialization, if compensation is paid at all, some claim must be created. But this claim may be either against the assets or earnings of the undertaking, or against the State. It may seem, therefore, to make no difference which form the claim takes. It used to be urged that a claim valid against the State would be more secure than a claim against any particular undertaking, and that accordingly the State could acquire an industry more cheaply by issuing Government debt than by any other method. But there are now objections to direct State borrowing because of the great increase in the size of the National Debt and the necessity for frequent conversion operations, which have depressed State credit. The State is therefore reluctant to borrow in order to pay compensation in cash; and it is urged that this can be avoided if share and bond holders in any undertaking that is taken over are allowed to retain their shares or bonds, or issued new shares or bonds in exchange. The continuance of private shareholding seems, however, to imply the continuance of private ownership, and is objected to by Socialists on that ground. This objection applies less to redeemable bonds than to perpetual shares; for it is possible to urge that the bonds should be gradually paid off, until the entire undertaking is publicly owned. Moreover, the continuance of shareholding would be more likely to lead to a demand that the holders should share in control than a continuance of bonds. I conclude, then, provisionally, that private shareholding is not compatible with socialization.

II

Does it make any difference whether such a claim, if it exists, takes the form of a claim to a fixed rate of interest or to a variable dividend?

Socialists used to argue in favour of fixed interest rates, in order that the public might get the advantage of the State's superior borrowing power and appropriate all profit above a low fixed rate of interest. But, of late years, the danger to industry of increasing fixed interest charges, which form part of the cost of production, has become more and more evident. This does not matter greatly where an industry or service is of such a sort as to be able to rely on earning a regular profit irrespective of trade fluctuations, though even in such a case, if the general level of prices falls, the effect may be to make an unnecessary present to the *rentiers* (and vice versa if prices rise). But it matters far more in any industry which is liable to fluctuating trade conditions, or open to outside competition. Thus, it may not matter much in the case of a London traffic monopoly; but it would matter greatly in the case of railways, or coal, or steel. There is, accordingly, a prima facie case for making the return to the providers of the capital required, even for a socialized undertaking, vary with the fluctuations in its earning capacity. But this, it may be said, involves giving the providers of capital the status of shareholders rather than bondholders; for herein lies the essential difference between the two. This is true, according to capitalist ideas; but there is no reason why we should accept these ideas. The State could give to the private providers of capital bonds secured, cumulatively or not, solely against the net earnings of the undertaking – i.e. a sort of income debenture without power of foreclosure, analogous in some respects to existing types of income debentures and in others to preference shares, but without even nominal rights of ownership. This is virtually the position of preference shareholders in many private undertakings today.

I conclude, provisionally, that the form of compensation should be an exchange of existing shares for income bonds secured only against the net earnings of the socialized undertaking, and bearing a limited, but not a fixed, rate of dividend rather than a fixed rate of interest.

III

Does it make any difference whether the claim, fixed or not in amount, is valid only against the net earnings of the undertaking, or is guaranteed in whole or in part by the State?

If the return on capital is to be made only out of the net earnings of the undertaking, it is to be presumed that the commission managing the industry will be instructed so to conduct it as to secure a reasonable dividend, and that any powers of price-control exercised by the State will be employed with this idea in mind, as under the Railways Act of 1921, the various Electricity Acts as applying to private undertakings, the Gas Acts, and so on. In other words, the socialized undertaking will be allowed and instructed to charge prices sufficient to pay what is regarded as a reasonable return on capital, provided that the trade will bear such prices. Such a method would preclude running the socialized service at a loss, or at less than the 'reasonable return', except with the aid of a direct State subsidy, as long as a profit could be made by raising prices. But it would exempt the State from guaranteeing dividends or interest on capital embarked in an undertaking which could not earn a reasonable return even by raising its prices. In other words, it would leave the owners of the capital to bear losses due to a real depreciation in the earning value of the undertaking. It would also avoid burdening either the State or the undertaking with heavy fixed charges. It will be objected that it would leave the providers of the capital to risk their money without having any control over its use. But this is already their position in large joint-stock undertakings; and they would have, even from the capitalist point of view, no real grievance if the price-fixing authority were definitely instructed to permit prices sufficient to yield a reasonable return, as long as this could be done.

My conclusion is that, ordinarily, claims should be valid only against the net earnings of the undertaking, but that this should not preclude the State, in order to encourage new investment, from guaranteeing a fixed or minimum return upon such investment for a limited period of years. This has, of course, been done in certain cases, e.g. for the London Tube Railways under the Trade Facilities Act. It is a matter for discussion whether the claims should be cumulative or not. I am inclined to think that they should not.

IV

If share or stockholders continue to exist, is it consistent with socialization to give them any share in the control of the undertaking, or any representation on the directorate?

This question has already been answered inferentially under section I. The answer is 'No'.

V

Is it consistent with socialization that the directors should be appointed for a period of years, and be irremovable during that period, or ought the State, or other appointing body, to have a continuous right to recall?

It is assumed that, in any case, directors will be removable for misconduct. The question is whether they are, or are not, to be removable on grounds of policy. This raises several difficult questions. It is bound up, in the first place, with the question of political control. How far are the directing bodies of socialized undertakings to be autonomous, or under Government control? I hold strongly that they must be ultimately under the orders of the Government in matters of policy, however little it may be desirable for the Government to interfere with their day-to-day management of the undertaking. This is best secured by giving them a large measure of autonomy, but leaving them removable at any time at the Government's pleasure. This is proposed in the London Passenger Transport Bill, whereas the Central Electricity Board's members are irremovable during their period of office.

But another question is also involved. If, and in as far as, members of the directing body are nominees of groups or interests other than the State, how far are they to be removable by these groups or interests? Representation is apt to become unreal if the representative becomes a full-time salaried servant of the State, and is not subject to recall by those whom he is supposed to represent, save at the end of a period of years. One remedy would be to make the period of appointment of such members short; but this might mean that they would carry less weight, and be less effective, than State

77

nominees serving for longer periods. Power of a represented body to recall its representative at any moment would be liable to abuse. I am inclined to suggest that (*a*) State representatives should be appointed for three years, subject to recall at any time, (*b*) representatives of outside bodies should be appointed by the State on the nomination of such bodies for three years, subject to recall at any time by the State, but not by the nominating body. This rule might, of course, be varied in particular cases. I am only laying it down as a broad generalization.

VI

Ought consumers to be represented on the directing body? Or ought Local Authorities to be represented on any other ground than as representing the consumers?

The case for consumers' representation is that the policy of socialized undertakings deeply affects their interests. It is, however, doubtful if direct representation of consumers on the *managing* body is the right way of protecting these interests. There is far more to be said for providing (as in the Labour schemes of 1919 and 1925 for the coal industry) something in the nature of a Consumers' Advisory Council, on which various interests can be represented, and for giving this body, subject to the final decision of the Government, a power to object to the policy of the managing body. The London Traffic Advisory Committee has powers of this order conferred upon it in the London Passenger Transport Bill. Clearly, consumers' interests ought to be represented in some form. We can best, however, return to this question at a later stage.

In the case of localized undertakings, there is evidently a case for the representation in some form of the local authority or authorities concerned. In as far as the local authority claims to represent the consumers, what has just been said applies to its claim. But the situation may appear different where an undertaking previously conducted by a local authority is being taken over by a Statutory Board or Commission (as in the case of the L.C.C. trams). In such a case, the local authority is really in the same position as the body of shareholders in a private undertaking that is socialized; and I do not see why it should be represented on that ground. There may, however, be a special case for representation of the local authority on the Statutory Board where, as in the instance of a Local Port Commission or Authority, there is need for close collaboration in the conduct of related services by the two bodies.

I conclude, then, that in general consumers should be represented, not on the managing Board, but in some other way, and that the question of local authority representation must be settled, not on general principles, but in each particular case.

VII

Ought the workers engaged in the undertaking to be represented, as a matter of principle, on the directing body, or given any statutory share in its control? If so, what form should their representation take?

I do not propose to argue over again the case for workers' control, in the sense of participation by workers' representatives in the control of socialized industry. I propose to assume that such control ought to exist, and to discuss what form it ought to take. If, as I think, the Board or Commission actually managing an industry must be kept small, if it is to work efficiently, and must consist largely of persons chosen on account of their technical qualifications and managerial abilities, it follows that there can be no room for any considerable number of persons chosen by, or as representing, the workers engaged in the industry. There may be room for one or two, but not more. Moreover, the managing body must be full-time; and it is doubtful how far a man chosen originally as representing the workers can continue to represent them if he becomes a salaried servant of the State or the enterprise, and is not subject to recall at any time by those whom he is supposed to represent. I conclude, therefore, that real representation of the workers on the managing body is impracticable in any full sense. This should not prevent Labour men from being appointed to the managing body when they have the right qualities; but men so appointed should not be regarded as satisfying the working-class demand for representation, which must be provided for in some other way.

I think the solution lies in the German system of the so-called 'double directorate'. The German Joint Stock Company has two executive organs: a *Vorstand*, or Managing Board, and an *Aufsichtrat* (or Council of Control). The former consists usually of full-time managing directors, and the latter of part-time representatives of interests and groups concerned in the conduct of the undertaking. I should favour the adoption of this form of organization for socialized enterprises in this country. There should be, first, a Board or Commission, consisting of full-time officers, and chosen on grounds of technical or managerial competence, and not as representatives of any interest, and, secondly, a part-time Council of Control, composed mainly of representatives of the groups concerned. On this Council, the workers should have a substantial representation, and there should also sit on it representatives of related industries and services with which close coordination is desirable, of local authorities, when they are closely concerned, and of consumers, while at least one member should have the specific function of representing the Government as the holder of a watching brief. There should, of course, be no representation of shareholders. The Council, I think, should meet often enough to exert a real influence on policy, and the report of the Managing Board should require its approval. There should, however, be a limited right for the Managing Board to appeal to the responsible Minister in case of differences between it and the Council over certain defined questions. There should be, further, in many industries, Regional Councils, related to the regional management; but it is doubtful if these ought, in most cases, to have more than advisory functions. The precise structure necessary can evidently be settled only in relation to each particular industry or service. A structure appropriate to railways might be largely unsuitable for building or coal-mining.

Workers' and other representatives on the Council could be either appointed for quite short periods or be subject to recall at any time. They would receive not a full-time salary, but only fees for work done, and would thus be able to preserve their really representative position. Workers' representatives should, I think, be chosen by the Trade Unions chiefly concerned in the industry.

The Essentials of Socialization

This section is not intended to be a complete treatment of the question of workers' control. It does not touch at all on control locally, or in each particular works or workshop. It relates only to the form of the controlling agencies for the socialized industry as a whole, and should be read strictly in this light.

VIII

Should the State reserve to itself the right to appoint some or all of the directing body, and, if so, what principles should it follow in making its appointments?

This question has largely been answered already. I think all appointments either to the Managing Board or to the Council of Control should be made by the State. But in the former case the State would appoint absolutely, subject only to such consultation with outside interests as it might deem desirable, whereas in the latter it would be appointing largely on the basis of nominations made by other bodies (as it does now in the case of workers' and employers' representatives on the I.L.O., and in many other instances). In the case of the Managing Board, the chief consideration should be to get the best possible technical and managerial ability combined with real belief in socialization. It is obviously wrong to appoint a Board that disbelieves in its job, however good its technical and managerial qualifications may otherwise be. Stress should be laid on the needs for appointing a reasonable proportion of men with first-class technical knowledge, and for having some members with special ability and sympathy in the handling of personnel.

In the case of the Council of Control, the State should accept the nominations of the bodies entitled to representation, while reserving the right to dismiss a representative, and call for a fresh nomination. In certain cases, when there is no one body plainly entitled to nominate, and the bodies concerned cannot agree, the State may have to choose between the nominations sent in; and in certain other cases an unorganized interest may have to be represented by direct State appointment. But as far as possible, nominating bodies should be chosen, and left free to

81

make nominations which the State would accept without question.

I am disposed to prefer appointments for a specified period to appointments for life or for an indefinite tenure, subject to the provisions for recall outlined in an earlier section.

IX

How, and in what forms, should new capital be raised for the development of the industry or undertaking?

There appear to be three possibilities. (1) direct provision by the State, or by some special body, such as a National Investment Board, acting as an organ of the State; (2) raising of capital by the industry or undertaking itself, backed by a State guarantee; (3) raising of capital by the industry or undertaking itself without State guarantee. There appears to be no sufficient reason for ruling out any of these methods. Their relative advantages depend on the circumstances of each case. Thus, method (3) would probably be unworkable in the case of depressed industries, or whenever there was not enough confidence on the part of the investing public to get the capital taken up. Moreover, it would become increasingly difficult if, as seems probable, the supply of funds available for investment in the hands of the public were to fall off. It has already been suggested that, where method (2) is employed, the State guarantee of dividends should be given only for a limited number of years. On the whole, method (1) seems likely to become of increasing importance in the course of the transition to Socialism. I do not, however, propose to discuss here how a National Investment Board would work. That is a subject large enough for separate treatment.

The above conclusions relate only to cases in which capital has to be raised from outside the industry. It is anticipated that normal capital developments will in the main be financed out of reserves accumulated by socialized undertakings out of surplus incomes, just as many joint stock concerns are accustomed to finance normal developments out of reserves. It is therefore suggested that socialized undertakings should be free to build up reasonable reserve funds, and that their surpluses should not be automatically appropriated by the Exchequer. This, of course, would not preclude the taxation of such surpluses, either at the standard rate of income tax, or at any other rate that might be fixed, or the lending of surpluses in the hands of one socialized undertaking to another, with the consent of the State (e.g., through the National Investment Board).

This method of financing development out of reserves seems to me an integral part of any real system of socialization, in which presumably the final aim is the complete elimination of the private investor from the sphere of socialized industries and services.

x

Should the undertaking aim at rendering service at cost price, or at making a profit (over and above capital charges)? If the latter, how should the profit be disposed of?

The chief reason why Socialists have usually been opposed to socialized services being run at a profit is (*a*) that this tends to depress wages and salaries in the service and (*b*) that, incomes being unequal and socialized services usually catering largely for poor people, the profit will be made largely at poor people's expense. Both these contentions are true; but neither would apply under a system based on economic equality. As we approach such a system, by far the easiest way of financing capital development will be for State services to be run at a profit, and for surplus funds to be used as capital in the ways described in the previous section. In other words, the community will distribute on wages and salaries only the amounts it means people to be free to spend, and not also the sums it wants them to invest; and funds for investment will be provided directly out of the product of industry before incomes are distributed to individuals. It is even worth while to make an approach to this system in the case of any industry which we may now decide to socialize. A reasonable wage should of course be fixed for the employees; and no surplus should be deemed to exist until the wage-charge has been fully met. But over and above this there is no reason why sums should go to the employees. The claim of the consumer to reduced charges is strong, in the case of consumers' services, while great inequalities of income continue to exist; but this is not a valid argument in the case of industries producing producers' goods, or selling services, or producing luxuries. On the whole, there is a strong case for extending the sphere within which socialized undertakings are to be allowed to charge enough to have a surplus.

The question of the disposal of this surplus has been answered in the previous section. Any surplus should go (*a*) to building up reasonable reserves in order to finance developments, or (*b*) in loans to other socialized undertakings – subject in both cases to such taxation as the State may decide to exact. The point is that surpluses should normally be retained by the socialized industry, and should not pass automatically to the Exchequer.

We have now attempted to answer all the questions raised at an earlier stage. How far have we succeeded, in the process, in defining the essentials of socialization? We have suggested that it is not compatible with the continuance of private shareholding, at least in any form which will give the shareholder any sort of control over the socialized undertaking. But we have urged that this does not preclude the existence of stock bearing not a fixed, but a variable, dividend, as long as this dividend is subject to a maximum, and is secured only against the earnings of the undertaking.

In relation to the form of control, it has been suggested that the difficulties can best be met by the creation of two distinct bodies – a full-time Managing Board or Commission on a non-representative basis, composed mainly of technical and managerial experts; and a part-time Council of Control, consisting of representatives from interested groups and parties, and including a strong representation of the workers engaged in the service.

Further, it has been urged that these directing bodies must be appointed by, and subject to recall by, the State, and must not be accorded power which will make them independent of the Government in matters of policy. This last point, however, is so important as to deserve some further argument.

Socialists presumably stand for a coordinated control of the economic life of the nation in the interests of all. This involves that the various industries and services must be subject, in matters of high policy as distinct from day-to-day management, to a common authority. This authority may be either the State itself, or a supreme economic organ created by the State (e.g., a representative National Economic Council or Economic Parliament). But it is simply inconsistent with socialization to set up a directing body for a single industry or service, and to make that body independent both of other industries and services and of the Central Government of the country. Unless and until a separate Economic Parliament or Council is created, each socialized service must be managed and directed by a body subject to Parliament and the Government, however wide its autonomy in day-to-day matters of management may be made. This, it has been suggested, can best be done by making all members of such bodies subject to recall at any time by the Minister responsible for them to Parliament.

This, however, is no reason why the directing bodies should not be given very wide autonomous powers, provided that their members are subject to recall, and that disputes on matters of principle between the Managing Board and the Council of Control can be referred to the Minister for decision. Indeed, it is obviously expedient, subject to the power of removal, to leave the directing bodies the fullest freedom in the execution of policy, while reserving to the Government the power to initiate or approve the policy itself. It would not be difficult in most cases to draw the line between matters which the directing bodies might do on their own responsibility, and matters requiring the Minister's sanction. Broadly, the distinction is that between laying down a policy, and taking the expert measures needed to give effect to it.

This paper has been written in the belief that we ought to be as precise as possible in trying to clear our minds about the essentials of socialization, and in drawing a line between the types of scheme we are prepared to accept as measures of socialization and those we are not. According to the principles here laid down, the creation of the Central Electricity Board was, I think, an act of socialization, though by no means firm in all its features. The creation of the Imperial Cables and Communications Company was definitely not an act of socialization. On Mr Morrison's London Passenger

Transport Bill final judgement must be deferred until it has emerged from the ordeal of a Joint Committee of both Houses of Parliament, with a clear Conservative majority.

July 1931

THE DILEMMA
OF MODERN SOCIALISM

J. M. Keynes

BESIDES two arms and two legs for oratory, gesticulation and movement, socialism has two heads and two hearts which are always at war with one another. The one is ardent to do things because they are economically sound. The other is no less ardent to do things which are admitted to be economically unsound. I mean by economically sound, improvements in organization and so forth which are desired because they will increase the production of wealth; and by economically unsound things which will, or may, have the opposite effect.

And there is a further distinction to make. Things which are economically unsound are advocated for two widely different sorts of reasons. The first set are in pursuance of the ideal. Those who are influenced by them are ready to sacrifice economic wealth for the attainment of higher goods – justice, equality, beauty, or the greater glory of the republic. The second set are political – to get up steam, to bribe political supporters, to stir up the embers of the class war, to irritate and exasperate the powers that be and to make their task more difficult and perhaps impossible, so that the mere force of events may compel their deposition and replacement. Thus some things may be advocated *in spite of* their being economically unsound, and other things may be advocated *because of* their being economically unsound.

These three motifs exist, variously compounded, in the breast of every socialist. They are seen magnified, and therefore clearer, in the *politik* of the Bolshevists, the changes and vacillations in which are due to the fluctuating preponderance of one or the other motif. The Marxian creed, I take it, is that the third motif, the revolutionary, should preponderate in the first phase, the phase of attaining power; that the first, the practical, should preponderate in the second phase, when power has been used to prepare the way; and that the second, the ideal, should preponderate when the socialist republic emerges out of the blood and dust and travail, fully fledged. The Revolution, the Five-Year Plan, the Ideal – that is the progression. But the distinction between the phases is not clear cut – all three motifs are present in some degree all the time. For English purposes one might perhaps sum the motifs up as the political, the practical and the ideal.

Now it is, I suggest, enormously important to know what one is doing, in what phase one is dwelling and in what proportions the motifs are mixed.

For my part I should like to define the socialist programme as aiming at political power, with a view to doing in the first instance what is economically sound, in order that, later on, the community may become rich enough to *afford* what is economically unsound.

My goal is the ideal; my object is to put economic considerations into a back seat; but my method at this moment of economic and social evolution would be to advance towards the goal by concentrating on doing what is economically sound. But there are others, I know, who would prefer, even today, to advocate what is economically unsound, because they believe that this is the best way to gain political power (which in any case is the first step), and that to render the existing system unworkable is the only means of reaching a new system. In my judgement both these notions are false; because the ruin of the old system, so far from making the construction of the new technically easier, may, on the contrary, make it impossible. For it will have to be on the basis of increased resources, not on the basis of poverty, that the grand experiment of the ideal republic will have to be made. I do not overlook the difficulty of getting up steam when things are going reasonably well. But I consider that precisely *that* is the problem to be solved. To be sufficiently deep-founded on the best intelligences and finest and strongest emotions of the community, to be able to keep up steam when things are going reasonably well; to thrive, not on the vapours of misery and discontent, but on the living energy of the passion for right construction and the right building up of a worthy society – that is the task.

This leads me to the daily perplexity of British socialism, and perhaps of socialism everywhere, as I see it. The practical problem, the problem of how to do what is economically sound, is mainly an intellectual problem and, as it happens, a very difficult intellectual problem, about which there is much disagreement. But intellectually a large element, probably the predominant element, of the Labour Party is old fashioned and even anti-intellectual. It has been the trouble for years past that the leaders of the Labour Party have differed from the leaders of the other parties chiefly in being more willing to do or to risk things which in their hearts they have believed to be economically unsound. They have not fundamentally disagreed with the other parties as to *what* is economically sound or unsound. Mr Thomas's ideas, for example, of what is economically sound are, and always have been, almost exactly the same as those of the Tory Nationalists, Mr Neville Chamberlain or Mr Amery; and Viscount Snowden's ideas have been just the same as those of liberal economists and deflationists such as Mr Runciman or Sir Herbert Samuel or Lord Grey. They have been totally out of sympathy with those who have had new notions of what is economically sound, whether the innovator has been right or wrong. And this condition of affairs goes deep into the bowels of the Labour Party. For the same is true, on the whole, of many others of the party's most respected pillars.

Now this puts the Labour Party into a feeble position when – as it happened last summer as a result of the deflation – the country has got into such a pickle that there is an overwhelming and universal demand for a practical solution, when everyone is determined that, for the time being at least, we must ensure what is economically sound. For it means that in such a conjuncture most of the Labour Leaders agree at heart with their opponents; so that having a bad conscience, they become exceedingly ineffective for the practical purposes of government. The Labour Cabinet was in a hopeless position last August, because most of them conscientiously believed in the Gold Standard and in deflation by economy, and were not prepared to throw these things overboard. Yet at the same time they were equally unprepared to sacrifice the political and the ideal motifs in which they had been brought up.

Therefore the first task of the Labour Party, if it is to be effective is, as I see it, to become intellectually emancipated as to what is economically sound, without losing either its political strength and its political organization, which goes so deep into the social and economic life of England, or its ideals and ultimate goals. For in the modern world it has to be one thing or the other. Either the revolutionary motif must prevail or the practical motif. Nothing lands you in a sillier position or one which will draw down more certainly or more justly the contempt of the British people than not to know, when you propose something, whether the object of proposing it is because it is economically sound or because it is economically unsound. No one knew at the last election which leg the Labour Party was standing on, least of all the party itself.

For my own part I would argue that we stand at a point in economic evolution when it is desirable to concentrate on what is economically sound. There are two good and sufficient reasons for this. In the first place it happens that the most pressing reforms which are economically sound do not, as perhaps they did in earlier days, point away from the ideal. On the contrary they point towards it. I am convinced that those things which are urgently called for on practical grounds, such as the central control of investment and the distribution of income in such a way as to provide purchasing power for the enormous potential output of modern productive technique, will also tend to produce a better kind of society on ideal grounds. There is probably less opposition today between the practical aim and the ideal than there has been hitherto.

In the second place there is so much to be hoped today from doing what is economically sound, that it is our duty to give this motif its opportunity. For it may be capable of solving once for all the problem of poverty. At present the world is being held back by something which would have surprised our fathers – by a failure of economic technique to exploit the possibilities of engineering and distributive technique; or, rather, engineering technique has reached a degree of perfection which is making obvious defects in economic technique which have always existed, though unnoticed, and have doubtless impoverished mankind since the days of Abraham. I mean by economic technique the means of solving the problem of the *general* organization of resources as distinct from the *particular* problems of production and distribution which are the province of the individual business technician and engineer. For the next twenty-five years in my belief, economists, at present the most incompetent, will be nevertheless the most important, group of scientists in the world. And it is to be hoped – if they are successful – that after that they will never be important again. But during this horrid interval, when these creatures matter, it is of vast importance that they should be free to pursue their problem in an environment – for they, with their mixed subject-matter, are, of all men, the least independent, as the history of their theory shows, of the surrounding atmosphere – uninfluenced, as far as possible, by the bias of the other motifs.

All this has been brought to a head, or at least brought to notice, by the radical changes in modern technique, especially in the last ten years, which are so brilliantly described in Mr Fred Henderson's 'Economic Consequences of Power Production'. Immemorially man's muscles have been, for the vast majority of purposes and operations, the source of power, sometimes aided by wind, water and domestic beasts. *Labour*, in the literal sense, has been the prime factor of production. It made a vast difference when, for transport and for certain limited operations, other sources of power were added. But even the addition of steam and electricity and petrol have not made, in themselves, so radical a change, as has the character of the new processes of production which have, in latter years, grown up with them. For until these latter years, the chief effort of new machines was to render *labour*, i.e. man's muscles, more efficient. Economists could plausibly argue that machinery was cooperative, not competitive with labour. But the effect of the latest types of machinery is increasingly, not to make man's muscles more efficient, but to render them *obsolete*. And the effect is twofold, first to furnish us with the ability to produce consumption goods, as distinct from services, almost without limit; and secondly to use so little labour in the process that an ever-increasing proportion of human employment must be occupied either in the field of supplying human services or in meeting the demand for durable goods which, if the rate of interest were low enough, would be still far from satisfied.

Thus the apparatus of economic organization is faced with a problem of readjustment of unusual difficulty in itself. If it is true that this apparatus has always been misunderstood and badly operated, if the supposed inner harmony and self-balancing characters of the economic system, in reliance on which our fathers were ready to surrender the system to *laissez-faire*, are an illusion, it is a natural result that events should be finding out where our intellectual weakness lies. Our prime task, therefore, is to discover, and then to do, what is economically sound. This temporary concentration on the practical is the best contribution which we of today can make towards the attainment of the ideal.

April 1932

THE CHOICE BEFORE THE LABOUR PARTY

R. H. Tawney

I

Now that the dust has settled, it is possible to examine the landscape left by the earthquake. The election of 1931 was, by general consent, a considerable sensation. But neither the preliminary manoeuvres described by Lord Passfield, nor the methods adopted during the contest itself, are the phenomena on which today it is most profitable for a member of the Labour Party to reflect. Political coroners may sit on the corpse of the late Cabinet, but the ordinary citizen is more concerned with its behaviour before life was extinct. What matters to him, and what is likely to determine his attitude when next the Labour Party appeals for his support, is less the question of the circumstances in which the last Government went out, than that of what it did, attempted, and neither did nor attempted to do, when it was in. It is possible that his verdict on its death, if at this time of day he paused to consider it, would be, neither murder nor misadventure, but pernicious anaemia producing general futility.

For the events of the late summer of 1931 were the occasion, rather than the cause, of the débâcle of the Labour Party. In spite of the dramatic episodes which heralded its collapse, the Government did not fall with a crash, in a tornado from the blue. It crawled slowly to its doom, deflated by inches, partly by its opponents, partly by circumstances beyond its control, but partly also by itself. The gunpowder was running out of it from the moment it assumed office, and was discovered, on inspection, to be surprisingly like sawdust. Due allowance must be made, no doubt, for the cruel chance which condemned it to face the worst collapse in prices of modern history; and due credit must be given for the measures which it introduced, but failed, through no fault of its own, to pass into law. But, granted the inexorable limits, can it seriously be argued that it was audacious in working up to them?

The commonest answer to that question was given in two words: Minority Government. To the writer it appeared at the time, and appears today, unconvincing. When the Cabinet took office, two alternatives were open to it. It could decide to live dangerously, or to play for safety. It could choose a short life, and – if the expression be not too harsh – an honest one; or it could proceed on the assumption that, once a Labour Government is in office, its primary duty is to find means of remaining there. If it acted on its principles, it could not hope to survive for more than twelve months. It could postpone its execution, but only at the cost of making its opponents the censors of its policy. It would invite them, in effect, to decide the character of the measures which it should be permitted to introduce, and to determine the issues of the next election.

The late Government chose the second course. It chose it, it must in fairness be admitted, with the tacit approval of the great majority of the party, including, as far as is known, those trade union elements in it which afterwards revolted against the results of the decision. The effects of its choice were, however, serious. Parts in life, once adopted, develop their consequences with a logic of their own, overriding the volition of the actors cast for them; however repulsive, if played at all, they must be played with gusto. Once convinced that discretion was their cue, ministers brought to the practice of the golden mean a conscientious assiduity almost painful to contemplate. They threw themselves into the role of The Obsequious Apprentice, or Prudence Rewarded, as though bent on proving that, so far from being different from other governments, His Majesty's Labour Government could rival the most respectable of them in cautious conventionality.

Industrial and social reconstruction, the favourite theme of Labour orators, owed little to the existence of a Labour Cabinet. It doubtless felt itself precluded, till the Macmillan Committee had reported, from making up its mind on the questions of currency and credit which were to prove its undoing. Even in matters, however, where delay was not imposed by circumstances, its action did not err on the side of trenchancy. It found coal, cotton and steel with one foot in the nineteenth century; it left them there. What passed in its inner councils is, of course, unknown; but it gave few outward symptoms of realizing that, if the modernization of the major industries is to be handled at all, it must be planned as a whole, or of grasping the necessity of creating a permanent organ to press it steadily forward, or of appreciating the importance of devoting attention to the long-range aspects of unemployment, as distinct from monthly fluctuations in the number of unemployed. It had even to be stimulated by the protests of its followers in the House into proceeding – too late – with its little Education Bill. In one sphere, indeed, that of international policy, it achieved, in the opinion of good judges, solid and genuine successes. Apart from that important exception, and from the fact that, if King Log was bad, King Stork would be worse, what strong reason could be advanced for desiring its survival?

The degeneration of socialist parties on assuming office is now an old story. If it is worth while to recall the latest British version of it, it is not in order to visit on individuals collective shortcomings. It is because, till its lessons are learned, the wretched business will go on. If the laments of some ex-ministers at the 'conspiracy', which 'stabbed them in the back' – as though a Titan, all energy and ardour, had been felled at his forge by the hand of assassins – were merely undignified, they would properly be ignored. Unfortunately, they are worse. What Labour most needs is not self-commiseration, but a little cold realism. These plaintive romancers would dry its tears with a tale of Red Riding Hood and the wicked wolf. They retard the recovery of the party by concealing its malady. They perpetuate the mentality which requires to be overcome before recovery can take place. The sole cure for its disease is sincerity. They offer it scapegoats.

If it is sincere, it will not be drugged by these opiates. It will not soothe the pain of defeat with the flattering illusion that it is the innocent victim of faults not its own. It is nothing of the kind. It is the author, the unintending and pitiable author, of its own misfortunes. It made a government in its own image; and the collapse of that government was the result neither of accident – though that played its part – nor of unfavourable circumstances – though luck was against it – nor, least of all, it must be repeated, of merely personal failings. It was in the logic of history; for 1929–31 repeated 1924. It sprang from within, not without; for it had begun within six months of the Government's return, and the flight from principles was both earlier and more precipitate than the flight from the pound. It was the consequence, not of individual defects, but of a general habit of mind and outlook on affairs which ministers had acquired long before they could anticipate that power would be their lot. What was tried, and found wanting, in short, in 1929–31, was, not merely two years of a Labour Cabinet, but a decade of Labour politics.

Such, and not merely the events of a few weeks last summer, were the cause of the débâcle. If these are the realities, to make the conduct of individuals, however odious in itself, the main target of criticism is to exaggerate their importance. To expel a person is not to exorcize a spirit. The truth is simpler and more serious. In the swift growth of the movement since 1918, its inner flaws had been concealed. But they had not disappeared; indeed, some of them had deepened. At the moment when the reality of power seemed almost within its grasp, its old faults found it out. It now has an interval in which to meditate on its errors.

II

The gravest weakness of British Labour is one which it shares with the greater part of the world, outside Russia, including British capitalists. It is its lack of a creed. The Labour Party is hesitant in action, because divided in mind. It does not achieve what it could, because it does not know what it wants. It frets out of office and fumbles in it, because it lacks the assurance either to wait or to strike. Being without clear convictions as to its own meaning and purpose, it is deprived of the dynamic which only convictions supply. If it neither acts with decision nor inspires others so to act, the principal reason is that it is itself undecided.

This weakness is fundamental. If it continues uncorrected, there neither is, nor ought to be, a future for the Labour Party. A political creed, it need hardly be said, is neither a system of transcendental doctrine nor a code of rigid formulae. It is a common conception of the ends of political action, and of the means of achieving them, based on a common view of the life proper to human beings, and of the steps required at any moment more nearly to attain it. A movement, like an individual, cannot build its existence round an internal vacuum. Till the void in the mind of the Labour Party is filled – till interests are hammered by principles into a serviceable tool, which is what interests should be, and a steady will for a new social order takes the place of mild yearnings to make somewhat more comfortable terms with the social order of today – mere repairs to the engines will produce little but disillusionment.

There is much criticism at the moment of organization and programmes. Some of it, like that which ascribes the troubles of the party to its trade union connexions, is misconceived. It is obvious that the unions, like other elements in English society, including the intelligentsia, are most imperfectly socialized. It is obvious that the weight which is given them at party conferences by the card vote is an anomaly, which has a historical justification, but is not permanently defensible. The picture, however, of torpid and rapacious trade unionists impeding bold schemes of constructive statesmanship is a caricature; it cannot truly be said that the late Government was harassed by recurrent pressure to sacrifice the larger aims of the movement to the sectional interests of one element in it. Some of the criticism, again, like the recoil of some members of the party from the social services – as though to recognize unemployment pay for the sorry makeshift it is involved repudiating the communism of Public Health, Housing and Education – is a mood of reaction, engendered by defeat, which in time will pass. But much of it is justified. The only comment to be made on it is that it does not go far enough.

Of course the programme of the party needs to be modernized; of course its organization requires to be overhauled. No one who knows how the former is made and the latter works is likely to remain long on his knees before either. But, granted the obvious weaknesses of both – granted the intellectual timidity, conservatism, conventionality, which keeps policy trailing tardily in the rear of

D

realities, and over which, if one's taste is for brilliance on the cheap, it is so easy to make merry – the root of the matter is elsewhere. These defects are the symptoms, not the source, of the trouble. They are, not causes, but effects.

The characteristic vice of the programmes of the party, as set out in conference resolutions, is that too often they are not programmes. They sweep together great things and small; nationalize land, mines and banking in one sentence, and abolish fox-hunting in the next; and, by touching on everything, commit ministers to nothing. The characteristic defect of its practical procedure is its tendency to rely for success on the mass support of societies, and the mass vote of constituencies, of whom neither have been genuinely converted to its principles. It requires an army. It collects a mob. The mob disperses. That is the nature of mobs.

But why are Labour programmes less programmes than miscellanies – a glittering forest of Christmas trees, with presents for everyone, instead of a plan of campaign for what must be, on any showing, a pretty desperate business? Because the party is at present without any ordered conception of its task. Because it possesses in its own mind nothing analogous to what used to be called, in the days when it was necessary to put jobs through to time, a Scheme of Priorities. Because it has no stable standard of political values, such as would teach it to discriminate between the relative urgencies of different objectives. Because, lacking such a standard, it lacks also the ability to subordinate the claims of this section of the movement or that to the progress of the whole, and to throw its whole weight against the central positions, where success means something, and failure itself is not wholly a disaster, instead of frittering away its *moral* in inconclusive skirmishes.

And why is the Labour Party's organization, in spite of its admirable *personnel*, stronger in numbers than in quality? For precisely the same reason. Because the finest individuals are nothing till mastered by a cause. Because the party, being itself not too certain what that cause is, has found it difficult to present it in a form convincing to plain men, of whom the majority, in England as elsewhere, are not politicians. Because, instead of stating its faith, undiluted and unqualified, and waiting for their support till, with the teaching of experience, which today teaches pretty fast, they come to share it, it tried to buy their votes with promises, whether they shared that faith or not. Because it appealed to them, on the ground, not that a Labour Government would be different from other governments, but that it would be a worthy successor to all British governments that had ever been. Because, when it ought to have called them to a long and arduous struggle, it too often did the opposite. It courted them with hopes of cheaply won benefits, and, if it did not despise them, sometimes addressed them as though it did. It demanded too little, and offered too much. It assured them that its aim was the supersession of capitalism, but that, in the meantime, the two-hooped pot should have four hoops. Is it surprising if they concluded that, since capitalism was the order of the day, it had better continue to be administered by capitalists, who, at any rate – so, poor innocents, they supposed – knew how to make the thing work?

These, it will be replied, are hard sayings. They are; but, unfortunately, they are true. The inner state of the movement has been concealed from itself by the glamour of a word. That word is Socialism. In 1918 the Labour Party finally declared itself to be a Socialist Party. It supposed, and supposes, that it thereby became one. It is mistaken. It recorded a wish, that is all; the wish has not been fulfilled. If it now disciplines itself for a decade, it may become a Socialist Party. It is not one at present. Until it recognizes that it is not Socialist, it is not likely to become Socialist.

Like any other creed, socialism has two aspects. It implies a personal attitude and a collective effort. The quality of the latter depends on the sincerity of the former. The collective effort involves three essentials: agreement as to the kind of society which it is desired to establish; agreement as to the nature of the resistance to be overcome in establishing it; agreement as to the technique, the methods and machinery, required for its establishment. The history of British socialism, during the present century, is largely the story of the concentration of attention on the third requirement, to the neglect of the two first.

The effort devoted to questions of method has, in itself, been admirable. But expedients require, in order that they may be applied, and produce, when applied, the results intended, a situation in which their application, their continuous application on a large scale, is possible. Such a situation can exist only if socialists come to power, not as diffident agents of policies not their own, but as socialists, and, having done so, are prepared to deal with the opposition which they will encounter. They must have created behind them, before they assume office, a strong body of opinion, which 'knows what it fights for, and loves what it knows'. They must have measured coolly the forces which will be mobilized against them. The Labour Party has done neither.

The reasons are partly historical. The British Labour movement was offered in its youth a foreign, and peculiarly arid, version of Marxian socialism. It very sensibly rejected it – very sensibly, not because the doctrine was Marxism, but because, in its pedantry and lack of historical realism, it was anything but Marxian. Then the unexpected happened. The seed sown by the pioneers began to bear fruit. The movement became a political power. Whole battalions were shepherded into it, much as the troops of Feng-husiang, 'the Christian general', were baptized with a hose. Thanks to the judges, the unions were the first wave. The war brought another; the election of 1923 a third; the events of 1926 a fourth. By that time a generation had grown up to which it seemed as easy to be a socialist – as easy, if you please! – as it had seemed difficult in 1900.

The result was that the British Labour Party, like British industry, was for a time too prosperous. It behaved, as the latter had behaved, as though summer would last for ever. It had inherited from the nineteenth century the economic psychology of an age of expansion. In the flush of success, its political psychology assumed for a time the same florid complexion. It deceived itself both as to its own condition, and as to the character of the forces on its side and against it. It mistook luck for merit; treated votes, which were clearly indispensable, as equivalent to convictions, as to the practical value of which it was not equally certain; and drugged itself with the illusion that, by adding one to one, it would achieve the millennium, without the painful necessity of clarifying its mind, disciplining its appetites, and training for a tough wrestle with established power and property. It touched lightly on its objectives, or veiled them in the radiant ambiguity of the word socialism, which each hearer could interpret to his taste. So it ended by forgetting the reason for its existence. It has now to rediscover it.

Yet the objective of a socialist party, and of the Labour Party in so far as it deserves the name, is simplicity itself. The fundamental question, as always, is: Who is to be master? Is the reality behind the decorous drapery of political democracy to continue to be the economic power wielded by a few thousand – or, if that be preferred, a few hundred thousand – bankers, industrialists and land-owners? Or shall a serious effort be made – as serious, for example, as was made, for other purposes, during the war – to create organs through which the nation can control, in cooperation with other nations, its own economic destinies; plan its business as it deems most conducive to the general well-being; override, for the sake of economic efficiency, the obstruction of vested interests; and distribute the product of its labours in accordance with some generally recognized principles of justice? Capitalist parties presumably accept the first alternative. A socialist party chooses the second. The nature of its business is determined by its choice.

That business is not the passage of a series of reforms in the interests of different sections of the working classes. It is to abolish all advantages and disabilities which have their source, not in differences of personal quality, but in disparities of wealth, opportunity, social position and economic power. It is, in short – it is absurd that at this time of day the statement should be necessary – a classless society. It is not a question, of course, either of merely improving the distribution of wealth, or of merely increasing its production, but of doing both together. Naturally the methods required to attain that objective are various, complex and tedious. Naturally, those who accept it may do so for more than one reason – because they think it more conducive to economic efficiency than a capitalism which no longer, as in its prime, delivers the goods; or merely because they have an eccentric prejudice in favour of treating men as men; or, since the reasons are not necessarily inconsistent, for both reasons at once. In either case, they are socialists, though on matters of technique and procedure they may be uninstructed socialists. Those who do not accept it are not socialists, though they may be as wise as Solon and as virtuous as Aristides. Socialism, thus defined, will be unpleasant, of course, to some persons professing it. Who promised them pleasure?

The elements composing the Labour Party are extremely miscellaneous. If variety of educational experience and economic condition among its active supporters be the test, it is, whether fortunately or not, as a mere matter of fact, less of a class party than any other British party. That variety means that the bond of common experience is weaker than in parties whose members have been taught at school and college to hang together. Hence it makes the cohesion which springs from common intellectual convictions all the more indispensable. There is room for workers of all types in it, but on one condition. It is that, in their public capacity, they put their personal idiosyncrasies second, and their allegiance to the objectives of the party first. If they accept titles and such toys, without a clear duty to the movement to do so; or think that their main business is not fundamental reconstruction, but more money for the unemployed; or suppose that such reconstruction, instead of being specially urgent in the circumstances of today, must be kept in cold storage till the automatic occurrence of a hypothetical trade revival; or, like thirty-six Labour members in the last House of Commons, regard the defence of the interests, or fancied interests, of denominational schools as more important than to strike a small blow at class privilege in education, they may be virtuous individuals, but they are not socialists. To the Labour Party they are a source, not of strength, but of weakness. They widen the rift between its principles and its practice.

The programme of the party, again, covers a wide range. Nor need that be regretted, but, again, on one condition. It is that the different proposals contained in it should be rigorously subordinated to the main objective. Clearly, class-privilege takes more than one form. It is both economic and social. It rests on functionless property, on the control of key-positions in finance and industry, on educational inequalities, on the mere precariousness of proletarian existence, which prevents its victims looking before and after. Clearly, therefore, a movement seeking to end class-privilege must use more than one weapon; and clearly, also, the Labour Party's programme, like all socialist programmes, from the Communist Manifesto to the present day, must include measures which are secondary as well as measures which are primary. The essential thing is that it should discriminate between them. What will not do is that a programme should be built up by a process of half-unconscious log-rolling, this measure being offered to one section of workers, and that, because no one must be left in the cold, being promised to another.

The Labour Party can either be a political agent, pressing in Parliament the claims of different groups of wage-earners; or it can be an instrument for the establishment of a socialist commonwealth, which alone, on its own principles, would meet those claims effectively, but would not meet them at once. What it cannot be is to be both at the same time in the same measure. It ought to tell its supporters that obvious truth. It ought to inform them that its business is to be the organ of a peaceful revolution, and that other interests must be subordinated to that primary duty. It is objected that, by taking that course, it will alienate many of them. It may, for the time being; New Models are not made by being all things to all men. But it will keep those worth keeping. And those retained will gather others; of a kind who will not turn back in the day of battle.

To formulate from time to time, amid swiftly changing complexities, international and domestic, a Labour policy which is relevant and up to date, is a task for the best brains that politics can command. But, when policy has been determined, two facts are as certain as political facts can be. The first is that, if a Labour Government, when it gets the opportunity, proceeds to act on it, it will encounter at once determined resistance. The second is that it will not overcome that resistance, unless it has explained its aims with complete openness and candour. It cannot avoid the struggle, except by compromising its principles; it must, therefore, prepare for it. In order to prepare for it, it must create in advance a temper and mentality of a kind to carry it through, not one crisis, but a series of crises, to which the Zinoviev letter and the Press campaign of last year will prove, it is to be expected, to have been mere skirmishes of outposts. Onions can be eaten leaf by leaf, but you cannot skin a live tiger paw by paw; vivisection is its trade, and it does the skinning first. If the Labour Party is to tackle its job with some hope of success, it must mobilize behind it a body of conviction as resolute and informed as the opposition in front of it.

To say this is not at all to lend countenance to a sterile propaganda of class hatred, or to forget that both duty and prudence require that necessary changes should be effected without a breakdown, or to ignore the truism that the possibility of effecting them is conditioned by international, as much as by domestic, factors. It is curious, in view of the historical origins of the Liberal movement, and, indeed, of such recent history as the campaign of 1909 against 'the peers and their litter', that Liberals, of all people, should find a rock of offence in the class connexions of the Labour Party. The reason for facing with candour the obvious and regrettable fact of the existence of a class struggle is not, of course, to idolize class, but to make it less of an idol than in England it is. It is to dissolve a morbid complex in the only way in which complexes can be dissolved, not by suppressing, but by admitting it. It is to emphasize that the dynamic of any living movement is to be found, not merely in interests, but in principles, which unite men whose personal interests may be poles asunder, and that, if principles are to exercise their appeal, they must be frankly stated. The form which the effort to apply them assumes necessarily varies, of course, from one society to another. Any realist view of the future of British socialism must obviously take account of the political maturity and dependence on a world economy of the people of Great Britain. It does not follow, however, that the struggle to be faced is less severe on that account. Intellectually and morally it may be more exacting.

If there is any country where the privileged classes are simpletons, it is certainly not England. The idea that tact and amiability in presenting the Labour Party's case – the 'statesmanship' of the last Government – can hoodwink them into the belief that it is also theirs is as hopeful as an attempt to bluff a sharp solicitor out of a property of which he holds the title-deeds. The plutocracy consists of agreeable, astute, forcible, self-confident, and, when hard-pressed, unscrupulous people, who know pretty well which side their bread is buttered, and intend that the supply of butter shall not run short. They respect success, the man or movement that 'brings it off'. But they have, very properly, no use for cajolery, and laugh in their sleeves – and not always in their sleeves – at attempts to wheedle them. If their position is seriously threatened, they will use every piece on the board, political and economic – the House of Lords, the Crown, and Press, disaffection in the army, financial crises, international difficulties, and even, as newspaper attacks on the pound last summer showed, the émigré trick of injuring one's country to protect one's pocket – in the honest conviction that they are saving civilization. The way to deal with them is not to pretend, as some Labour leaders do, that, because many of them are pleasant creatures, they can be talked into the belief that they want what the Labour movement wants, and differ only as to methods. It is, except for the necessary contacts of political warfare, to leave them alone till one can talk with effect, when less talking will be needed, and, in the meantime, to seize every opportunity of forcing a battle on fundamental questions. When they have been knocked out in a straight fight on a major economic issue, they will proceed, in the words of Walt Whitman, to 're-examine philosophies and religions'. They will open their eyes and mend their manners. They will not do so before. Why should they?

III

If such are the objectives of the Labour Party, and such the forces against it, what are the practical conclusions? They are four, relating respectively to programmes, propaganda, discipline, and tactics.

The conclusion of an article is not the proper place for even the outline of a policy, which, with the world sliding as it is, may be out of date in six months. But certain points are clear. The business of making programmes by including in them an assortment of measures appealing to different sections of the movement must stop. The function of the party is not to offer the largest possible number of carrots to the largest possible number of donkeys. It is, while working for international peace and cooperation abroad, to carry through at home the large measures of economic and social reconstruction which, to the grave injury of the nation, have been too long postponed, and with that object to secure that the key-positions of the economic system are under public control.

That task must, of course, be interpreted in a broad sense. It is not for Labour to relapse into the Philistinism of the May Report, with its assumption that all but economic interests, and those interpreted *à la* capitalist, are of secondary importance. Side by side with action of a strictly economic character, such as the transference to public ownership of foundation services, including the banks; the establishment of machinery to bring the supply of capital to industry under public control; the creation of a permanent Industrial Development Commission to press steadily forward the modernization of industrial organization; and such other measures of the same order as may be adopted, must go a policy for the improvement of education, health, and the system of local government, which themselves, it may be remarked, are matters not irrelevant to economic prosperity. It is monstrous that services vital to the welfare of the great majority of the population, and especially to that of the young, should be crippled or curtailed, while the *rentier* takes an actually larger percentage than in the past of the national income. If that income is too small to permit of our ensuring that all children have proper opportunities of health and education, it is clearly too small to allow us other luxuries, including the continued payment of £300,000,000 odd a year to holders of war debt. A Labour Government should not wait till circumstances are favourable to a voluntary conversion, nor should it deal with war debt alone. It should follow the example set by Australia and other countries, and, indeed, as far as a disregard for the sanctity of contractual obligations is concerned, by the highly respectable Cabinet at present in power. It should compulsorily reduce fixed interest charges.

Of the general considerations which arise in planning a programme, the most important are three. The essentials must be put first, and sectional claims must not be permitted to conflict with them. The transference of economic power to public hands must take precedence over the mere alleviation of distress. It must be recognized that any serious attempt to give effect to such a policy will provoke a counter-attack, including action to cause economic embarrassment to the government of the day, and measures to meet it must be prepared in advance. The present government has shown that wealth can be redistributed, and existing contracts broken, by the convenient procedure of Orders in Council. The precedent should be remembered. An Emergency Powers Act is on the statute-book. Labour must be prepared to use it, and, if the powers which it confers are insufficient, to pass another.

What a Labour Government can do depends on what, when in opposition, it has taught its supporters to believe will be done. 'Never office again without a majority' is the formula of the moment. But quality of support is as important as quantity. The Labour Party deceives itself, if it supposes that the mere achievement of a majority will enable it to carry out fundamental measures, unless it has previously created in the country the temper to stand behind it when the real struggle begins. Much of its propaganda appears to the writer – himself the least effective of propagandists – to ignore that truism. What is needed, is not merely the advocacy of particular measures of socialist reconstruction, indispensable though that is. It is the creation of a body of men and women who, whether trade unionists or intellectuals, put socialism first, and whose creed carries conviction, because they live in accordance with it.

The impressive feature of Russia is not that, apart from agriculture, the items in its policy are particularly novel. It is that, whether novel or not, they are being carried out. The force which causes them to be carried out is, not material, but spiritual. It is the presence of such a body, at once dynamic and antiseptic, the energumens, the zealots, the Puritans, the Jacobins, the religious order, the Communist Party – call it what you please – which possesses, not merely opinions, but convictions, and acts as it believes. Its existence does not depend on political forms; it is as compatible with Parliamentary, as with any other, machinery. Till something analogous to it develops in England, Labour will be plaintive, not formidable, and its business will not march.

The way to create it, and the way, when created, for it to set about its task, is not to prophesy smooth things; support won by such methods is a reed shaken by every wind. It is not to encourage adherents to ask what they will get from a Labour Government, as though a campaign were a picnic, all beer and sunshine. It is to ask them what they will give. It is to make them understand that the return of a Labour Government is merely the first phase of a struggle the issue of which depends on themselves. It is objected that such methods involve surrendering for a decade the prospect of office. It may be replied that, if so, impotence out of office is preferable, at any rate, to impotence in it. It does not prejudice the future, or leave a record to be lived down. But is it certain that, had the late Government spoken in that sense before coming to power, and then fallen in 1930 in the attempt to carry a measure of first-class importance, it would have been less likely to supply an alternative government in 1936?

Talk is nauseous without practice. Who will believe that the Labour Party means business as long as some of its stalwarts sit up and beg for social sugar-plums, like poodles in a drawing-room? On this matter there is at the moment a good deal of cant. The only test is the practical one; what behaviour is most conducive to getting on with the job? A distinction may be drawn, no doubt, between compliance with public conventions and conduct in matters of purely personal choice. If one is a postman, one can wear a postman's uniform, without thereby being turned into a pillar of sealing-wax. And, if Privy Councillors make up for the part, when duty requires it, by hiring official clothes from a theatrical costume-maker, who will let them for the day at not unreasonable rates, there is nothing to shed tears over, except their discomfort. The thing, all the same, though a trifle, is insincere and undignified. Livery and an independent mind go ill together. Labour has no need to imitate an etiquette. It can make its own.

It is one thing to bow down in the House of Rimmon, for practical reasons, when necessity requires it. It is quite another to press, all credulity and adoration, into the inner circle of his votaries. But the criticism on the snobbery of some pillars of the party, though just as far as it goes, does not go far enough. Those who live in glass houses should not throw stones. The truth is that, though the ways of some of the big fish are bad, those of some of the smaller fry are not much better. Five-pounders and fingerlings, we insist on rising, and – shades of Walton! – to what flies!

The Choice Before the Labour Party

It will not do. To kick over an idol, you must first get off your knees. To say that snobbery is inevitable in the Labour Party, because all Englishmen are snobs, is to throw up the sponge. Either the Labour Party means to end the tyranny of money, or it does not. If it does, it must not fawn on the owners and symbols of money. If there are members of it – a small minority no doubt, but one would be too many – who angle for notice in the capitalist Press; accept, or even beg for, 'honours'; are flattered by invitations from fashionable hostesses; suppose that their financial betters are endowed with intellects more dazzling and characters more sublime than those of commen men; and succumb to convivial sociabilities, like Red Indians to fire-water, they have mistaken their vocation. They would be happier as footmen. It may be answered, of course, that it is sufficient to leave them to the ridicule of the world which they are so anxious to enter, and which may be trusted in time – its favourites change pretty quickly – to let them know what it thinks of them. But, in the meantime, there are such places as colliery villages and cotton towns. How can followers be Ironsides if leaders are flunkies?

One cannot legislate for sycophancy; one can only expose it, and hope that one's acquaintances will expose it in oneself. The silly business of 'honours' is a different story. For Labour knighthoods and the rest of it (except when, as in the case of civil servants and municipal officers, such as mayors and town clerks, they are recognized steps in an official career) there is no excuse. Cruel boys tie tin cans to the tails of dogs; but even a mad dog does not tie a can to its own tail. Why on earth should a Labour member? He has already all the honour a man wants in the respect of his own people. He can afford to tell the tempter to take his wares to a market which will pay for them and himself to the devil. While the House of Lords lasts, the party must have spokesmen in it. Peerages, therefore, have very properly been undergone, as an unpleasant duty, by men who disliked them. It should in future, be made clear, beyond possibility of doubt, that that reason, and no other, is the ground for accepting them. When it is necessary that a Labour peer should be made, the victim required to play the part of Jephtha's daughter should be designated by a formal vote of the Parliamentary Party meeting. It is not actually essential that the next Annual Conference should pass a resolution of sympathy with him and his wife, but it would be a graceful act for it to do so. What odious Puritanism! Yes, but the Puritans, though unpleasant people, had one trifling merit. They did the job, or, at any rate, their job. Is the Labour Party doing it?

If there is the right spirit in the movement, there will not be any question of the next Labour Government repeating the policy of office at all costs which was followed by the last. Whether it takes office without an independent majority is a matter of secondary importance compared with its conduct when it gets there. Its proper course is clear. The only sound policy for a minority government is to act like a majority government. It is not to attempt to enact the less controversial parts of its programme; for its opponents give nothing away, and will resist a small measure of educational reform as remorselessly as a bill for the nationalization of the land. It is to fight on large issues, and to fight at once. It is to introduce in the first three months, while its prestige is high and its *moral* unimpaired, the measures of economic reconstruction which it regards as essential. It will, of course, be defeated; if it is in a minority, in the Commons, if it is in a majority, in the Lords. In the second case, it can use the Parliament Act, supposing it to be still law, and go to the country on the abolition of the House of Lords; in the first, it must demand a dissolution. In either, it will do better for the nation and itself by forcing the issue, than by earning as its epitaph the answer which Sièyes gave to the question what he had done during the Terror: '*J'ai vécu*': 'I kept alive.'

It is objected that such a policy involves sacrificing opportunities for useful work, particularly in the field of international affairs. It may – for the time being; had the late government acted on it, Sir John Simon would have succeeded Mr Henderson after one year, instead of after two. On a long view, however, the dilemma is less absolute than that argument suggests. The League is what the rulers of the Great Powers, and the interests behind them, permit it to be. In the light of the history of the last thirteen years, and not least of 1931–2 – in the light, for example, of their attitude in the test case of Manchuria and of the tragic farce of the Disarmament

Conference – can it seriously be argued that they are eager that it should itself be a power, or that even a Labour Government, if it holds office at the mercy of its opponents and the League's, can succeed, during a brief spell of precarious authority, in making it one? It is obvious that, as the world is today, no nation can save itself by itself; we must cooperate, or decline. But is it probable that international cooperation can be built on a foundation of states dominated, in their internal lives, by ideals antithetic to it? Those who cannot practise their creed under their own roof can practise it nowhere, and one contribution, at least, which a Labour Government can make to that cause is to be made at home. It is to apply to the affairs of its own country the principles which, it believes, should govern those of the world. It is to extend the area of economic life controlled by some rational conception of the common good, not by a scramble, whether of persons, classes, or nations, for individual power and profit.

Sir Arthur Salter, in contrasting the frank individualism of the nineteenth century with the improvised, half-conscious experiments in collective control of the post-war world, observes that 'we have, in our present intermediate position between these two systems, lost many of the advantages of both, and failed to secure the full benefits of either'. In the sphere of international, as of domestic, policy, the attempt to give a social bias to capitalism, while leaving it master of the house, appears to have failed. If capitalism is to be our future, then capitalists, who believe in it, are most likely to make it work, though at the moment they seem to have some difficulty in doing so. The Labour Party will serve the world best, not by doing half-heartedly what they do with conviction, but by clarifying its own principles and acting in accordance with them.

July 1932

THE REPORT OF
THE COMMITTEE ON MINISTERS'
POWERS

William A. Robson

I

M. BARTHÉLEMY, the Dean of the Faculty of Law in the University of Paris, relates that thirty years ago he was spending a weekend with the late Professor Dicey. In the course of conversation M. Barthélemy asked a question about administrative law in this country. 'In England,' replied Dicey, 'we know nothing of administrative law; and we wish to know nothing.'

This episode illustrates the attitude of mind which has characterized the political intelligentsia of Great Britain towards one of the most vital subjects of the day during the present century. The late Professor Dicey was not a legal pedant or a man of narrow outlook. He was, on the contrary, distinguished by a remarkable breadth of vision; and it was his extraordinary insight into the organic relation between law and public opinion, into the connexion between constitutional law and traditional convention, which placed him high above his contemporaries as an exponent of the English system of government. But despite all his insight, Dicey suffered from one immense delusion until almost the end of his life. He believed that in England the rule of law is supreme, and that under it 'every official, from the Prime Minister down to a constable or a collector of taxes, is under the same responsibility for every act done without legal justification as any other citizen'.[1] He believed that there was nothing to be found in England even remotely resembling the system of *droit administratif* in France, whereby wrongful acts alleged to have been committed by public officials in the course of their duty are tried by special administrative courts. In contrasting the French system with our own he described it as one in which the

[1] *Law of the Constitution*, 8th Ed., p. 189.

state is given exceptional and extensive privileges: a misreading of the position in France almost as complete as that famous misreading of the English Constitution which occurs in Montesquieu's *Esprit des Lois* (Ch. 6, Book xi).

In a very narrow sense Dicey was right in declaring that in England there is no precise equivalent to the French system. But in proving that he proved too much; and his accuracy over a small matter obscured the larger truth. In exorcizing from the British Constitution all doctrines having even the most remote connexion with the hated *droit administratif*, he at the same time excommunicated from the field of his vision a series of administrative institutions which, while peculiar to the English polity, are impossible to reconcile with the constitutional principles which he had announced. As each year passed, Dicey's *Law of the Constitution* found increasing favour with the governing classes both in England and throughout the Empire. The suggestion it contained, that in England the Rule of Law and Liberty prevail, whereas the barbarians of the continent have perforce to endure all the misery and oppression of a lawless tyranny imposed by a privileged state, brought unction to the soul even when it was most clearly at variance with the facts. The work became the standard textbook for students of law and politics at the older universities, at the Inns of Court, at the solicitors' law schools. It matured into a classic; and finally became almost part of the Constitution itself. It is not too much to say that 'Dicey on the Constitution' dominated political and legal thought among educated Englishmen at home and abroad for more than thirty years. Yet with each succeeding edition the phenomena it ignored grew more insistent both in numbers and in strength; until at last its author, near the end of his long life, gave voice to the unquiet doubts which had at last come upon him.[1]

It is probably true to say that the acquisition by departments of state of legislative and judicial powers has proceeded more easily and more rapidly during the past half-century by reason of the fact that scarcely anyone was aware of what was occurring, than would otherwise have been the case. It was not until several years after the

---

[1] See the article he wrote entitled, 'The Development of Administrative Law in England', *Law Quarterly Review*, Vol. xxxi, p. 148.

war of 1914–18, when the advent of the Defence of the Realm Act had made people conscious of the extreme lengths to which the hegemony of the executive had been pushed, that systematic inquiry began to be made here and there into the position which had arisen. The judges commenced to introduce caustic observations into their judgements in cases where Ministers of the Crown were officially concerned. Lawyers began to denounce 'the bureaucrats'. And in 1929 the Lord Chief Justice took the unusual step of publishing a series of newspaper articles, afterwards issued in book form under the title *The New Despotism*, in which he made a violent and undisguised attack upon the Civil Service.

There is, Lord Hewart pointed out, a persistent influence at work which, whatever the motives or intentions that support it, undoubtedly has the effect of placing a large and increasing field of departmental authority and activity beyond the reach of the ordinary law. Thus, what he called a despotic power was being produced which places government departments above the sovereignty of Parliament and beyond the jurisdiction of the courts. He then remarked that the growth of the system of delegating legislative power to government departments had proceeded side by side with a great increase in the number of public officials, and suggested that it was 'the officials in the departments concerned who initiate the legislation by which the arbitrary powers are conferred upon them'.[1] Thus, in short, Parliament is hoodwinked by the Cabinet, the Cabinet is directed by the officials, and the officials are guilty of a vast conspiracy to deprive the commonwealth of the hard-earned constitutional liberties which have been won through centuries of strife and sacrifice.

This simple denunciation won immediate support in the Press, on the platform and in Parliament. It is not too much to say that Lord Hewart's attitude represents ninety-nine per cent of the opinion of the bench, the bar and the solicitors' profession. The reason, of which they are entirely unconscious, is interesting. An opposition has for long existed in Britain between the idea of 'law' and the idea of 'government'. This is a heritage from the conflict in the seventeenth century between, on the one side, a sovereign

[1] *The New Despotism*, p. 52.

claiming to rule by divine right and to exercise an undisputed prerogative in all matters of government, and on the other side a nation claiming a supreme law to which even the sovereign should be subject. That struggle between King and Commons has become transformed in our own day into a conflict between the Executive on the one hand and the Judiciary and the legal profession on the other. The lawyers still regard themselves as champions of the popular cause; but there can be little doubt that the great departments of state administering or supervising public health, public education, pension schemes, unemployment and health insurance, housing and all the other modern social services, are not only essential to the well-being of the great mass of the people, but also the most significant expressions of democracy in our time. Considerations of this kind, however, could scarcely be expected to weigh with the predominantly upper middle-class, Forsytic and conservative legal mind.

What may be accounted an influence of some importance is the injury to the livelihood and prestige of the legal profession threatened by the new development. Just as the rank and file of the medical profession have displayed for decades an uncompromising hostility towards the public health movement and the modern science of preventive medicine; just as in the sixteenth century the practitioners of the Common Law Courts fought desperately to avert the shifting of the living law to the King's Council, to the Court of Requests, the Court of Chancery and the Star Chamber[1] – all of them what we should now call Administrative Tribunals – so today it requires no great effort of the mind or will to enable a lawyer or a judge to persuade himself that a development which removes disputes from the courts, which will provide a mode of adjudication wherein the practising lawyer has but little part, in which a rival technique and a new jurisdiction will outstrip the waning popularity of the established courts, is a Machiavellian tendency which the public good requires to be stamped out like an evil pest.

This was the setting in which the Donoughmore Committee on Ministerial Powers was appointed in 1929. It is worthy of note that

[1] Cf. Roscoe Pound: *The Spirit of the Common Law*, p. 73.

although the Committee was set up by the Lord Chancellor of a Labour government, the personnel of the Committee was almost exactly what might have been expected from a Conservative ministry. Out of the seventeen members originally appointed, six are eminent practising barristers or solicitors, and another two are lawyers of highly Conservative views – a majority of the entire Committee. Three of the remaining members are Conservative ex-ministers; and the only persons from whom progressive ideals might reasonably be expected were Sir John Anderson, Professor Laski and three Labour members of Parliament. A reforming Lord Chancellor appears to be an impossibility at the present time.

The terms of reference are of great significance. In them the Committee is directed to consider the powers exercised by or under the direction of (or by persons or bodies appointed specially by) Ministers of the Crown by way of (*a*) delegated legislation and (*b*) judicial or quasi-judicial decision, 'and to report what safeguards are desirable or necessary to secure the constitutional principles of the sovereignty of Parliament and the supremacy of the Law'. Here we have the curious spectacle of the conclusions at which the Committee is expected to arrive being embodied in its terms of reference. The Committee started life with the dead hand of Dicey lying frozen on its neck.

II

All things considered, the Committee has done a far better piece of work than might have been expected in view of the unpropitious circumstances attending its birth.

The Report[1] starts by observing that in the British Constitution there is no such thing as the absolute separation of legislative, executive and judicial powers. In practice it is inevitable that they should overlap. Formal denial is thus given at the outset to that doctrine of the separation of powers which has for generations confused the minds of men both at home and abroad. The divine right of powers to be separated, insisted upon so strongly in the constitutional law of the United States, and ignored so flagrantly in con-

[1] Cmd. 4060/1932. 2/6 net. H.M. Stationery Office.

stitutional practice, springs at bottom from the attitude of suspicion and hostility towards government which was well justified in the days when the rulers consisted of a sovereign and a small group of self-interested noblemen and royal favourites, but is utterly unsuited to the efficient conduct of government in the modern democratic state, when what is required is not a system of checks and balances to stultify the effectiveness of each organ of government, but a cooperative effort between all the powers of the state directed towards the common welfare.

It has been suggested, the Committee states, that the practice of delegating legislative and judicial powers to administrative organs is bad, and should be forthwith abandoned. This, however, is not the Committee's own view, nor that of most persons who have considered the problem. Delegation is inevitable today. But apart from its inevitability, 'We see nothing to justify any lowering of the country's high opinion of its Civil Service or any reflection on its sense of justice, or any ground for a belief that our constitutional machinery is developing in directions which are fundamentally wrong.' What is needed, in fact, is a series of safeguards against possible abuse. If the right precautions are taken, the Committee expressly declares, 'there is no ground for public fear'. With these preliminary observations the grisly spectre of executive tyranny is banished to the theatrical property-room from which it was so unwisely permitted to wander, and the sensational phrases used to describe it are shown to be little more than journalistic devices for misleading the ignorant. The suggestion that the statutory provisions conferring powers on the departments are due directly or indirectly to an attempt on the part of civil servants to secure arbitrary power for themselves is disposed of as being 'unsupported by the smallest shred of evidence'.

The Report describes at some length the enormous variety of delegated legislation which now exists; the diverse procedures which are prescribed; and the haphazard way in which such safeguards as laying before Parliament and antecedent publicity are sometimes required and sometimes omitted. In all these matters the Committee seeks to introduce a measure of systematization and rationalization. Nomenclature is to be simplified, the Rules Publication Act should be amended, the practice of departmental consultation with interests affected should be pursued, the method of appending explanatory notes to rules or regulations extended, and a uniform procedure in regard to laying regulations before Parliament adopted. The improved drafting of delegated legislation should be secured either by enlarging the staff of the Parliamentary Counsel's office or by providing the departments with properly qualified draftsmen.

All this relates to the exercise by ministers of their legislative functions. The principles which should guide Parliament in delegating such functions are also laid down. The normal type of delegated legislation is marked by two characteristics: first, the limits of the power conferred are so clearly defined by statute as to be plainly known to Parliament, the executive, the public and the judiciary. Second, the powers delegated do not include power to legislate on matters of principle, to impose taxation, or to amend Acts of Parliament. The exceptional type involves not only power to do all these things, but the delegated powers confer so wide a discretion on a minister that it is almost impossible to know what limit Parliament intended to impose; and control by the courts is in some instances expressly excluded. It is worth noticing that the most conspicuous examples of these abnormal types have occurred within the past year, e.g. the Gold Standard (Amendment) Act, 1931, the National Economy Act, 1931, the Foodstuffs (Prevention of Exploitation) Act, 1931, the Horticultural Products (Emergency Customs Duties) Act, 1931, and the Import Duties Act, 1932. The Committee utters a warning that exceptional measures should be reserved for exceptional emergencies; and recommends that Parliament should not depart from the normal into the exceptional type of delegated legislation without special need, nor without conscious consideration of the special grounds on which the need is said to be founded. The so-called Henry VIII Clause, by which a dispensing power is given to a minister to modify the provisions of a statute, should never be employed except for the sole purpose of bringing an Act into operation, and should be subject to a time limit of one year for the period of its operation.

Most important of all is the proposal to set up a small Standing

Committee of each House of Parliament for the dual purpose of considering and reporting on every Bill containing a proposal to confer law-making power on a minister, and of scrutinizing every rule and regulation made by a department in the exercise of delegated legislative power. These Committees would be required to consider the form only and not the merits of a Bill submitted to them. They would report on its form, and state whether it contained any exceptional features from a constitutional point of view. In particular, the Committees would inquire whether the limits of the powers conferred on the executive were clearly defined; whether any power to legislate on matters of principle, or to impose a tax, were involved; whether immunity from challenge in the courts were asked for in respect of any regulation to be made; whether any clause of the Henry VIII type were inserted; and finally, whether the proposals contained in the Bill in this connexion were properly and adequately explained by the minister in an explanatory memorandum which is to accompany all such measures in future.

These recommendations appear to combine practical common sense with theoretical wisdom. They avoid the danger of attempting to lay down inflexible dogmas to guide the orthodox for all eternity, while at the same time they are based on recognizable principles. They distinguish between the normal and the abnormal; they embody the indispensable feature of perpetual scrutiny by members of the legislature; they observe the need for expert assistance to aid the Parliamentary Committees in their task; they emphasize the importance of good drafting, publicity, uniformity of procedure and rationalization of method. They endeavour to make Parliament more conscious of what it is doing or about to do than to persuade it to accept self-denying penances in the future. Inevitably, there are obvious doubts which arise in connexion with some of the recommendations. One wonders, for instance, how a single Committee of each House will manage to cover the whole vast field of delegated legislation without missing the significance of many of the statutory rules and orders. One questions the ability of the Committees to report on form while avoiding judgement on the substance. But these and similar criticisms are purely hypothetical.

Taken as a whole, the recommendations of the Committee on delegated legislation seem to be exceedingly good.

III

The second half of the Report, dealing with 'Judicial or Quasi-Judicial Decision', covers a field which presents problems that are harder to grasp intellectually and more difficult to solve from a practical point of view.

'The supremacy or rule of the law of the land,' we are told, 'is a recognized principle of the English Constitution.' The Committee accepts the exposition of this rule of law given by Dicey, who declared it to have with us three different meanings. First, it means (according to this exposition), the absolute supremacy of regular law as opposed to the influence of arbitrary power, and excludes the existence of arbitrariness, of prerogative or even of wide discretionary authority on the part of the Government. It means, second, equality before the law, or 'the equal subjection of all classes to the ordinary law of the land administered by the ordinary law courts'. Thirdly, it means that our constitutional law is not the source but the consequence of the rights of the individual as defined and enforced by the courts.

The first of these conditions is so manifestly remote from the state of affairs which has existed at any rate for the past century that it is obviously untrue in any large sense. Every government possesses, and must possess, 'wide discretionary authority'; and the importance of the prerogative can scarcely be over-emphasized in England of all countries, where the entire field of foreign affairs, to take only one instance, falls within its scope. But it is the second condition which is of chief significance in connexion with the present discussion. (The third condition is not of particular moment.)

The doctrine that all classes in this country are subject equally to the ordinary law of the land, administered by the ordinary courts of law, can be maintained only if at the same time it is admitted that 'the ordinary law of the land' makes such colossal distinctions between administrative departments of government and private individuals that the former carry on their activities under what is virtually a special code or dispensation. The immunity of the Crown from liability in tort, which applies not merely to the ministers and departments of state, but extends right down the hierarchy to such relatively humble figures as a borough constable, has now become so glaring an instance of state privilege that even the blindest advocates of the orthodox theory are compelled to denounce it as an 'anomaly'; and the present Report goes out of its way, and even outside its terms of reference, to commend a Bill to fill 'this lacuna in the rule of law'. But quite apart from this notorious scandal, there are a whole series of other privileges given to the executive in the courts of law: by statutory measures such as the Public Authorities Protection Act; by common law doctrines founded on ancient prejudices, such as nonfeasance, whereby a public authority cannot be made liable for damages for the non-fulfilment of a public duty, even though injury results to one or more citizens; by the self-limitation of the courts of law, which impels them to refuse to investigate entire fields of executive action; by the archaic forms of procedure which have usually to be adopted whenever the activity of the Government is questioned in the courts of law.

The net result of all this is twofold. In the first place, there is almost no equality before the law, as between government and citizen, in the ordinary courts of justice, for the simple reason that a special body of law and procedure applies exclusively to public authorities. In the second place this body of law operates so as to deprive the citizen of a remedy against the state in nearly all the cases where he most requires it, and at the same time enables the most important administrative decisions to escape any shadow of review by the courts of law.

The English legal system has, in fact, shown the most remarkable incapacity to expand in accordance with the needs of the modern state. The liability of the individual official for wrongdoing committed in the course of his duty, on which so much praise has been bestowed by English writers, is essentially a relic from past centuries when government was in the hands of a few known, prominent, independent and substantial persons called Public Officers, who were in no way responsible to ministers or elected legislatures or councils.[1] Such a doctrine is utterly unsuited to the twentieth-century state, in which the Public Officer has been superseded by armies of anonymous and obscure Civil Servants acting directly under the orders of their superiors, who are ultimately responsible to an elected body. The exclusive liability of the individual officer is a doctrine typical of a highly individual common law. It is of decreasing value today, and is small recompense for an irresponsible state. The doctrine has been abandoned, in whole or in part, by the more intelligent legal systems on the Continent.

English jurists have, unfortunately, for the most part been so preoccupied with the mote in the eye of the executive that they have failed to notice the beam in their own. Their concern at the judicial functions acquired by administrative departments has dominated the discussion of public law questions for the past decade and has diverted the attention of both lawyers and the general public from the defects of the courts of justice as instruments for controlling, wisely and effectively, the relations between the citizen and the state.

IV

With these considerations in mind, we can now turn to the section of the Report dealing with the judicial powers of ministers.

For more than half a century Parliament has made a practice of conferring, with increasing frequency, judicial powers on ministers of state. The legislation relating to public health, education, local

---

[1] An interesting passage on this subject occurs in an excellent monograph recently published entitled, *Responsible Bureaucracy: A study of the Swiss Civil Service* by Carl Joachim Friedrich and Taylor Cole (Harvard University Press, 1932): 'Because of the peculiar conditions under which English government developed, there is a widespread belief in English-speaking countries to the effect that a clear line of distinction can and must be drawn between political responsibility of the government enforceable through Cabinet responsibility or general elections on the one hand and personal responsibility of the agents of the Government, the civil servant (or servants of the Crown), enforceable through the courts. Such a distinction, which historically speaking is a feudal heritage, is totally inadmissible under modern conditions . . .', p. 5.

government, health insurance, unemployment insurance, pensions and other social services is teeming with provisions in which disputes between administrative authorities and householders, parents, employers, insured persons, approved societies, doctors, druggists, and other sections of the community are determined, not by the courts of law, but by departments of state or by administrative tribunals appointed by ministers of the Crown. This tendency was not the result of a well thought out constitutional principle. It was haphazard and sporadic and unsystematic. Yet it was not, on the other hand, due to a fit of absent-mindedness. Parliament did not merely overlook the courts of law. But the possibility of setting up new organs of adjudication which would do the work more rapidly, more cheaply, more efficiently than the ordinary courts; which would possess greater technical knowledge and fewer prejudices against government; which would give greater heed to the social interests involved and show less solicitude for private property rights; which would decide the dispute with a conscious effort at furthering the social policy embodied in the legislation: this prospect offered solid advantages which no doubt induced Parliament to extend the administrative jurisdiction of government departments so as to include judicial functions affecting the social services. In doing so Parliament was only repeating a process which had happened again and again in the history not only of England but of many civilized countries.

The Committee thus came to be faced with a *fait accompli*. Broadly speaking, three courses were open to it. It could (in theory at least) have recommended a return to the eighteenth-century position, illustrated by the Lord Chief Justice when he expressed the hope that 'the worst of the offending sections' in Acts of Parliament be repealed or amended. It could have accepted the proposals which I put forward to rationalize and institutionalize the administrative jurisdiction in a boldly conceived system of administrative courts separated to a large extent from the ordinary routine of departmental administration and free from indirect ministerial interference. Or thirdly, it could accept the patchwork quilt of ill-constructed tribunals which at present exists, and endeavour to remedy some of the more obvious defects.

It is this last-named alternative which the Committee has adopted. The Report contains no recommendations which drastically disturb the existing structure, nor is it suggested that in practice any injustice or hardship has resulted from the present arrangements. Indeed, the Committee explicitly declares that 'there is nothing radically wrong about the existing practice of Parliament in permitting the exercise of judicial and quasi-judicial powers by Ministers and of judicial power by Ministerial Tribunals'. There are, however, a number of proposals intended to safeguard the interests of the citizen. Thus, every party to a dispute should be given an opportunity to state his case, and also of knowing the case which he has to meet. Every minister or administrative tribunal should be required to give the reasons on which their decision is based, and this document should be available to the parties. A précis of leading decisions should be published at regular intervals. Wherever a public inquiry is held in connexion with the exercise of judicial functions by ministers, the Inspector's report should be published in all save the most exceptional circumstances.

These recommendations are good so far as they go; and constitute in most cases a definite advance on established practice. The disappointing feature of the Report is its failure to make any significant contribution to the structure of the system. Instead of endeavouring to increase the sense of responsibility and independence of the administrative tribunals, the Report relies on a hostile judiciary to provide 'checks and balances'. It recommends, accordingly, that the supervisory jurisdiction of the High Court to compel ministers and administrative tribunals to keep within their powers and to hear and determine according to law be maintained; and further, that anyone aggrieved by a decision should have an absolute right of appeal to the High Court on any question of law.

This is the means by which the rule of law is to be perpetuated and the liberty of the subject protected for all eternity. It sounds admirable. But when one looks a little deeper doubts begin to arise. In the first place, it is often extraordinarily difficult to discover any essential difference between a question of law and a question of fact. A question of fact in one generation sometimes becomes a question of law in the next; and a vast body of precedents is almost certain to arise on hair-splitting distinctions between questions of law and questions of fact in the field of public administration. When the courts want to interfere they will seek to find that a question of law is involved; and vice versa. Second, the procedure for getting a decision reviewed on a question of law by the courts is, to quote the Report, 'too expensive and in certain respects archaic, cumbrous and too inelastic'; and the Committee recommends a cheaper and more simple procedure. One must consider the implications of this criticism. Here are the judges and the lawyers complaining that they are not empowered in all cases to interfere with judicial decisions by administrative tribunals, and clamouring for more power. Yet in the large sphere where the right of judicial control over the executive *does* exist, the courts have done absolutely nothing to modernize, to cheapen or to bring into accord with modern needs a fantastic procedure which has been obsolete for at least a century. Yet this is a matter entirely within the control of the Rules' Committee of the Supreme Court! It is difficult to believe that the legal profession retains any considerable capacity for reforming either the law or the practice of the courts.

It is, indeed, the very backwardness of the court process which enables the departments of state to use the right of access to the courts as a weapon of the most tyrannous character. Compare, for instance, the cheap, informal and entirely admirable system of Income Tax Appeals before the Special Commissioners of Income Tax, an example of a true administrative tribunal, which the Committee admits 'gives general satisfaction by its impartiality', with the oppressive costliness and lengthiness of the system of appeals from the Special Commissioners on questions of law to the High Court, the Court of Appeal, and the House of Lords. Only the wealthiest persons or corporations can afford to continue a dispute with the Inland Revenue once the threat of litigation has been made.

Fortunately, however, in the case of judicial decisions by administrative departments, there is no incentive for the government department to challenge its own decision in the courts, so that the vicious element to which I have just referred will be absent. Fortunately, again, the Committee has discovered a very remarkable method of leaving undisturbed the present allocation of functions.

The method consists of distinguishing judicial from quasi-judicial functions by a process of reasoning which appears to me entirely misleading. A 'true judicial decision', they say, involves four requisites: (1) the presentation of their case by the parties to a dispute; (2) the ascertainment of the facts by evidence adduced by the parties; (3) the submission of argument on the law; (4) 'a decision which disposes of the whole matter by a finding on the facts in dispute and an application of the law of the land to the facts is found, including where required a ruling upon any disputed question of law'. A quasi-judicial decision, continues the Report, involves the first two elements; it does not necessarily involve the third; and it never involves the fourth, which is replaced by 'administrative action, the character of which is determined by the minister's free choice'. In a later passage, in which an example is given of quasi-judicial functions from the field of public health, the Committee emphasizes that, after examining the evidence and so forth, and taking into consideration medical policy in local administration, 'In the end the minister makes up his mind what is *best* to do, and does it.'

There is something almost naïve in the distinction here drawn. The conception of 'the law of the land' as being a complete and perfect structure ready to be applied to every controversy immediately it arises is one of those copy-book maxims which one thought had disappeared generations ago. Did the Committee take into account the view of the judicial process put forward by Mr Justice Cardozo? Did they consider the discussion about 'free judicial decision' which has been agitating the Continent for years? Can we be told just when and how the Chancery jurisdiction, for centuries a purely discretionary interference on moral grounds, became 'truly judicial'? When did the *Conseil d'Etat* become judicial? Surely not when it began to follow precedents, for no court of law on the Continent is bound by previous decisions. Did not the House of Lords do precisely what it thought 'best' to do in *Sorrell v. Smith*, or the *Taff Vale* case, or *Quinn v. Leathem*? Have not both the common law and equity been developed to an enormous extent by the judges doing what they thought 'best' to do in the cases before them?

These and a hundred other questions spring to the mind in protest against the false view of history, of legal evolution and of the judicial process which the Committee's analysis involves. But they may be permitted to die away unanswered when we realize that this false analysis is the very instrument which enables the Committee to escape from the fetters of its terms of reference. By the simple device of declaring that 'true' judicial functions must reside with the courts except in special circumstances, but that quasi-judicial functions may be given to administrative tribunals, the Committee in effect recommends that decisions which require consideration of high state policy in the field of social administration shall, as hitherto, remain within the scope of ministerial action. In the way a false analysis is turned to good purpose in distinguishing the things which are Caesar's from those which are not. Once again we are muddling through!

Will anyone ever say again that we[1] have no administrative law in this country?

July 1932

---

[1] The great significance of administrative law is much more widely recognized in the United States than in England. Not only do the leading American law schools provide for extensive teaching and research in the subject but there is a steadily growing body of literature on administrative law of original quality and high value. Two recent publications deserve special mention. One of these is Professor Sharfman's excellent treatise, *The Interstate Commerce Commission*, published by the Commonwealth Fund; the other is the exceedingly useful source book, *Cases and other Materials on Administrative Law*, edited by Felix Frankfurter and J. Forrester Davison (C.C.H. University Casebook Series, Chicago, 1932). One finds in this volume the careful scholarship and wide range of interest usually found in works in which Professor Frankfurter has participated or of which he is the author.

IS STALIN WEAKENING
OR THE SOVIETS?

Leon Trotsky

THE writer of this article is being plied on all sides with the question – now gleefully ironical, now genuinely perplexed: why is the ruling group in the Soviet Union at this time wholly engrossed in historic research? While Japan masters Manchuria, and Hitler makes ready to master Germany, Stalin is inditing extensive dissertations on the policies of Trotsky in the year 1905 and other questions equally up to date. Three years have passed since Stalin and Molotov announced that 'Trotskyism' was dead and buried, and now a new campaign – a fifth or sixth campaign – against this same 'Trotskyism' has sprung up in the pages of the Soviet Press. The unexpectedness of this – for what is the sense of fighting corpses? – and the unusual viciousness of the attack, have caused something of a sensation in the European Press. Both English and French papers have published disclosures of a mighty conspiracy of 'Trotskyists' in the U.S.S.R. They are receiving 60,000 roubles monthly from abroad; they have captured the most important positions in the industrial, administrative and educational fields, etc., etc. Most captivating is the accuracy with which the amount of the foreign subsidy is reported.

With all its absurdity this report rests upon an authority sufficiently precise in its own way – the authority of Stalin himself. Stalin quite recently announced that 'Trotskyism' is not a movement within the Communist Party, as the party members in spite of everything still continue to believe, but is 'the vanguard of the bourgeois counter-revolution'. If this statement be taken seriously, a number of inferences follow. The goal of the counter-revolution is to re-establish capitalism in the Soviet Union, a goal which can be achieved only by overthrowing the Bolshevik power. If the 'Trotskyists' are the vanguard of the counter-revolution, that can only mean that they are preparing the destruction of the Soviet

regime. From this it is but a step to the conclusion that the interested capitalist circles of Europe must be generously financing their
work. To speak plainly, it is just this interpretation of his words
that Stalin is counting on. Just as in 1917 Miliukov and Kerensky
felt obliged to assert that Lenin and Trotsky were agents of the
German militarism, so now Stalin is trying to get it on record that
Trotsky and the Opposition are agents of the counter-revolution.

Some months ago a widely circulated Polish newspaper printed
over my signature a forged article – not the first of its kind – about
the complete breakdown of the five-year plan and the inevitable
fall of the Soviets. Although the crudeness of the forgery was
obvious even to an inexperienced eye, Yaroslavsky, the official
historiographer of the Stalin faction, published a facsimile of the
article in the Moscow *Pravda*, giving it out as an authentic document and drawing the corresponding inferences in regard to 'Trotskyism'. A formal declaration from me that the article was a falsi-
fication from beginning to end was refused publication in *Pravda*.
The Stalin faction considered it more expedient to support the
tale that a powerful group among the Bolsheviks, a group led by the
closest associates of Lenin, considers inevitable the downfall of the
Soviet power and is working to that end.

The same game has been played before. Government circles
must have been surprised four years ago when they read that
Rakovsky, who so forcefully and brilliantly defended the interests
of the Soviet Union during the Franco-Soviet negotiations, is in
reality a most vicious enemy of the Soviet power. They doubtless
said to themselves at that time: 'Things must be going badly with
the Soviet Republic, if even Rakovsky has turned up among the
counter-revolutionaries.' If the French Government has hesitated
of late years to develop economic relations with the Soviets, or, on
the other hand, to break off diplomatic relations, the banishment
of Rakovsky has contributed to this hesitation.

The present campaign against the Opposition, arming itself with
cruder exaggeration even than the preceding ones, is against placing
a weapon in the hands of the most implacable enemies of the
Soviet Union in all countries. 'Evidently' – they are saying – 'the
situation in the country is getting extremely bad if the inner

struggle has again become so bitter.' It is this fact that the struggle against 'Trotskyism' is being waged with methods deeply injuring the interests of the Soviet Union which impels me to take up a subject which otherwise I would prefer to let alone.

If the 'Trotskyists' are in reality 'the vanguard of the bourgeois counter-revolution' – so the man in the street must reason – then how explain the fact that the European governments, including even the government of the brand-new Spanish republic, have one after the other refused asylum to Trotsky? Such an inhospitable attitude towards one's own 'vanguard' is difficult to explain. The European bourgeoisie has had enough experience to be able by this time to distinguish its friends from its enemies.

The so-called 'Trotskyists' – the older generation at least – took part in the revolutionary struggle against tsarism, in the October revolution of 1917, in the building of the Soviet Republic, in the creation of the Red Army, in the defence of the land of the Soviets against innumerable enemies during three years of civil war, and they played an intimate and frequently a leading part in the economic revival of the country. During these recent years, under the blows of the repression, they have remained completely loyal to those tasks which they set themselves long before 1917. It is needless to say that at a moment of danger to the Soviets the 'Trotskyists' would be found in the first line of defence, a position familiar to them in the experience of the past years.

The Stalin faction knows and understands this better than anybody else. If it puts into circulation accusations which are obviously damaging to the Soviet Union, and thus at the same time compromising to itself, the explanation lies in the political situation in which the course of events and its own preceding policies have placed the Stalin faction.

STALINISM, THE POLICY OF A CONSERVATIVE BUREAUCRACY

The first campaign against 'Trotskyism' was opened in 1923, while Lenin was on his death-bed, and during a protracted illness of Trotsky. The second and more violent attack developed in 1924, shortly after the death of Lenin. These dates speak for themselves.

The members of the old Politbureau, the body which actually governed the Soviet Republic, were: Lenin, Trotsky, Zinoviev, Kamenev, Stalin, Rykov and Tomsky (or Bukharin). In the present Politbureau only Stalin is left of the old staff, although all its members, except Lenin, are living. The selection of leaders of a great historic party is no accidental process. How can it happen that the leaders of the party during the heavy years preceding the revolution, and during the years when the foundations of the Soviets were laid, and the building in construction was being defended with the sword, have suddenly turned out to be 'inner enemies', at a time when the daily Soviet work has become to a certain degree a matter of bureaucratic routine?

These shifts and replacements which stand out at a glance in the Politbureau or the Council of People's Commissars have also been taking place during the recent period in all storeys of the party building, right down to the village councils. The present staff of the Central Executive Committee of the Soviets, the personnel of the provincial party secretariats, of the industrial, military and diplomatic bodies – all of them with but few exceptions are men of the new crowd. A majority of them took no part in the October revolution. A very considerable number were in the camp of its open enemies. To be sure, a small minority of the new ruling layer did belong to the Bolshevik party before October; but these were all revolutionary figures of the second or third magnitude. Such a combination is wholly according to the laws of history. A new bureaucratic stratum requires an 'authoritative' covering. This covering has been created by those among the old Bolsheviks who in the period of storm and assault were pushed to one side, those who felt a little out of place, who found themselves in silent semi-opposition to the actual leaders of the insurrection, and became able to enjoy their authority as 'old bolsheviks' only in the second stage of the revolution.

It has never yet happened in history that a stratum which achieved a revolution and guided and defended it in the most diffi-cult circumstances, suddenly, when the work of its hands was assured, turned out to be a 'counter-revolutionary' stratum, and that a few years after the revolution a new genuinely revolutionary stratum arrived to take its place. Indeed, the opposite fact is to be observed in the history of all great revolutions: when the victory is assured and has brought forth a new ruling stratum with its own interests and pretensions, and when this more moderate stratum, reflecting the demand for 'law and order', has pushed aside the revolutionists of the first draft, it always accuses its predecessors of a lack of revolutionism. The most conservative bureaucracy which might issue from a revolution could not otherwise defend its right to power except by declaring its opponents moderate, half-hearted and even counter-revolutionary. The methods of Stalin present nothing new whatever. We must not think, however, that Stalin is consciously plagiarizing anybody. He does not know enough history for that. He is simply obeying the logic of his own situation.

ECONOMIC DISAGREEMENTS

In order to get the sense of Stalin's present political difficulties, it is necessary to recall briefly the essence of those disagreements which lay at the bottom of the dispute between us and the Stalin faction. The Opposition demonstrated that the bureaucracy was underestimating the possibilities of industrialization and collectivization; that the economic work was being carried on empirically in a hand-to-mouth manner; that it was necessary to adopt a broader scale and a faster tempo. The Opposition demanded the abandonment of the one-year for the five-year plan, and asserted that a yearly twenty per cent growth of industrial production presented nothing unattainable with a centralized leadership. The Stalin bureaucracy accused the Opposition at that time of super-industrialism and utopianism. Kow-towing to the individual peasant proprietor, preparation to abandon the nationalization of the land, defence of a tortoise tempo in industry, and mockery of the planning principle – such was the platform of the Stalin faction from 1923 to 1928. All the present members of the Politbureau without a single exception answered our demand for an increased tempo of industrialization with the stereotyped question: where shall we get the means? The first draft of the five-year plan, upon which the government institutions got to work in 1927 under pressure from the prosecuted 'Trotskyists', was constructed on the principle of the descending curve: the growth of production was charted to fall from nine to four per cent. This draft was subjected to a withering criticism by the Opposition. The second variant of the five-year plan, the one officially ratified by that Fifteenth Congress of the Party which condemned the industrial 'romanticism' of the Opposition, called for an average growth of nine per cent.

How far Stalin himself fell short of the scale of the present five-year plan a year before its ratification, may be seen in the mere fact that in April 1927, answering Trotsky – who was then President of the Dnieprostroy Commission – he declared at a meeting of the Central Executive Committee: 'For us to build the Dnieprostroy (the mighty electrical power plant on the Dnieper) would be just the same as to buy the mouzhik a gramophone instead of a cow.' In the stenographic report of the Central Committee those words are inscribed as the most authentic opinion of Stalin. Subsequent attempts to explain his struggle against industrialization with references to the 'prematureness' of the proposals of the Opposition are meaningless, since it was not a question of a particular task of the moment but of the general prospects of industry and the five-year programme. The trial of the engineer-conspirators, publicly staged a year or so ago, showed that the actual leadership was in the hands of the irreconcilable enemies of the socialist economy. In defending his plans for a 'tortoise tempo' Stalin employed methods of repression against the Opposition.

With its usual shortsighted empiricism the Stalin bureaucracy under the influence of successes began in 1928 to increase uncritically the tempo of industrialization and collectivization. Here the roles were exchanged. The Left Opposition came out with a warning: with a too swift pace, not tested out by previous experience, disproportions may arise between the cities and the country, and between the different branches of industry, creating dangerous crises. Moreover – and this was the chief argument of the Opposition – a too rapid investment of capital in industry will cut off excessively the share allotted to current consumption, and fail to guarantee the necessary rise of the standard of living of the people. Although cut off from the whole world in his exile in Barnaoul,

Christien G. Rakovsky sounded the alarm: it is necessary, he said, even at the cost of a lowered tempo, to better the material condition of the worker-masses. Here too the Stalin bureaucracy has been ultimately compelled to listen to the voice of the Opposition. Quite recently a separate Commissariat of Manufacturing Industries was formed out of the staff of the Supreme Council of National Economy. Its task is to take care of the current needs of the population. At the present stage this reform has a purely bureaucratic character, but its goal is clear: to create in the government mechanism certain guarantees that the daily needs of the masses will not be too much sacrificed to the interest of the heavy industries. Here, too, the Stalin faction, lacking perspective and creative force, is compelled to bless today what it was cursing yesterday.

'SPICY DISHES'

Early in 1928 mass raids against the Opposition were carried out (expulsions, arrests, banishments). During that same year a new five-year plan was put into force, following upon all essential questions the platform of the Left Opposition. This volte-face was so sharp that the bureaucracy directly contradicted everything that it had defended during the first four years after Lenin's death. The accusation of super-industrialism lost all meaning, and active repressions against Left Opposition still more so.

But here the interest of the new ruling stratum in its own self-preservation stepped to the front. If the Opposition was right in its judgements and proposals, so much the worse for the Opposition. If yesterday's arguments against it are worthless, we must have new ones – and in order to justify repressions we must have extraordinary bitter ones. It is just in this sphere, however, that Stalin is especially gifted. In 1921, when Stalin was first elected general secretary of the party, Lenin remarked warningly to a small circle: 'This cook will give us nothing but spicy dishes.' In his death-bed letter to the party, commonly called his 'Testament', where he insisted on the removal of Stalin from his position as general secretary, Lenin pointed to the crudeness of his methods, his disloyalty and inclination to misuse of power. All these personal traits of Stalin, subsequently developed to a high degree, have been especially well manifested in his struggle against the Opposition.

It was not enough, however, to bring forward fantastic accusations; it was necessary that people should believe them, or at least be afraid to object. In its struggle for self-preservation, the Stalin bureaucracy was, therefore, compelled to begin by suppressing all criticism. Along this line, accordingly, the Opposition opened its most fervent struggle – a struggle for a democratic regime in the party, in the trade unions, in the soviets. We were defending one of the basic traditions of Bolshevism.

In the very heaviest years of the past – in the period of the underground struggle under tsarism, in 1917 when the country passed through two revolutions, during the following three years when twenty armies were fighting on a front 7,000 miles long – the party lived a seething inner life. All questions were freely discussed from the top of the party to the bottom; the freedom of judgement within the party was unqualified. The Stalin apparatus directed its chief efforts to the destruction of this embarrassing party democracy. Tens of thousands of so-called 'Trotskyists' were excluded from the party. More than ten thousand were subjected to various forms of criminal repression. Several were shot. Many tens of thousands of fighting revolutionists of the first draft were retained in the party only because they turned away and kept their mouths shut. Thus, in the course of these years, not only the membership of the ruling stratum has completely changed, but also the inner regime of the Bolshevik party.

Whereas Lenin, to say nothing of his closest comrades in arms, was subjected hundreds of times to the most furious blows of intra-party criticism, at the present time any communist who ventures to doubt the absolute correctness of Stalin upon every question whatever, and, moreover, who does not express a conviction as to his innate sinlessness, is expelled from the party and suffers all the consequences which flow from that. The shattering of the Opposition has become at the same time a shattering of the party of Lenin.

This shattering has been promoted by deep, although transitory causes. The years of the revolutionary earthquake and the civil war left the masses in a desperate need of rest. The workers, oppressed with need and hunger, wanted a revival of economic life at any price. In the presence of considerable unemployment the removal of a worker from a factory for Oppositional views was a fearful weapon in the hands of the Stalin faction. Political interests fell away. The workers were ready to give the bureaucracy the broadest powers, if only it would restore order, offer an opportunity to revive the factories and furnish provisions and raw material from the country. In this reaction of weariness, quite inevitable after every great revolutionary tension, lies the chief cause of the consolidation of the bureaucratic regime and the growth of that personal power of Stalin in which the new bureaucracy has found its personification.

TROTSKYIST CONTRABAND

When living voices had been finally suppressed it turned out that in the libraries, in the clubs, in the Soviet bookstores, on the shelves of students and workers, old books were standing, which continued to talk the same language they had talked in the days when the names of Lenin and Trotsky were inseparable. It is this barricade of hostile books that the Stalin bureaucracy has now come up against.

After nine years of uninterrupted struggle against the Opposition, the leaders have suddenly discovered that the fundamental scientific works and textbooks – on questions of economics, sociology, history – and above all the history of the October revolution and the Communist International – are chock-full of 'Trotskyist contraband', and that the most important chairs of social science in many institutions of learning are occupied by 'Trotskyists' or 'semi-Trotskyists'. Worst of all, those have been found guilty of Trotskyism who up to now had been its chief prosecutors.

In order to show how far this thing has gone it is sufficient to adduce an example touching the history of Bolshevism. Immediately after the death of Lenin a history of the party hastily written by Zinoviev was put into circulation, its sole purpose being to portray the whole past as a struggle between two principles, the good and the evil, in the persons of Lenin and Trotsky. But since this history accorded to Zinoviev himself a place in the camp of the good, and what is still more horrible, said nothing whatever about the providential role of Stalin, Zinoviev's history was placed on the index as early as 1926, the date of the open conflict between Zinoviev and Stalin.

The man designated to write an authentic history of the party was now Yaroslavsky. In the order of the party hierarchy it fell to Yaroslavsky, a member of the Praesidium of the Central Control Commission, to captain the whole struggle against the Left Opposition. All the indictments leading to arrests and explusions, and also a majority of the articles lighting up the repressions against 'Trotskyists' in the Soviet Press, came from the pen of Yaroslavsky. It was he, indeed, who reprinted in *Pravda* the forged article from a Polish newspaper. To be sure, the scientific-literary standing of Yaroslavsky was not wholly adequate, but he made up for this with his complete willingness to rewrite all history, including that of ancient Egypt, according to the demands of the bureaucratic stratum led by Stalin. A more reliable historiographer the Stalin bureaucracy could not possibly desire.

The result, however, was a completely unexpected one. In November of last year Stalin found himself compelled to come down on the fourth volume of Yaroslavsky history with a severe article. This too, it seems, was filled with 'Trotskyist contraband'. If Stanley Baldwin, in one of his speeches, should accuse Winston Churchill of a sympathy for Bolshevism, this would hardly create a greater sensation in England than did Stalin's accusing Yaroslavsky of abetting 'Trotskyism' in the Soviet Union. That accusatory article of Stalin served as an introduction to this last campaign. Obeying the signal, hundreds and thousands of functionaries, professors, journalists, distinguished in nothing but their zeal, rushed out to rummage through all the Soviet publications. Horrors! 'Trotskyism' at every step! There is no escape from 'contraband'!

But, after all, how could such a thing happen? Every new stratum as it rises to power shows an inclination to embellish its own past. Since the Stalin bureaucracy cannot, like other ruling classes, find reinforcement among the high places of religion, it is compelled to create its own historic mythology. It paints in black colours the past of all those who resisted it, while brushing up its own past with the brightest tints of the spectrum. The biographies of the leading actors of the revolutions are made over from year to year in accordance with the changes in the staff of the ruling stratum and the growth of its pretensions. But the historic material puts up some resistance. No matter how great is the zeal of the official historians, they are held in leash by the archives, the periodic Press of past years, and by the old articles – among them the articles of Stalin himself. That is the root of the evil!

Under the leadership of Yaroslavsky a number of young historians have been working over the history of the party. They have done all they could. But running into certain unsubmissive facts and documents, they found themselves unable, in spite of their zeal, either to crowd Trotsky out of the October revolution or provide Stalin with a sufficiently imposing role in it. It was just along this line that Yaroslavsky fell under indictment for circulating 'Trotskyist contraband': he did not carry the re-making of history clear through to the end. Woe to him who leaves his job half done.

In many cases the accusation of harbouring contraband has another source. Thousands of the less resolute partisans of the Opposition formally renounced their views during the last years, and were replaced in the party and set to work. It soon became evident, however, that the Opposition school had been for them an invaluable school for scientific thinking. Former 'Trotskyists' have occupied prominent positions in the sphere of economics, science, literature and educational activities. They are submissive, as frightened functionaries know how to be, but they also know the facts. In their brain-convolutions a number of critical habits have got stuck. The agents of Stalin, spying upon them from all sides, have had no difficulty in discovering in their books and lectures the poison of 'Trotskyist contraband'.

There is also a third source of this poison, no less dangerous. Serious young investigators, not at all bound up in the past with the Opposition, to a considerable extent non-political, but also free from careerist motives, frequently become victims of the scientific material they are working on and their own conscientiousness.

Upon a whole series of questions, without ever suspecting it, they fall into the tracks laid down by the Left Opposition. The system of opinions which the Stalin bureaucracy imposes has come into more and more serious conflict, not only with the traditions of the party, but also with any somewhat serious independent investigations in the various spheres of historic and social science, thus giving rise to Opposition moods. As a result it has suddenly been discovered that highly important branches of the social work in the Soviet Union are in the hands of the 'vanguard of the bourgeois counter-revolution'!

THE STRENGTHENING OF THE SOVIET ECONOMY WEAKENS STALIN

The bitter character of the present campaign against 'Trotskyists' has inspired the Russian emigrant Press to new prophecies of the coming downfall of the Soviet power. And these voices, in spite of the discouraging experience of the last fourteen years, have found an echo even in the great European and American newspapers. This is not, after all, surprising: not only does the Stalin bureaucracy stubbornly identify itself with the Soviet regime, but its enemies also, in search for comforting illusions, become victims of the same political aberration.

As a matter of fact, there is not the slightest foundation for this talk of the approaching long-awaited 'end'. The development of the productive forces of the Soviet Union is the most colossal phenomenon of contemporary history. The gigantic advantage of a planned leadership has been demonstrated with a force which nothing can ever refute. The near-sightedness and zigzagging of the Stalin bureaucracy only the more clearly emphasizes the power of the methods themselves. Only the maniacs of the restoration can imagine that the toiling masses of Russia want to turn back to the conditions of backward Russian capitalism.

But it is no less an error to imagine that the economic successes in strengthening the new industrial regime have also automatically reinforced the political position of Stalin and his faction. Up to a certain moment it was so. But at present a process of exactly the opposite kind is developing. A people who have achieved a mighty revolution may temporarily, in difficult circumstances, hand over the guidance of their destinies to a bureaucracy. But they are not able to renounce politics for long. It would be blindness not to see that the very strengthening of the economic situation of the country sets the toiling masses in more and more hostile opposition to the omnipotence of a bureaucracy. The workers, not without justification, attribute to themselves the achieved successes, and follow the bureaucracy with more and more critical eyes. For the masses see from below not only the successes and the possibilities flowing from them, but also the crude mistakes of the leaders and their continuous tendency to shift the responsibility for these mistakes from themselves to their agents. In raising the pride of the workers the successes have also raised their political demands.

The lessons of the economic zigzags, especially the astounding exposures of the trials of the sabotagers, have taken deep root in the consciousness of the population and greatly undermined even the prestige of Stalin. The inference comes of itself: 'It seems as though the Opposition was right!' The ideas of the Opposition, although not showing themselves on the surface, have long been laying down hidden roads. A critical period is now opening. The workers desire not only to obey but to decide. They intend to change many things. It is more than ever demanded of them, however, that they merely ratify decisions adopted without them. The workers are discontented – not with the Soviet regime, but with the fact that a bureaucracy is replacing the Soviets. In various workers' councils the 'Trotskyists' are lifting their heads, sometimes very courageously. They are being expelled. This has opened a new chapter in the life of the ruling party. Critical voices can no longer be silenced.

Whereas the former party crises reflected directly the difficulties and contradictions of the development of the Soviet republic under bureaucratic leadership, what comes to view in the present period is the contradiction in the position of the Stalin section, and above all of Stalin himself.

When these lines see the light the seventeenth conference of the party will already be ending in Moscow, a conference which is nothing but a meeting of the apparatus – that is, the centralized

Stalinist faction. Without a doubt the conference will pass off sufficiently well for the present leadership. But no matter how strong the Stalin faction is, it will not decide. The decision will be made in the last analysis by industrial processes on the one side, and on the other – by deep political processes taking place in the consciousness of the masses.

The campaign against 'Trotskyism' now developing signalizes the twilight of the omnipotence of the Stalin bureaucracy. But therewith it foretells, not the fall of the Bolshevik power, but on the contrary a new rise of the Soviet regime – not only its industry, but its politics and culture. That movement to which the author belongs is firmly confident of finding its place in the gigantic work to come.

July 1932

THE REVOLT AGAINST REASON

Bertrand Russell, F.R.S.

WHEN we compare our age with that of (say) George I, we are conscious of a profound change of intellectual temper, which has been followed by a corresponding change of the tone of politics. In a certain sense the outlook of two hundred years ago may be called 'rational', and that which is most characteristic of our time may be called 'anti-rational'. But I want to use these words without implying a complete acceptance of the one temper or a complete rejection of the other. Moreover, it is important to remember that political events very frequently take their colour from the speculations of an earlier time: there is usually a considerable interval between the promulgation of a theory and its practical efficacy. English politics in 1860 were dominated by the ideas expressed by Adam Smith in 1776; German politics today are a realization of theories set forth by Fichte in 1807; Russian politics since 1917 have embodied the doctrines of the Communist Manifesto, which dates from 1848. To understand the present age, therefore, it is necessary to go back to a considerably earlier time.

A widespread political doctrine has, as a rule, two very different kinds of causes. On the one hand, there are intellectual antecedents: men who have advanced theories which have grown, by development or reaction, from previous theories. On the other hand, there are economic and political circumstances which predispose people to accept views that minister to certain moods. These alone do not give a complete explanation when, as too often happens, intellectual antecedents are neglected. In the particular case that concerns us, various sections of the post-war world have had certain grounds of discontent which have made them sympathetic to a certain general philosophy invented at a much earlier date. I propose first to consider this philosophy, and then to touch on the reasons for its present popularity.

The revolt against *reason* began as a revolt against *reasoning*. In the first half of the eighteenth century, while Newton ruled men's minds, there was a widespread belief that the road to knowledge consisted in the discovery of simple general laws, from which conclusions could be drawn by deductive ratiocination. Many people forgot that Newton's law of gravitation was based upon a century of careful observation, and imagined that general laws could be discovered by the light of nature. There was natural religion, natural law, natural morality, and so on. These subjects were supposed to consist of demonstrative inferences from self-evident axioms, after the style of Euclid. The political outcome of this point of view was the doctrine of the Rights of Man, as preached during the American and French Revolutions.

But at the very moment when the Temple of Reason seemed to be nearing completion, a mine was laid by which, in the end, the whole edifice was blown sky-high. The man who laid the mine was David Hume. His *Treatise of Human Nature*, published in 1739, has as its sub-title 'An attempt to introduce the experimental method of reasoning into moral subjects'. This represents the whole of his intention, but only half of his performance. His intention was to substitute observation and induction for deduction from nominally self-evident axioms. In his temper of mind he was a complete rationalist, though of the Baconian rather than the Aristotelian variety. But his almost unexampled combination of acuteness with intellectual honesty led him to certain devastating conclusions: that induction is a habit without logical justification, and that the belief in causation is little better than a superstition. It followed that science, along with theology, should be relegated to the limbo of delusive hopes and irrational convictions.

In Hume, rationalism and scepticism existed peacefully side by side. Scepticism was for the study only, and was to be forgotten in the business of practical life. Moreover, practical life was to be governed, as far as possible, by those very methods of science which his scepticism impugned. Such a compromise was only possible for a man who was in equal parts a philosopher and a man of the world; there is also a flavour of aristocratic toryism in the reservation of an esoteric unbelief for the initiated. The world at large refused to accept Hume's doctrines in their entirety. His followers rejected his scepticism, while his German opponents emphasized it as the inevitable outcome of a merely scientific and rational outlook. Thus, as the result of his teaching, British philosophy became superficial, while German philosophy became anti-rational – in each case from fear of an unbearable agnosticism. European thought has never recovered its previous whole-heartedness; among all the successors of Hume, sanity has meant superficiality, and profundity has meant some degree of madness. In the most recent discussions of the philosophy appropriate to quantum physics, the old debates raised by Hume are still proceeding.

The philosophy which has been distinctive of Germany begins with Kant, and begins as a reaction against Hume. Kant was determined to believe in causality, God, immortality, the moral law, and so on, but perceived that Hume's philosophy made all this difficult. He therefore invented a distinction between 'pure' reason and 'practical' reason. 'Pure' reason was concerned with what could be proved, which was not much; 'practical' reason was concerned with what was necessary for virtue, which was a great deal. It is, of course, obvious that 'pure' reason was simply reason while 'practical' reason was prejudice. Thus Kant brought back into philosophy the appeal to something recognized as outside the sphere of theoretical rationality, which had been banished from the schools ever since the rise of scholasticism.

More important even than Kant, from our point of view, was his immediate successor Fichte, who, passing over from philosophy to politics, inaugurated the movement which has developed into National Socialism. But before speaking of him there is more to be said about the conception of 'reason'.

In view of the failure to find an answer to Hume, 'reason' can no longer be regarded as something absolute, any departure from which is to be condemned on theoretical grounds. Nevertheless, there is obviously a difference, and an important one, between the frame of mind of (say) the philosophical radicals and such people as the early Mohammedan fanatics. If we call the former temper of mind reasonable and the latter unreasonable, it is clear that there has been a growth of unreason in recent times.

I think that what we mean in practice by reason can be defined by three characteristics. In the first place, it relies upon persuasion rather than force; in the second place, it seeks to persuade by means of arguments which the man who uses them believes to be completely valid; and in the third place, in forming opinions, it uses observation and induction as much as possible and intuition as little as possible. The first of these rules out the Inquisition; the second rules out such methods as those of British war propaganda, which Hitler praises on the ground that propaganda 'must sink its mental elevation deeper in proportion to the numbers of the mass whom it has to grip'; the third forbids the use of such a major premise as that of President Andrew Jackson apropos of the Mississippi, 'the God of the Universe intended this great valley to belong to one nation', which was self-evident to him and his hearers, but not easily demonstrated to one who questioned it.

Reliance upon reason, as thus defined, assumes a certain community of interest and outlook between oneself and one's audience. It is true that Mrs Bond tried it on her ducks, when she cried 'come and be killed, for you must be stuffed and my customers filled'; but in general the appeal to reason is thought ineffective with those whom we mean to devour. Those who believe in eating meat do not attempt to find arguments which would seem valid to a sheep, and Nietzsche does not attempt to persuade the mass of the population, whom he calls 'the bungled and botched'. Nor does Marx try to enlist the support of capitalists. As these instances show, the appeal to reason is easier when power is unquestioningly confined to an oligarchy. In eighteenth-century England, only the opinions of aristocrats and their friends were important, and these could always be presented in a rational form to other aristocrats. As the political constituency grows larger and more heterogeneous, the appeal to reason becomes more difficult, since there are fewer universally conceded assumptions from which agreement can start. When such assumptions cannot be found, men are driven to rely upon their own intuitions; and since the intuitions of different groups differ, reliance upon them leads to strife and power politics.

Revolts against reason, in this sense, are a recurrent phenomenon in history. Early Buddhism was reasonable; its later forms, and the Hinduism which replaced it in India, were not. In ancient

Greece the Orphics were in revolt against Homeric rationality. From Socrates to Marcus Aurelius, the prominent men in the ancient world were, in the main, rational; after Marcus Aurelius, even the conservative Neo-Platonists were filled with superstition. Except in the Mohammedan world, the claims of reason remained in abeyance until the eleventh century; after that, through scholasticism, the renaissance, and science, they became increasingly dominant. A reaction set in with Rousseau and Wesley, but was held in check by the triumphs of science and machinery in the nineteenth century. The belief in reason reached its maximum in the sixties; since then it has gradually diminished, and it is still diminishing. Rationalism and anti-rationalism have existed side by side since the beginning of Greek civilization, and each, when it has seemed likely to become completely dominant, has always led, by reaction, to a new outburst of its opposite.

The modern revolt against reason differs in an important respect from most of its predecessors. From the Orphics onwards, the usual aim in the past was salvation – a complex concept involving both goodness and happiness, and achieved, as a rule, by some difficult renunciation. The irrationalists of our time aim, not at salvation, but at power. They thus develop an ethic which is opposed to that of Christianity and of Buddhism; and through their lust of dominion they are of necessity involved in politics. Their genealogy among writers is Fichte, Carlyle, Mazzini, Nietzsche – with supporters such as Treitschke, Rudyard Kipling, Houston Chamberlain and Bergson. As opposed to this movement, Benthamites and Socialists may be viewed as two wings of one party; both are cosmopolitan, both are democratic, both appeal to economic self-interest. Their differences *inter se* are as to means, not ends, whereas the new movement, which culminates (as yet) in Hitler, differs from both as to ends, and differs even from the whole tradition of Christian civilization.

The end which statesmen should pursue, as conceived by almost all the irrationalists out of whom fascism has grown, is most clearly stated by Nietzsche. In conscious opposition to Christianity as well as to the utilitarians, he rejects Bentham's doctrines as regards both happiness and the 'greatest number'. 'Mankind,' he says, 'is much more of a means than an end . . . mankind is merely the experimental material.' The end he proposes is the greatness of exceptional individuals: 'The object is to attain that enormous *energy of greatness* which can model the man of the future by means of discipline and also by means of the annihilation of millions of the bungled and botched, and which can yet avoid *going to ruin* at the sight of the suffering *created* thereby, the like of which has never been seen before.' This conception of the end, it should be observed, cannot be regarded as in itself contrary to reason, since questions of ends are not amenable to rational argument. We may *dislike* it – I do myself – but we cannot *disprove* it any more than Nietzsche can prove it. There is, none the less, a natural connexion with irrationality, since reason demands impartiality, whereas the cult of the great man always has as its minor premise the assertion: 'I am a great man.'

The founders of the school of thought out of which fascism has grown all have certain common characteristics. They seek the good in *will* rather than in feeling or cognition; they value power more than happiness; they prefer force to argument, war to peace, aristocracy to democracy, propaganda to scientific impartiality. They advocate a Spartan form of austerity, as opposed to the Christian form; that is to say, they view austerity as a means of obtaining mastery over others, not as a self-discipline which helps to produce virtue, and happiness only in the next world. The later ones among them are imbued with popular Darwinism, and regard the struggle for existence as the source of a higher species; but it is to be rather a struggle between races than one between individuals, such as the apostles of free competition advocated. Pleasure and knowledge, conceived as ends, appear to them unduly passive. For pleasure they substitute glory, and for knowledge the pragmatic assertion that what they desire is true. In Fichte, Carlyle and Mazzini, these doctrines are still enveloped in a mantle of conventional moralistic cant; in Nietzsche they first step forth naked and unashamed.

Fichte has received less than his due share of credit for inaugurating this great movement. He began as an abstract metaphysician, but showed even then a certain arbitrary and self-centred disposition. His whole philosophy develops out of the proposition 'I am I', as to which he says:

'The Ego *posits itself* and it *is* in consequence of this bare positing by itself; it is both the agent and the result of the action, the active and that which is produced by the activity; *I am* expresses a deed (*Thathandlung*). The Ego is, because it has posited itself.'

The Ego, according to this theory, exists because it wills to exist. Presently it appears that the non-Ego also exists because the Ego so wills it; but a non-Ego so generated never becomes really external to the Ego which chooses to posit it. Louis XIV said *l'état, c'est moi*; Fichte said 'the universe is myself'. As Heine remarked in comparing Kant and Robespierre, 'in comparison with us Germans, you French are tame and moderate'.

Fichte, it is true, explains, after a while, that when he says 'I' he means 'God'; but the reader is not wholly reassured.

When, as a result of the battle of Jena, Fichte had to fly from Berlin, he began to think that he had been too vigorously positing the non-Ego in the shape of Napoleon. On his return in 1807, he delivered his famous 'Addresses to the German Nation', in which, for the first time, the complete creed of nationalism was set out. These addresses begin by explaining that the German is superior to all other moderns, because he alone has a pure language. (The Russians, Turks and Chinese, not to mention the Eskimoes and the Hottentots, also have pure languages, but they were not mentioned in Fichte's history books.) The purity of the German language makes the German alone capable of profundity; he concludes that 'to have character and to be German undoubtedly mean the same'. But if the German character is to be preserved from foreign corrupting influences, and if the German nation is to be capable of acting as a whole, there must be a new kind of education, which will 'mould the Germans into a corporate body'. The new education, he says, 'must consist essentially in this, that it completely destroys freedom of the will'. He adds that will 'is the very root of man'.

There is to be no external commerce, beyond what is absolutely unavoidable. There is to be universal military service; everybody is to be compelled to fight, not for material well-being, not for freedom, not in defence of the constitution, but under the impulsion of 'the devouring flame of higher patriotism, which embraces the nation as the vesture of the eternal, for which the noble-minded man joyfully sacrifices himself, and the ignoble man, who only exists for the sake of the other, must likewise sacrifice himself'.

This doctrine, that the 'noble' man is the purpose of humanity, and that the 'ignoble' man has no claims on his own account, is of the essence of the modern attack on democracy. Christianity taught that every human being has an immortal soul, and that, in this respect, all men are equal; the 'rights of man' was only a development of Christian doctrine. Utilitarianism, while it conceded no absolute 'rights' to the individual, gave the same weight to one man's happiness as to another's; thus it led to democracy just as much as did the doctrine of natural rights. But Fichte, like a sort of political Calvin, picked out certain men as the elect, and rejected all the rest as of no account.

The difficulty, of course, is to know who are the elect. In a world in which Fichte's doctrine was universally accepted, every man would think that he was 'noble', and would join some party of people sufficiently similar to himself to seem to share some of his nobility. These people might be his nation, as in Fichte's case, or his class, as in that of a proletarian communist, or his family, as with Napoleon. There is no objective criterion of 'nobility' except success in war; therefore war is the necessary outcome of this creed.

Carlyle's outlook on life was, in the main, derived from Fichte, who was the strongest single influence on his opinions. But Carlyle added something which has been characteristic of the school ever since: a kind of socialism and solicitude for the proletariat which is really dislike of industrialism and of the *nouveau riche*. Carlyle did this so well that he deceived even Engels, whose book on the English working class in 1844 mentions him with the highest praise. In view of this, we can scarcely wonder that many people were taken in by the socialistic façade in National Socialism.

Carlyle, in fact, still has his dupes. His 'hero worship' sounds very exalted; 'we need,' he says, 'not elected parliaments, but Hero-kings, and a whole world not unheroic.' To understand this, one must study its translation into fact. Carlyle, in *Past and Present*, holds up the twelfth-century Abbot Samson as a model; but whoever does not take that worthy on trust, but reads the Chronicle of Jocelin of Brakelonde, will find that the abbot was an unscrupulous ruffian, combining the vices of a tyrannous landlord with those of a pettifogging attorney. Carlyle's other heroes are at least equally objectionable. Cromwell's massacres in Ireland move him to the comment: 'But in Oliver's time, as I say, there was still belief in the Judgements of God; in Oliver's time there was yet no distracted jargon of "abolishing Capital Punishments", of Jean-Jacques Philanthropy, and universal rose-water in this world still so full of sin. . . . Only in late decadent generations . . . can such indiscriminate mashing-up of Good and Evil into one universal patent-treacle . . . take effect in our earth.' Of most of his other heroes, such as Frederick the Great, Dr Francia and Governor Eyre, all that need be said is that their one common characteristic was a thirst for blood.

Those who still think that Carlyle was in some sense more or less liberal should read his chapter on democracy in *Past and Present*. Most of it is occupied with praise of William the Conqueror, and with a description of the pleasant lives enjoyed by serfs in his day. Then comes a definition of liberty: 'The true liberty of a man, you would say, consisted in his finding out, or being forced to find out the right path, and to walk thereon' (p. 263). He passes on to the statement that democracy 'means despair of finding any heroes to govern you, and contented putting up with the want of them'. The chapter ends by stating, in eloquent prophetical language, that when democracy shall have run its full course, the problem that will remain is 'that of finding government by your Real-Superiors'. Is there one word in all this to which Hitler would not subscribe?

Mazzini was a milder man than Carlyle, from whom he disagreed as regards the cult of heroes. Not the individual great man, but the nation, was the object of his adoration; and while he placed Italy highest, he allowed a role to every European nation except the Irish. He believed, however, like Carlyle, that duty should be placed above happiness, above even collective happiness. He thought that God revealed to each human conscience what was right, and that all that was necessary was that everybody should obey the moral law as felt in his own heart. He never realized that different people may genuinely differ as to what the moral law enjoins, or that what he was really demanding was that others should act according to *his* revelation. He put morals above democracy, saying: 'The simple vote of a majority does not constitute sovereignty, if it evidently contradicts the supreme moral precepts ... the will of the people is sacred, when it interprets and applies the moral law; null and impotent, when it dissociates itself from the law, and only represents caprice.' This is also the opinion of Mussolini.

Only one important element has since been added to the doctrines of this school, namely, the pseudo-Darwinian belief in 'race'. (Fichte made German superiority a matter of language, not of biological heredity.) Nietzsche, who, unlike his followers, is not a nationalist or an anti-semite, applies the doctrine only as between different individuals; he wishes the unfit to be prevented from breeding, and he hopes, by the methods of the dog-fancier, to produce a race of supermen, who shall have all power, and for whose benefit alone the rest of mankind shall exist. But subsequent writers with a similar outlook have tried to prove that all excellence has been connected with their own race. Irish professors write books to prove that Homer was an Irishman; French anthropologists give archaeological evidence that the Celts, not the Teutons, were the source of civilization in Northern Europe; Houston Chamberlain argues at length that Dante was a German and Christ was not a Jew. Emphasis upon race has been universal among Anglo-Indians, from whom imperialist England caught the infection through the medium of Rudyard Kipling. But the anti-semitic element has never been prominent in England, although an Englishman, Houston Chamberlain, was mainly responsible for giving it a sham historical basis in Germany, where it had persisted ever since the Middle Ages.

About race, if politics were not involved, it would be enough to say that nothing politically important is known. It may be taken as probable that there are genetic mental differences between races; but it is certain that we do not yet know what these differences are.

In an adult man the effects of environment mask those of heredity. Moreover, the racial differences among different Europeans are less definite than those between white, yellow and black men; there are no well-marked physical characteristics by which members of different modern European nations can be certainly known apart, since all have resulted from a mixture of different stocks. When it comes to mental superiority, every civilized nation can make out a plausible claim, which proves that all the claims are equally invalid. It is *possible* that the Jews are inferior to the Germans, but it is just as possible that the Germans are inferior to the Jews. The whole business of introducing pseudo-Darwinian jargon in such a question is utterly unscientific. Whatever we may come to know hereafter, we have not at present any good ground for wishing to encourage one race at the expense of another.

The whole movement, from Fichte onwards, is a method of bolstering up self-esteem and lust for power by means of beliefs which have nothing in their favour except that they are flattering. Fichte needed a doctrine which would make him feel superior to Napoleon; Carlyle and Nietzsche had infirmities for which they sought compensation in the world of imagination; British imperialism of Rudyard Kipling's epoch was due to shame at having lost industrial supremacy; and the Hitlerite madness of our time is a mantle of myth in which the German ego keeps itself warm against the cold blasts of Versailles. No man thinks sanely when his self-esteem has suffered a mortal wound, and those who deliberately humiliate a nation have only themselves to thank if it becomes a nation of lunatics.

This brings me to the reasons which have produced the wide acceptance of the irrational and even anti-rational doctrine that we have been considering. There are at most times all sorts of doctrines being preached by all sorts of prophets, but those which became popular must make some special appeal to the moods produced by the circumstances of the time. Now the characteristic doctrines of modern irrationalists, as we have seen, are: emphasis on *will* as opposed to thought and feeling; glorification of power; belief in intuitional 'positing' of propositions as opposed to observational and inductive testing. This state of mind is the natural reaction of those who have the habit of controlling modern mechanisms such as aeroplanes, and also of those who have less power than formerly, but are unable to find any rational ground for the restoration of their former preponderance. Industrialism and the war, while giving the habit of mechanical power, caused a great shift of economic and political power, and therefore left large groups in the mood for pragmatic self-assertion. Hence the growth of fascism.

Comparing the world of 1920 with that of 1820, we find that there had been an increase of power on the part of: large industrialists, wage-earners, women, heretics and Jews. (By 'heretics' I mean those whose religion was not that of the government of their country.) Correlatively, there had been a loss of power on the part of monarchs, aristocracies, ecclesiastics, the lower middle classes, and males as opposed to females. The large industrialists, though stronger than at any previous period, felt themselves insecure owing to the threat of socialism, and more particularly from fear of Moscow. The war interest – generals, admirals, aviators and armament firms – were in the like case: strong at the moment, but menaced by a pestilential crew of Bolsheviks and pacifists. The sections already defeated – the kings and nobles, the small shopkeepers, the men who from temperament were opponents of religious toleration, and the men who regretted the days of masculine domination over women – seemed to be definitely down and out; economic and cultural development, it was thought, had left no place for them in the modern world. Naturally they were discontented, and collectively they were numerous. The Nietzschean philosophy was psychologically adapted to their mental needs, and, very cleverly, the industrialists and militarists made use of it to weld the defeated sections into a party which should support a medievalist reaction in everything except industry and war. In regard to industry and war, there was to be everything modern in the way of technique, but not the sharing out of power and the effort after peace that made the socialists dangerous to the existing magnates.

Thus the irrational elements in the Nazi philosophy are due, politically speaking, to the need of enlisting the support of sections which have no longer any *raison d'être*, while the comparatively sane elements are due to the industrialists and militarists. The former elements are 'irrational' because it is scarcely possible that the small shopkeepers, for example, should realize their hopes, and fantastic beliefs are their only refuge from despair; *per contra*, the hopes of industrialists and militarists might be realized by means of fascism, but hardly in any other way. The fact that their hopes can only be achieved through the ruin of civilization does not make them irrational, but only Satanic. These men form intellectually the best, and morally the worst, element in the movement; the rest, dazzled by the vision of glory, heroism and self-sacrifice, have become blind to their serious interests, and in a blaze of emotion have allowed themselves to be used for purposes not their own. This is the psycho-pathology of Nazidom.

I have spoken of the industrialists and militarists who support fascism as sane, but their sanity is only comparative. Thyssen believes that, by means of the Nazi movement, he can both kill socialism and immensely increase his market. There seems, however, no more reason to think him right than to think that his predecessors were right in 1914. It is necessary for him to stir up German self-confidence and nationalist feeling to a dangerous degree, and unsuccessful war is the most probable outcome. Even great initial successes would not bring ultimate victory; now, as twenty years ago, the German government forgets America.

There is one very important element which is on the whole against the Nazis although it might have been expected to support reaction – I mean organized religion. The philosophy of the movement which culminates in the Nazi is, in a sense, a logical development of Protestantism. The morality of Fichte and Carlyle is Calvinistic, and Mazzini, who was in life-long opposition to Rome, had a thoroughly Lutheran belief in the infallibility of the individual conscience. Nietzsche believed passionately in the worth of the individual, and considered that the hero should not submit to authority; in this he was developing the Protestant spirit of revolt. It might have been expected that the Protestant churches would welcome the Nazi movement, and to a certain extent they did so. But in all those elements which Protestantism shared with Catholicism, it found itself opposed by the new philosophy. Nietzsche is emphatically anti-Christian, and Houston Chamberlain gives an impression that Christianity was a degraded superstition which grew up among the mongrel cosmopolitans of the Levant. The rejection of humility, of love of one's neighbour, and of the rights of the meek, is contrary to Gospel teaching; and anti-semitism, when it is theoretical as well as practical, is not easily reconciled with a religion of Jewish origin. For these reasons Nazidom and Christianity have difficulty in making friends, and it is not impossible that their antagonism may bring about the downfall of the Nazis.

There is another reason why the modern cult of unreason, whether in Germany or elsewhere, is incompatible with any traditional form of Christianity. Inspired by Judaism, Christianity adopted the notion of Truth, with the correlative virtue of Faith. The notion and the virtue survived in 'honest doubt', as all the Christian virtues remained among Victorian free-thinkers. But gradually the influence of scepticism and advertising made it seem hopeless to discover truth, but very profitable to assert falsehood. Intellectual probity was thus destroyed. Hitler, explaining the Nazi programme, says:

The national state will look upon science as a means for increasing national pride. Not only world-history, but also the history of civilization, must be taught from this point of view. The inventor should appear great, not merely as an inventor, but even more so as a fellow-countryman. Admiration of any great deed must be combined with pride because the fortunate doer of it is a member of our own nation. We must extract the greatest from the mass of great names in German history and place them before the youth in so impressive a fashion that they may become the pillars of an unshakable nationalist sentiment.

The conception of science as a pursuit of truth has so entirely disappeared from Hitler's mind that he does not even argue against it. As we know, the theory of relativity has come to be thought bad because it was invented by a Jew. The Inquisition rejected Galileo's doctrine because it considered it untrue; but Hitler accepts or rejects doctrines on political grounds without bringing in the notion of truth or falsehood. Poor William James, who invented this point of view, would be horrified at the use which is made of it; but when once the conception of objective truth is abandoned, it is clear that the question 'what shall I believe?' is one to be settled, as I wrote in 1907, by 'the appeal to force and the arbitrament of the big battalions', not by the methods of either theology or science. States whose policy is based upon the revolt against reason must therefore find themselves in conflict, not only with learning, but also with the churches wherever any genuine Christianity survives.

An important element in the causation of the revolt against reason is that many able and energetic men have no outlet for their love of power, and therefore become subversive. Small States, formerly, gave more men political power, and small businesses gave more men economic power. Consider the huge population that sleeps in suburbs and works in great cities. Coming into London by train, one passes through great regions of small villas, inhabited by families which feel no solidarity with the working class; the man of the family has no part in local affairs, since he is absent all day submitting to the orders of his employers; his only outlet for initiative is the cultivation of his back garden at the week-end. Politically, he is envious of all that is done for the working classes; but, though he feels poor, snobbery prevents him from adopting the methods of socialism and trade unionism. His suburb may be as populous as many a famous city of antiquity, but its collective life is languid, and he has no time to be interested in it. To such a man, if he has enough spirit for discontent, a fascist movement may well appear as a deliverance.

The decay of reason in politics is a product of two factors: on the one hand, there are classes and types of individuals to whom the world as it is offers no scope, but who see no hope in socialism because they are not wage-earners; on the other hand, there are able and powerful men whose interests are opposed to those of the community at large, and who, therefore, can best retain their influence by promoting various kinds of hysteria. Anti-communism, fear of foreign armaments, and hatred of foreign competition, are the most important bogeys. I do not mean that no rational man could feel these sentiments; I mean that they are used in a way to preclude intelligent consideration of practical issues. The two things the world needs most are socialism and peace, but both are contrary to the interests of the most powerful men of our time. It is not difficult to make the steps leading up to them *appear* contrary to the interests of large sections of the population, and the easiest way of doing this is to generate mass hysteria. The greater the danger of socialism and peace, the more governments will debauch the mental life of their subjects; and the greater the economic hardships of the present, the more willing the sufferers will be to be seduced from intellectual sobriety in favour of some delusive will-o'-the-wisp.

The fever of nationalism which has been increasing ever since 1848 is one form of the cult of unreason. The idea of one universal truth has been abandoned; there is English truth, French truth, German truth, Montenegrin truth, and truth for the principality of Monaco. Similarly, there is truth for the wage-earner and truth for the capitalist. Between these different 'truths', if rational persuasion is despaired of, the only possible decision is by means of war and rivalry in propagandist insanity. Until the deep conflicts of nations and classes which infect our world have been resolved, it is hardly to be expected that mankind will return to a rational habit of mind. The difficulty is that, so long as unreason prevails, a solution of our troubles can only be reached by chance; for while reason, being impersonal, makes universal cooperation possible, unreason, since it represents private passions, makes strife inevitable. It is for this reason that rationality, in the sense of an appeal to a universal and impersonal standard of truth, is of supreme importance to the well-being of the human species, not only in ages in which it easily prevails, but also, and even more, in those less fortunate times in which it is despised and rejected as the vain dream of men who lack the virility to kill where they cannot agree.

January 1935

MEDITATION ON ABYSSINIA

Leonard Woolf

THE world has not, at the moment, 'liquidated' the Abyssinian affair, to borrow a useful word of great significance which we have all adopted from the Communist vocabulary. It is a post-war word and it is significant because it indicates the extent to which the post-war world has adopted or accepted violence as a normal method of settling political and economic problems. It means what we used to mean by such a phrase as 'finally settle a question', but it implies that the question or persons liquidated were finally, summarily, and violently settled. In Russia the monarchy, the White generals, the interventionists, the bourgeoisie, the kulaks, and the Trotskyists have all been successfully liquidated. In Germany Herr Hitler has already liquidated the Communists, Social-Democrats, Jews, and a considerable number of those who helped to place him in power and is now attempting to liquidate the Evangelical and Roman Catholic Churches. Socialism has been pretty thoroughly liquidated in Austria, Spain, and Italy. Signor Mussolini, having 'cleaned up' (to use another technical phrase of contemporary political science) the inside of Italy, then decided to liquidate Abyssinia with an army which has turned out to be about three times too large for accomplishing the task. And now the League of Nations, in the opinion of many people, is engaged in an attempt to liquidate Signor Mussolini, while Sir Samuel Hoare and M. Laval are doing their best to liquidate the League.

The process in Abyssinia has not yet worked itself out to a definite conclusion, but it is worth while remarking in parenthesis that this is also true of the general process of liquidation as a world technique for regulating social relations. The trouble about the use of force or violence as the primary instrument of a government or society is the inordinate difficulty of stopping or stabilizing it. It does not matter whether the units be individuals, classes, or nations, the more they rely upon force to determine their relations,

the more difficult it becomes to stabilize relations. That is the profound truth which has appealed to so many, Christians and non-
Christians, as underlying the flash of intuition in the famous
statement that those who take the sword perish by the sword. The
whole of history proves it. The intolerable instability of a society in
which individuals are allowed to regulate their private and personal
relations by force is now recognized over the greater part of the
earth, though it took thousands of years to abolish this elementary
system of 'liquidation'. Another instance of the same cause producing a similar effect can be observed in the fact that nearly all revolutions follow the same curve of instability and violence: they begin
with a government established bloodlessly but violently; there
follows instability with the government compelled to rely on force
against threats and acts of violence from right and left of it, and
again and again the curve of violence and instability has risen
steadily or rapidly through blood to dictatorship. Another instance
is the intolerable instability and anarchy in the society of nations
which produced the war and, after the war, the world-wide movement for ending it through the system of a League of Nations.

The previous paragraph is a parenthesis, but is not, as we shall
see, an irrelevant parenthesis. But let us return to Ethiopia. Signor
Mussolini has not yet liquidated Ethopia and the League has not
yet liquidated Signor Mussolini. It is impossible, therefore, to
know how the adventure will end and what must be the final judgement on its historical significance. But it has reached a stage at
which the outlines of the final figure which it will cut in history
may perhaps be discerned and meditation upon some of its aspects
may therefore be useful.

The British 'National' Government and most people in this
country are now, at the present stage, agreed that we are engaged
in a test case, probably the final test, in case of failure, of the
League of Nations and of what is called a system of collective
security. I propose first to consider the attitude of the government
and of various important sections of public opinion towards the
events which have led us into the existing situation, but before
doing so it is necessary to recall some elementary facts about the
League and recent history, for there seem to be many people in

positions of power and authority who have either no knowledge or no understanding of them. The League of Nations is not a super-state; it has not even that fictitious entity which is usually ascribed to nations. It is an organization of existing states for certain specific purposes. There is no mystery or doubt about its origin or its pur-pose. It was consciously and deliberately created, in answer to a world-wide demand, to make certain specific changes in the pre-war system of inter-state relations, to substitute for the claims and pretensions of sovereign states to settle things by war the right and obligation to have disputes settled peacefully.

There is, too, no mystery or doubt with regard to the difference between the inter-state organization which existed before 1918 and that which was created by agreement in the Covenant. In 1914 every state claimed to be and was judge in its own disputes; it claimed to be and was absolute arbiter in every case of whether there should be peace or war. So anarchical had the world of nations remained that, if a dispute arose between two states which, in fact, might involve the peace of the whole world, no other state or states could intervene in order to promote a peaceful settlement without danger that its action would be construed as what was called 'an unfriendly act' by one or other of the parties and there-fore without danger of itself becoming involved in a war – in other words, a neutral state could only in a crisis intervene to prevent war by making peace a *casus belli*. In such dangerous conditions every state looked for security to armies and armaments, des-perately endeavouring to make itself as strong as its resources allowed and stronger than its neighbour, and searching for alliances or understandings which would ensure that, when the inevitable war came, it was on the winning side.

The post-war world attempted through the League to bring into existence an entirely different system of international relations. By entering the League a state renounced the right of being judge in its own case and of settling its disputes by resort to force or war. In order to provide alternative methods to war for settling disputes the Covenant set up an elaborate system of conciliation and arbi-tration, a system of pacific settlement which in practice has been shown to be efficient whenever – a not unimportant proviso – the object of both disputants has been pacific settlement. (A system devised to ensure international peace cannot be expected to work if those who work it in fact want war.) Finally, the League system proposed to provide for the security of states, not by individual armaments or armed alliances, but by assuring every member of the League that if attacked all the other members would support the victim of aggression against the aggressor.

There can be no real doubts about the facts in the dispute between Italy and Abyssinia. The Emperor of Ethiopia rules over the only completely independent native state in Africa. Before the war it had been the subject of the usual imperialist manoeuvres and machinations of Great Powers seeking to acquire or control it. The Powers concerned were Italy, Great Britain, and France. It had been partitioned into 'spheres of interest', the inevitable prelude to conquest, and in 1896 Italy, who had in some way or other established her right to be the conqueror by squaring Great Britain, marched her armies into Abyssinia. Her armies were defeated, the partition of Africa failed so far as Abyssinia was concerned, and the Italian Government signed a treaty of peace recognizing 'the absolute and unreserved independence of the Ethiopian Empire as a sovereign and independent state'. But this by no means implied that either Italy or the other Great Powers had finally abandoned their intention to 'partition' Abyssinia. In 1906 Italy, Great Britain, and France again signed one of those treaties which have always been the prelude to an imperialist conquest in Africa; they first solemnly pledged themselves 'to maintain intact the integrity of Ethiopia' and then proceeded to carve it up into spheres of influence. The immediate protest of the Abyssinian Government showed that it was alive to the danger threatening it. In 1923, at the instance of France and Italy, and against the wishes of the British Government, Abyssinia was admitted a member of the League. That fact should have finally settled the 'Abyssinian question', so far as imperialism was concerned. By admitting that country to the League, all the other members pledged themselves to protect its independence and territorial integrity and to settle all disputes which might arise between them and the Abyssinian Government by the pacific procedure laid down in the Covenant. If this was to be a prelude to conquest or forceful partition of Abyssinia at the hands of those states which had admitted it into the League, they were not only reducing the League and its system to a farce, but were destroying all foundations for peace and civilized or ordered relations between states. There are after all limits to the cynicism with which states and statesmen can afford to break every elementary rule of truth and honesty in the dealings between nations, even though the dealings are between strong and weak nations, for if Great Powers, like Britain and France, regulate their relations with the small Powers by the methods and moralities of tricksters, gangsters, and thugs, it is inevitable that sooner or later they will begin to deal in the same way with one another. That, however, was apparently not the view of the Conservative Government of Mr Baldwin or of the Fascist Government of Signor Mussolini. These two governments, in 1925, two years after Abyssinia entered the League, exchanged notes in which once more, though in slightly different and more precise terms, they recorded their agreement upon the measures which they would take in order to exert pressure upon Abyssinia to accept the claims to concessions and spheres of influence enumerated in the 1906 treaty. The 1906 treaty and these notes were clearly incompatible with the obligations incurred by Great Britain and Italy to respect and protect the territorial integrity and independence of Abyssinia, as soon as she was admitted a member of the League, and Abyssinia rightly pointed this out at once and protested against it.

It has been necessary to recapitulate these historical facts, for except against their background it is impossible to understand either the course or significance of what has been happening during the last eleven months. Between 1926 and the second half of 1934 there was no indication of any move by Italy against Abyssinia. Between July 1934 and January 1935 evidence began to accumulate even in the Press that Signor Mussolini was contemplating, and indeed already preparing, a military expedition for the conquest of Abyssinia, and it is therefore certain that every Foreign Office in Europe must have had far more conclusive evidence of the military preparations. In January 1935 the Abyssinian Government formally brought the matter before the League under Article 11 of the

Covenant. It is important to understand what that means: it means that nine months before Italy invaded Abyssinia every Government in the League had been formally warned by Abyssinia that she was threatened with this invasion by Italy and that they were bound by their obligations under the Covenant immediately to take such 'wise and effectual' action as would 'safeguard the peace of nations'. For the next eight months the League Council, impelled by the British and French Governments, did nothing wise or effectual to safeguard the peace of nations. Those governments again and again during that time prevented the League from putting into operation the machinery of pacific settlement under Articles 10 and 15 of the Covenant, though they were repeatedly asked to do so by Abyssinia. Meanwhile, the Italian Government made no attempt to conceal its intentions and demands. It treated the League and the Council with contumely; it openly repudiated its obligations under the Covenant; it denied that it would be satisfied by any peaceful settlement – in fact, it never even took the trouble to formulate against Abyssinia any serious grounds for complaint or dispute; and finally it stated explicitly that nothing short of a war and the military conquest of Abyssinia would 'satisfy' it. Throughout that period Signor Mussolini made speeches to the Italian people informing them that he was going to war; he mobilized large numbers of troops; and he sent to the Italian East African colonies an immense army fully equipped for a first-class war. It was only in September, when it was obviously far too late to prevent a war, that the League was allowed to put into operation its procedure for preventing war laid down in Article 15 and within a week or two Italy invaded Abyssinia. So flagrant had been the behaviour of Signor Mussolini and his Government that the League unanimously declared Italy to be an aggressor under Article 16 and a discussion as to the application of sanctions immediately followed. About that discussion and the half-hearted application of sanctions I shall say more later.

I propose now to examine the attitude during the last twelve months of the Government, the Labour Party, and certain influential sections of what is called 'public opinion', vocal in the great newspapers, towards the course of events and policy recorded in the previous paragraphs. And it may as well be said at once that such an examination reveals on all sides a perilous confusion of mind and purpose with regard to even the most general lines of policy which this country should pursue in international affairs. The Foreign Secretary, the Prime Minister, and Mr Eden have informed us authoritatively on behalf of the Government that in their opinion the Italian–Abyssinian dispute has become, as was pointed out above, a test case of the League system and of the possibility of basing peace upon collective security. If the League fails in this case and Italy succeeds in reaping the fruits of aggression by acquiring possession of or control over Abyssinian territory, the League as an effective instrument of peace will be finally discredited. Most people agree with this view, but very few of them seem to understand what it really implies. There is for instance continual confusion between 'the League' or 'the League system' and what is called collective security. They are not the same thing. The League is an organization of states which attempts by agreement (*a*) to regulate inter-state relations, (*b*) to provide regular procedure for settling such disputes as may arise among states, and (*c*) to provide for the security of states, i.e. to protect their independence and territorial integrity. These three functions of the League are different, though they may be and are closely interconnected. Even if the League did not exist they would still be functions of the international system which took its place, for they must always be among the primary objects of policy of each individual state. An international 'system' existed before the war and, like the League system, it too, though in a different way, attempted to perform these three functions: it attempted (*a*) to regulate inter-state relations by diplomacy, the rules of international law, and treaties, (*b*) to settle disputes by negotiation, arbitration, or war, (*c*) to provide for security by military offensive or defensive alliances and by competitive armament. The League system differs in two vital respects from this system, because it attempts (*b*) to provide a regular and obligatory procedure for settling disputes without war and makes the settlement of any dispute without resort to war and the use of such procedure a concern not only of the states involved in the dispute but of all the members of the League, and (*c*) to provide collectively for the security of each state by disarmament and the assurance that in case of attack or aggression of one state against another all the other members of the League will come to the assistance of the victim. The important thing to observe is that 'collective security' is only a part of the whole system; it comes in only through the provisions, assurances, and obligations described above under (c); in practice it consists of the assurances and obligations defined in Article 10 of the Covenant, the reduction of armaments to be carried through under Article 8, and the assurance under Article 16 that if any state resorts to war in disregard of its obligations, the state which is attacked will have the assistance of all the other states in the League which are bound to apply certain specified sanctions against the aggressor.

Let us first examine the attitude and policy of the Government towards this League system in the Abyssinian dispute. The Government's actions in that dispute cannot be treated as unconnected with the general lines of their foreign policy in the past. The Ancient Mariner owing to one act had to go about with an albatross instead of a cross hung round his neck, for no one can disencumber himself from the effects of his actions; when the National Government at the end of 1934 were faced at Geneva with the truculent determination of Signor Mussolini to ignore the League, violate treaties, and make war upon Abyssinia, they entered the League Council their necks metaphorically encumbered with a whole necklace of albatrosses. The first albatross, though a little one, has throughout the last twelve months had a disastrous effect upon the mind and action of our Government; it is the 1906 treaty and the exchange of Notes. Our obligations to Italy implied in those documents are incompatible with our obligations to Abyssinia under the Covenant. They bound us in effect to help Italy to gain without war what she is now attempting to gain by war, control of Abyssinia, 'economic' control which in Africa always leads to political control. It is true that these obligations and understandings, in so far as they are inconsistent with the terms of the Covenant, are by Article 20 of the Covenant declared to be abrogated; but our Government has never publicly or openly admitted this or taken steps, in accordance with Article 20, 'to procure its release from such obligations'. On the contrary, up to October of this year in negotiations with Italy it showed that it still considered itself to be bound to these agreements, e.g., in September the British representative informed the Committee of Five that his Government was 'prepared to recognize a special Italian interest in the economic development of Ethopia'. And these same agreements inspired and are embodied in the Hoare–Laval 'peace' proposals, which astonished and outraged public opinion in nearly every country of the world. Owing to this there has been a fatal element of muddle and weakness in British policy. Here is a test case for the League system and the British Government proposes to be the protagonist in upholding the system against Mussolini's Government. And yet it never makes clear either to itself or to Mussolini or to the rest of the world whether it is really going to stand by the League and protect the integrity and independence of its fellow-member Abyssinia or whether it is going to stand by its agreement with Italy to give Italy economic and political control over Abyssinia. Is it to be wondered at that in these circumstances Mussolini obviously assumed until October that the British Government and the League never meant business, and that, as far as we were concerned, after a face-saving process of protest, he would be allowed to do what he liked in Ethiopia just as Japan had been allowed after due protest, to do what she liked in Manchuria? The old methods of imperialism are inconsistent and incompatible with the League system. There may be something to be said for a national policy based upon either the one or the other; there is nothing to be said for a policy which tries to poise itself impossibly on or between the two.

The mention of Manchuria introduces us to another of the British Government's albatrosses, a much larger and more disastrous bird. When the Italian–Abyssinian dispute became acute towards the end of 1934 – this 'test case of the League system' – the League system had all but been destroyed, and the British Government had played a leading part in destroying it. Adequately to prove this statement would require a long and minute examination of the whole foreign policy of the National Government, a task which is obviously impossible in this article. Happily such an examination has already been made, and the reader who wishes to have the evidence should read *Inquest on Peace* by Vigilantes. Some people may perhaps consider that the authors of that book are sometimes intemperate in language and politically biased in their judgements, but their facts remain documented and irrefutable. And the facts prove that at best the Government's foreign policy was muddle-headed, vacillating, inconsistent, paying lip-service to the League and its system, but continually in practice repudiating the obligations the fulfilment of which could alone give reality to the League system of peace, disarmament, and collective security. The effects of this policy can be observed over the whole field of international relations, but they were particularly marked in the Manchurian affair and in the Disarmament Conference, and it is essential to understand why the attitude of the Government in these two cases had undermined confidence in the League system and therefore had fatal repercussions in Italy and Ethiopia. The invasion of Manchuria by Japan was as clear a violation of the Covenant and a case of aggression as the invasion of Abyssinia by Italy. The action of Japan immediately presented to the League and to its members, indeed to the whole world, a choice between two different systems of regulating the relations between states. Was Japan, because she was stronger than China, to be judge in her own dispute and of her own claims and to enforce those claims by war? Or was the dispute between these two Powers to be remitted through the operation of the League and according to the provisions of its Covenant peacefully to impartial examination and decision? And further, if the stronger party took the law into its own hands, violated its obligations, and resorted to war as its instrument of national policy against the weaker party, were the other states to stand aside from a matter as of no concern to them or were they to maintain the system of 'collective security' to which they had all pledged themselves, i.e. – to quote the actual words of the treaty which every one of them had signed and had never denounced – 'to deem the resort to war by Japan against China an act of war against all other Members of the League' and to come to the assistance of China – that is the very gist and meaning of 'collective security' –

by immediately subjecting the aggressor to the 'sanctions', the severance of all trade or financial relations, etc., which they themselves had undertaken to impose.

There could be no real dispute about the horns of the British Government's dilemma. If it chose the first of these alternatives, it was repudiating the system of the League and of collective security and definitely returning to the pre-war system. But if it chose the second, it must meet its obligations and take the risks necessary for the establishment of peace and the resistance to aggression. That is to say, it must insist first, that the dispute be settled pacifically by mediation, conciliation, and arbitration of the League, and secondly, it must make plain from the outset that it stood by the system of collective security and would be ready to fulfil its obligation to resist aggression. And there can be no dispute which horn of the dilemma Sir John Simon and the National Government chose to sit on. They threw over the League and scoffed at the system of collective security. They made a pretence of trying to get Japan to accept a settlement without war, but they showed the Japanese Government from the first that so far as they were concerned, it could go ahead and treat the Covenant as a scrap of paper; the British Government would not under any circumstances fulfil its obligations under Article 16 towards China.

Japan went ahead, attacked China, and took from her the territory which she now calls Manchukuo. The result upon the whole international situation and upon the League was inevitable and instantaneous. The members of the League had repudiated their obligations, led by the British Empire. I say 'led' advisedly. Members of the Labour Party have repeatedly maintained during the last few years that the influence of the British Empire in shaping the course of international affairs is paramount, that if a British Government takes the lead in establishing the system of peace and collective security, the rest of the world will follow it, and that if that government stands by its obligations under the Covenant, the League system will work. The view has often been ridiculed as romantic and exaggerated and represented as an invitation to the Government to ride off on quixotic crusades all over the habitable globe. It is a view, however, which is shared by nearly every

foreigner concerned with foreign policy or conversant with international affairs. And it has now been proved to be correct by what
has happened in the Abyssinian question. As soon as Great Britain
stood by its obligations under the Covenant, the rest of the world
stood by Great Britain for the Covenant, and, even with a hesitant
or hostile France, the League system began once more to work as
an instrument for peace and collective security.

The attitude of Great Britain at the Disarmament Conference
repeated and confirmed its policy towards Japanese aggression; it
convinced other countries that we had abandoned the League
system, were not prepared to fulfil our obligations under the Covenant, and were now determined to look for our security to our own
armaments, re-establishing in Europe the old 'Balance of Power'
system which inevitably involves a competition in armaments.
Throughout the first part of the Conference, when it was still possible that something might have been achieved, the representatives
of Great Britain were either negative or obstructive to every concrete
proposal for limiting or abolishing armaments. The British Government was, in fact, taking the most prominent part in the business
of destroying the League and a system of collective security, and it
was doing so because it both misunderstood and mistrusted them.
This muddle and misunderstanding of their own policy and of
international affairs in the minds of British ministers is of the
greatest importance for it still infects their policy. On 23 November
1934 Mr Baldwin made the following statement of his own view of
the League system:

It is curious that there is growing among the Labour Party support
for what is called a collective peace system. Well now, a collective
peace system in my view is perfectly impracticable in view of the fact
that the United States is not yet, to our unbounded regret, a member
of the League of Nations, and that in the last two years two great
Powers, Germany and Japan, have both retired from it. It is hardly
worth considering when those are the facts.

There is no more honest politician in Europe than Mr Baldwin
and only muddle can explain the fact that, when he made that
speech, his Government and his country were deeply committed to
the collective peace system through the Covenant, and in parti-

cular by Articles 10 and 16, that he and his Government had never stated that they did not hold themselves bound by the obligations of those articles and had never given notice of intention to leave the League, and finally that within a year of that speech he himself as Prime Minister was saying precisely the opposite about the collective peace system from what he was saying in 1934 and was in fact taking the leading part in maintaining that system against Italy even to the point of the application of sanctions. The nature of the muddle is clearly shown in the debates in Parliament regarding this speech of Mr Baldwin and the whole of the Government's Manchurian policy. For instance, the Under-Secretary for Foreign Affairs in explaining the Government's views said that it is a mistake to think that the whole collective system is enshrined in Article 16 of the Covenant; 'the collective system is by no means confined', he said, 'to the imposition of sanctions. Personally, I deplore all this talk of war and of sanctions.' Here there is complete misunderstanding of the facts and psychology which determine international history. The whole of the League system is, of course, not enshrined in the articles dealing with sanctions, but those articles are a vital part of the system of collective peace, as the Under-Secretary of State is now learning in the Abyssinian question. The League or any other international 'system' is not an artificial, imaginary contrivance inscribed on waste paper and laid up safely out of the way in Heaven or the Foreign Office; it is a concrete method of dealing with international relations which ministers can use or refuse to use in shaping national policy. There are, I repeat, two great questions which every Prime Minister and Government have to decide with regard to the international system. First, how are they going to regulate their relations and settle any dispute which may arise between them and another nation? Is it to be by the old system of negotiation in which each side is judge in its own cause and ultimately may rely on war as the instrument of its policy or is it to be the League system of regular and compulsory pacific settlement through third-party conciliation or arbitration? That is one question, a practical, concrete question always looming over the head of a Foreign Secretary. But instantly and always he is faced by a second question: how in the world of today am I to provide for the security of my country against attack? Whether he rejects the League system or accepts it, he will have to answer that question. He may, like Lord Stanhope, 'deplore all this talk of war and sanction', but he will still have to answer that question and in answering it he will have to talk of war and sanctions. He is again faced with two alternatives. He can take the pre-war method of trusting to his own armaments and those of his allies and to a competition in armaments which will put preponderance of power in his hands. In that case he rejects the League system, for he is making a competition in armed forces and not pacific settlement the determining factor in international affairs. But if he accepts the League system of pacific settlement and renunciation of war, he still has to satisfy his own country *and every other member of the League* on the question of security. For every nation will say: If I enter the League and pledge myself to pacific settlement and renounce war and no longer try to make myself stronger than my neighbour, where is my guarantee of security against a breach of the Covenant, against an attack from my neighbour? And the answer, if you accept the League system, is plain and inescapable: a collective peace system implies a system of collective security: if a state enters the League of Nations, it must look for its security to common action by all members in its defence against attack and violation of the peace system: the members of the League pledge themselves to apply sanctions against the aggressor.

Thus the sanctions clauses are not the whole League or the whole collective peace system, but they are a vital part of it because the security of members depends upon their being carried out and the confidence of states in the League and in their own security depends upon their belief that other members will fulfil their obligations under those clauses. The fatal thing was at the beginning of the Abyssinian affair that that confidence, largely owing to the British Government, had been undermined. There was every excuse for the Italian Government to assume, in the light of such statements as those of Mr Baldwin and other ministers quoted above, that the British Government repudiated its obligations of collective security and sanctions and that Mussolini would be allowed to do in Abyssinia what Japan had done in Manchuria. And that assumption was confirmed by the attitude of the British Government and of France all through the negotiations about Abyssinia from January to September of this year. Great Britain worked with France to prevent the regular machinery of the League's pacific settlement being brought into operation. No resistance was offered to Italy's refusal to comply with her obligations and accept pacific settlement. The League was not allowed, therefore, to prevent war, yet no warning of any kind was given to Italy that if she did make war upon Abyssinia, the provisions with regard to collective security, the sanction clauses, would be put into operation against her, and no preparations of any kind were made for collective resistance to her aggression.

So much for the British Government. Let us examine very briefly the attitude of mind during this long drawn-out crisis of some non-official currents of public opinion. The case of Mr Garvin is the most remarkable. He is editor of one of the most important English newspapers; he writes every week upon politics; he has written books which show that he is not completely ignorant of history; he addresses an immense public and might be expected, therefore, by the canons of British journalism, to feel some measure of responsibility for what he writes. Yet week after week Mr Garvin pours out a flood of vituperative misrepresentation over every one who says a word on behalf of the League system or of trying to prevent Italy attacking and conquering Abyssinia. Those who wish to prevent war and resist aggression collectively are dismissed as 'jingo pacifists' and warmongers. The facts with regard to the League which have been given in the previous paragraphs are completely ignored and suppressed. The notion that states like Britain and Italy should respect and fulfil obligations which they have assumed by signing treaties, e.g. the Covenant, is ridiculed. Mr Garvin's policy is bleak, bare, and, as he says, based on realities (just like the Kaiser's and Admiral Tirpitz's between 1910 and 1918). Italy is a Great Power, Abyssinia is a small power; therefore, Italy has a right to do what she wills with Abyssinia. Abyssinia is a barbarous state, has no right to be in the League, has no right to the territory which she governs, has in fact only one right – to be conquered and ruled by Italy. Great Britain cannot oppose Italy, because Italy is stronger than Great Britain. Great Britain must therefore give way completely to Italy and rearm herself – presumably, though this is not stated, in order eventually to be able to fight Italy. Many people laugh at Mr Garvin, but he is really no laughing matter. When the Editor of a great English paper can take this view of the principles upon which British policy and international affairs should be based, not laughter, but terror is the appropriate emotion – terror at observing how little separates us from the chaos and barbarism which Mr Garvin foolishly imagines to be confined to Ethiopia.

As regards the Labour Party, it has always stood officially for the League system and has supported it in its entirety as the only hope of preventing war. But Abyssinia has revealed fundamental differences of opinion and considerable confusion of mind both among its leaders and supporters. The majority has endorsed the party's previous official policy, but in the minority two broad and deep currents of opposition may be detected. There is first the hundred per cent pacifist position which maintains that the use of force, and, therefore, the application of sanctions by a government, should never be supported in international affairs. It is an intelligible policy, but those who urge it upon Britain in the Abyssinian crisis should have made their position clear before the crisis arose; it is a policy incompatible with Britain remaining a member of the League – a fact which was as obvious before as it was after Italy invaded Abyssinia. Yet many of those who for pacifist reasons are opposed to the fulfilment of Britain's obligations under the sanction clauses had always previously urged that Britain should remain a member of the League and show her 'loyalty' to the Covenant. The second current of opposition is Marxism or socialist. The League, it is argued, is a League of capitalist states; capitalism inevitably implies imperialism and imperialism inevitably implies war; therefore, the League cannot prevent war and the application of sanctions will be only the camouflage of a quarrel between rival imperialist Powers. A socialist or a socialist party should refuse to have anything to do either with the League or with sanctions or with a war between capitalist states. I suggest that the social attitude to war, cruelty, and violence changes from age to age and, although influenced by economics, it is also influenced by other things. The opposition to and revulsion from them increased considerably in Europe for 150 years before the beginning of the present century. It manifested itself both within nations and also in the increasing demand among all classes and in many countries that the relations between states should be regulated and their differences settled without war. Such a revolutionary movement of feeling and opinion, as this against violence, is due to and influenced by a vast number of different factors, besides the economic factor, and its ebbs and flows through centuries. We are, therefore, spectators and participants in a long drawn-out struggle between two different methods of organizing relations between states, the method of violence and war and the method of settlement and agreement. It is true, I think, that without socialism the permanent elimination of war is impossible, but even a world of socialist national states would be faced with the choice of regulating their relations either in the one way or in the other. The outcome of this struggle is doubtful; it will not be determined either today or tomorrow, either by 'victory' or by 'defeat' of the League in Abyssinia; but it will be profoundly influenced in every incident and 'crisis' by the choice which each individual, party, class, and nation makes, and by its ability to distinguish without prejudice the instruments and methods of peace and civilization from those of war and barbarism.

January 1936

PUBLIC ORDER

W. Ivor Jennings

I

THE ordinary Englishman is law-abiding partly by social habit and partly because he fears the consequences. Social habit and fear are both produced by economic stability. It was not the Reform Act but constantly improving standards of life that made law and order the dominant characteristic of Victorian England. While half Europe was in revolution the Chartists' petition was brought to Parliament in a cab. For half a century afterwards profits and wages were rising, and it was not fundamentally important to the individual that the proportionate increases were by no means commensurate. During the present century social insurance and other public services have prevented industrial depression from producing riot and rebellion. The result of a long development since the Industrial Revolution is a highly complex class structure in which the members of every class have something to lose by chaos. The middle classes are all for the *status quo*. The working classes do not unite because they have much to lose besides their chains. The threat of economic disturbance is enough to prevent even serious economic reform; it is even more effective where the fear is not of a confiscating government but of no government at all. Rebellion means, in the first instance, loss of salaries, wages, bank deposits, and perhaps even movable and immovable property. There may be loot; but who will loot whom?

These considerations are conscious to few, though their importance is demonstrated by the attempt of some politicians to associate reform and revolution. Nevertheless, the fear that changes may be for the worst is often conscious and otherwise always subconscious. A 'red' among the middle classes – even a mild and pacific Fabian – is regarded as at best a crank and at worst a dangerous character. Communism had few adherents even among the working classes, and even during the depression; it becomes more influential as it becomes more law-abiding and more 'respectable'. Revolution in England is not practical politics. Though no doubt the Army considers that one of its tasks is to 'keep order', it is significant that the words 'throughout the British Empire' are always added.

Moreover, most people are not more than mildly interested in politics. In the modern sense of that word, man is not a political but a social animal. Indeed, if the phrase were permissible, it might be said that a political animal is a rare bird. Political enthusiasts are always in a minority. The representatives present at the annual conferences of the National Union of Conservative and Unionist Associations, or of the Labour Party, or of the Trade Union Congress, represent few save themselves. The ordinary man thinks primarily of himself, his family and his friends. His social sympathies are wide but not deep. He hates injustice and can be roused to indignation by oppression. He considers that something ought to be done about it but rarely thinks of doing anything himself. He can soon be induced to believe that it is none of his business. For his first task is to maintain and improve his social and economic status. The newspapers are aware of the comparative unimportance of politics. The *Daily Herald* achieved a two-million circulation by developing its 'features'. The readers of the *Daily Express* will stand Beaverbrook so long as they can read Beachcomber. Even Mr Garvin does not frighten away those who are willing to spend twopence on Torquemada and advertisements.

Successful dictators arise out of economic confusion. They secure a measure of popular support because it is believed that they can restore order and preserve economic advantages. Herr Hitler obtained his funds from big capitalists and his votes from the lower middle class. Once in power a dictator can maintain his authority because of the fear of change. He can pile up armaments at the expense of the standard of living because slow economic changes are not noticed and because order at least means stability. He can, too, suppress the politically minded minority, or distract its attention, or divert its enthusiasm. An elegant system of espionage, a little propaganda about the merits of concentration camps or the sinister activities of secret police, and an occasional dramatic flourish against some 'common enemy', real or imagined, are soon sufficient to render politics as taboo as religion. If in addition some economic carrot can be held before the nose of hungry donkeys, such as the possibility of ousting a minority like the Jews from effective competition, acquiescence among the donkeys may be converted into enthusiasm. Opposition can then arise only from 'intellectuals' or from what Charles Booth significantly described as 'the semi-criminal classes'. The former can be suppressed – 'whenever I hear the word "culture" I suspect treason'; the latter can be drilled in conscripted armies and labour corps. In such circumstances only an unmanageable economic crisis or a split in the higher command can give hope to the democrats.

The real case for Section 1 of the Public Order Act is not that political uniforms in themselves incite to violence, nor that disorders have occurred or might occur in Bethnal Green; it is, rather, that a disciplined body is one of the essential supports of a campaign of virulence against minorities and of appeals to economic greed that might, in time of industrial depression, obtain enough support to overthrow democracy. Uniforms are the symbol of discipline. They have psychological effects upon those who wear them as well as upon those who see them. They create on the one hand a feeling of security to those who wear them and of insecurity in those who see them. Both are necessary to the establishment of dictatorship. The prohibition of uniforms in section 1 of the Act hangs with the prohibition of organization and training in section 2.

There may be a successful dictatorship where there is no successful dictator. In concentrating our attention on those who dictate by talking, we forget that a large part of the world is governed by tongue-tied military officers. Democracies must, or think that they must, defend themselves against external aggression. So they create armies and hope that political control will prevent them from becoming instruments of internal aggression. A soldier is an expert; and all experts tend to assume that the whole of knowledge is comprised in their *expertise*. General officers are apt to assume that discipline is justice and force the ultimate reason. To command an army in time of peace is the easiest task in the world. The commander commands and thousands obey. There is one right, the right to command, and one duty, the duty to obey. It needs a long democratic tradition, such as has so far persisted in England and in France, to persuade army officers that their right to command some proceeds only from their duty to obey others. Even in democracies they can easily acquire an extravagant idea of their own powers and their own importance. They are necessarily surrounded by yes-men. They are subject to no criticism save that of ignorant leader-writers and 'fool politicians'. There is only one promotion from the control of an army – the control of a nation. In the circumstances it is not surprising that so many of the nations who, in the first fine flush of liberalism, rushed into democracy, have since sunk into military dictatorship. The military dictator is necessarily unstable. Others, too, want promotion. He can be overthrown by the sword as he overthrew by the sword – though indeed the weapons used are far more deadly. But it is the dictator, not the dictatorship, that is unstable. It needs a great and courageous people to fight an army. What are many against a few provided with the arms that modern science has invented?

English law assumes rather pathetically that the generals need to be protected against common soldiers, not that the people needs to be protected against the generals. The notion that soldiers can be made revolutionaries by communist leaflets – the notion behind the Incitement to Disaffection Act – is simply ludicrous. Any army – that is, the people who fight – becomes politically disaffected only when economic disturbance among the civil population has reached such a stage that civil revolution becomes practicable. The real problem, as Spain and South America have demonstrated, is to prevent the incitement of generals. Fortunately, in spite of some disquieting tendencies between 1912 and 1915, this problem has not been actual in England since the overthrow of James II. So long as peace is maintained, and so long as Parliament can be relied upon not to pass the Army and Air Force (Annual) Act automatically, the danger hardly exists.

II

The problem of public order thus becomes, with us, simply a

problem of preventing riot. Unless another war creates complete economic chaos, as it probably will, the chances of a revolution from below are negligible. So long as the State can maintain its social services through a depression and so long as the existence of trained gangs not under parliamentary control is strictly prohibited (and the Public Order Act, in its initial provisions, provides additional powers for that purpose), a Fascist revolution is not to be anticipated. So long as parliamentary control of the forces is maintained, the possibility of a military dictatorship is remote.

It is obvious that any government must possess the means for suppressing actual disorder. Riots have no necessary connexion with politics. They may arise merely from high spirits, as among academic and athletic 'toughs'. They may arise, though rarely in fact, from criminals intent upon loot. Normally, however, rioting is a political offence. A sense of injustice or inferiority, played upon by a skilful orator, may give rise to a sudden movement of disgust. Miners in the depressed areas, compelled to exist below the poverty line for reasons which they cannot understand and which cannot be explained to them, can easily be persuaded that there is a specific enemy and that he ought to be dealt with there and then. Men on strike may be convinced that the industrial weapon is ineffective. Where strong religious prejudices exist, oratory can turn peaceful citizens into frenzied mobs. Where economic motives can be combined with the ignorant man's dislike of 'foreigners', anti-Jewish feeling is easily aroused.

Where social injustices exist, the most effective remedy is to remove them. Education is a cure for prejudice and ignorance. No reasonable person objects to the association with these prophylactic remedies of legal prohibitions against incitement to violence. There is, too, another kind of incitement to violence which consists in the use of insulting words and gestures. This is peculiarly a fascist technique, though it has also been used by religious controversialists. It might appear to be a double-edged weapon; but those who use it are careful to direct it against minorities and to provide an adequate bodyguard. The riot is stimulated not for its own sake but for its publicity value and for the feeling of uncertainty which all rioting tends to create. It is sought to expand the area of prejudice and antipathy. Those who attend meetings are few; those who read about riots are many. The minority tends to lose its sense of security; the prejudiced tend to lose their fear of economic disorder; and the feeling of bewilderment out of which successful dictators arise is stimulated and propagated. Provision is contained in the Public Order Act for strengthening the law on this point. It may be doubted whether it is necessary. Indeed, the strengthening of the law is essentially dangerous. For the notion of 'insulting words' has been enormously extended in recent years. On one occasion the cry of, 'Give us bread,' was, in the circumstances, held to be insulting; the distribution of pacifist literature in the neighbourhood of militarist displays has been prosecuted; and generally the law has been used as an instrument for repressing what some democrats, at least, regard as legitimate propaganda.

Uniform and drill are used partly for the same purpose of creating fear and uncertainty. If there are two kings in Jerusalem the individual whose primary concern is with himself tends to render allegiance to both. If there are two churches the millions of vicars of Bray must join in communion with both. If two political parties contend for complete domination the political neutral, like the big industrialist, must insure himself by subscribing to both. The result is to create a state of uncertainty, a psychological momentum that can readily be increased by some outside impulse. If there are two forces, the gang and the police, must I not make my peace with both if peace is what I most desire?

There are, however, subsidiary motives. As the Salvation Army has shown, much publicity may be obtained by a uniform and a band. Publicity is essential to true democracy. Burke's doctrine of representative government was no doubt adequate for a period when only certain 'interests' were represented; it is inadequate for modern democracy. It is the business of the elected representative not only to forward the interests of his constituents and to take decisions on matters of public policy as they arise, but also to secure the carrying out of those views of public policy which are prevalent in his constituency and which he was elected to support. Since Peel's Tamworth manifesto the parties have appealed to the people to support their policies and to vote accordingly. It is essential, therefore, that the parties should have policies and the means of publicity for making them known.

The instruments for this purpose are varied. The Press is perhaps the most important. It suffers from a number of defects as an instrument of political education. It is essentially partial. It relies primarily on advertisers who, even if they do not dictate policy necessarily give it a bias. It can be bought either directly by wealthy syndicates or indirectly by subsidies. It can, moreover, rarely devote the space to effective political discussion; for the circulation of most of the newspapers depends essentially upon 'features'. In the educative sense the Press is much less valuable than the book and the pamphlet. These are the best of all methods because they can develop policies at length and because the reader has access to both sides. They are, however, expensive. Moreover, the primary problem is to induce the ordinary voter to take more than a mere passing interest, not to provide the material for the politically-minded who read books and pamphlets on political questions. The short and snappy leaflet is of little value because it is short and snappy. It says too much in too little space. No one would deny the importance of the freedom of the Press; but it is not the only method of publicity.

Of the newer methods the cinema and broadcasting are the most important. The cinema is even more biased than the Press and is, for practical purposes, in the hands of one party. Broadcasting has to make an attempt to be impartial; but, because of the difficulty of persuading the average politician that impartiality involves the possibility of somebody listening to the other side, it tends to fall into the safer atmosphere of the non-controversial.

We thus come to the oldest of the propaganda methods, the public meeting. Its proportionate efficacy has no doubt declined since the development of new resources of publicity. Yet its importance is not to be measured by the numbers who attend meetings; nor is its value to be deprecated because audiences usually consist of enthusiastic supporters and enthusiastic opponents. Politics in a democratic country is not taboo. There is more propaganda value in the private discussion, the casual discussion, and the sudden interjection than in the shrieking headline. It is not only the constant blaring of newspapers and loudspeakers but also the system of espionage which makes fascist propaganda so effective. No one can visit Germany without noticing the almost total absence of discussion of internal political affairs. A British Government may survive with all the newspapers against it; if the word goes round that its foundation is rotten, or its policy contemptible, or its personnel incompetent, it is doomed. The earnest party supporter, the man who voluntarily licks envelopes and stands on draughty doorsteps at election time, is he from whom there springs the fertile word. A party can survive if it has no money and no leaders; it cannot live if it has no members. The political meeting is the means by which the earnest party men are brought into contact with their leaders, are renewed in their faith, and are strengthened in their endeavour. It is, too, in the political meeting that interested doubters are turned into enthusiastic workers. No one can doubt the influence of the street-corner meeting in the development of the socialist movement. Here there were no favourable newspapers, no funds, and, for practical purposes, no national leaders. No one can doubt, either, the value of the great Conservative rallies which Disraeli used and Joseph Chamberlain elaborated.

Viewed from this angle, the public meeting holds a cardinal position in democratic government; and it is significant that in fascist countries the complete control of the Press and of broadcasting has not prevented the leaders from organizing bigger and better public meetings. Where two views of politics are permitted and opponents are not only expected to attend but are welcomed, a public meeting is a danger to public order because in a crowd both enthusiasm and opposition are infective. To prohibit or to destroy its utility by close restriction would be a mistake of the first order. It is, too, essential not to restrict too closely the means by which crowds may be attracted. A meeting summoned by poster has little appeal. The Salvation Army technique is interesting because it has been effective. Bands, uniforms, banners, cheerful tunes, attract the audience. A short street-corner meeting stimulates interest. The indoor meeting is for serious instruction. Uniforms apart, the Labour Party has used the same method. The speech at the street-corner is often the prelude to the formal indoor oration. Where no great funds are available, it is often the only means of propaganda available.

III

At a time when the English law of public meetings is being strengthened, it is wise to know what the law is and what it ought to be. As usual, it is easier to say what it ought to be than what it is. Dicey's classic statement is, like most of Dicey's statements, so partial as to be entirely misleading. The common law 'broadens down from precedent to precedent' – which means that it is very often what the courts choose to make it. Moreover, most of the decisions have been rendered by the Divisional Court on cases stated by justices. As such a case necessarily deals with a 'criminal cause or matter', no appeal has been possible, and the views of courts higher than the Divisional Court have never yet been expressed.

The first point is abundantly clear, though it is not mentioned by Dicey. Not only is there no right of public meeting in general, but it is definitely unlawful to hold a meeting in a public street and perhaps in any public place. The only right which a subject possesses in the highway is the right to pass and repass. Used for any other purpose is a trespass to the highway which is actionable by the owner of the soil. This is perhaps a small matter because even where the owner is known he never takes proceedings. In addition, however, it has to be remembered that any obstruction of the highway is a nuisance at common law. It is, moreover, an offence under section 72 of the Highway Act, 1835. It is immaterial that there is no effective obstruction to traffic. It has been so decided; and in any case any motorist knows that he may be liable for obstruction even if he leaves a car in a cul-de-sac. Usually the law is not rigidly enforced. Cars are permitted to remain parked for a period which the police think reasonable; costers are normally allowed to ply their trade subject to obedience to by-laws; and frequently street-corner meetings are permitted.

It is, however, entirely undesirable that the police should have a discretion to waive the strict requirements of the law. Either the law should be enforced or it should be altered. Under the present system if a police constable orders a speaker to take up his soap-box

183

and walk, the speaker has no lawful answer. If he refuses to move he is 'obstructing the police in the execution of their duty'. Nor does it matter if ten yards away a fashionable wedding, or even a rival political meeting, is obstructing the highway even more effectively. The police should have as little discretion in these matters as possible, partly because they cannot always be trusted not to discriminate, and partly because the law falls into disrepute when they are believed to discriminate, even if they do not.

One can be somewhat less positive about processions. Dicey fathered the extraordinary idea that if A has the right to go down the High Street then 'A, B, C, D and a thousand or ten thousand other persons' may also walk down the High Street. Statutory restrictions apart this is a very doubtful proposition (almost as doubtful as Dicey's statement that ten thousand people have a right to hold a meeting on a common: apart from the common law, see section 26 of the Commons Act, 1879). A's right is to pass along the highway in such a manner as not to interfere with the similar rights of others. If three undergraduates walking arm-in-arm after a bump supper had obstructed Professor Dicey's way to All Souls College he might have had different views about the common law – even if their purpose was the more effectively to discuss the treachery of the Grand Old Man in deciding to introduce the Home Rule Bill. In any case, though there is no decision on it, a procession of ten thousand people in column of fours (and Dicey says nothing about an orderly procession, so that according to him they might apparently straggle right across the road) would presumably come within the Highway Act. Nor, in fact, does the Highway Act matter much, because the police regulate processions either under the Metropolitan Police Act or under the Town Police Clauses Act; and where neither is in force the local police inspector passes his own Act.

Obviously there must be control. The Lord Mayor's Procession is, in ordinary language, a nuisance. A succession of long processions would try modern Oxford, if not the Oxford of Dicey's day, too high. The idea of a procession of ten thousand undergraduates marching down the High Street every day and in any sort of order, even crossing against the traffic lights, is ludicrous even if they were anxious to support the successors of Mr Joseph Chamberlain and Sir Edward Carson. If at the same time another ten thousand undergraduates (no doubt from another university) were to move in the opposite direction to support the successors of Mr Gladstone and Mr Asquith, it would be necessary to turn All Souls College and the Shelley Memorial into hospitals. The difficulty is to know who is to exercise the regulation. If the question had been raised in 1914, could the Oxford chief constable of the day have been trusted not to discriminate between the then Vinerian Professor and the then Attorney-General? Probably he could not: yet it is difficult to suggest an alternative. The local council would, in some cases, be better because it might contain at least some representatives of both sides; but the problem may arise at any moment, and it is not practicable to insist on the summoning of the council or even of the watch committee.

It is clear, however, that the right to prohibit meetings altogether, such as is provided by the Public Order Act, is a dangerous innovation. Neither the chief officer of police nor the local authority can be trusted with a power to prohibit for weeks, months or even years on end, all or any political processions. The fact that the consent of the Secretary of State has to be obtained is some protection; for, whatever his politics, he can always be heckled by the Opposition. Nor should the efficacy of such heckling be minimized. The function of an Opposition in such circumstances is to make a nuisance of itself, to give the Home Secretary a warm time. Ministers are all for peace unless war is inevitable; and, except in extreme cases, no minister is prepared to fight long for a cause with which he is not immediately concerned. Above all, the appeal of the Opposition is to the constituencies; and if they can make a case they are sure to find some support. A local injustice, properly presented, can be of substantial national importance; and a government exists, in the long run, by means of its majority. The provision is, nevertheless, dangerous to the (moral) right of public meeting. Combined with the impossibility of a lawful street meeting, it means that little is left of the right which is commonly regarded as existing. The fact upon which Dicey so much insists that a meeting which is not intended to become riotous is not an unlawful assembly merely because a gang of toughs proposes to break it up is of no importance. The youngest police constable has enough intelligence not to lay an indictment for unlawful assembly. He tells the meeting to disperse and, if it does not, summons assistance to arrest the leaders for obstructing the police in the execution of their duty. The right of public meeting, in other words, is a right to hold a peaceful meeting on private property if the necessary funds can be found or the necessary consents can be obtained. Meetings in the Carlton Club are still lawful provided that they do not put reasonable persons in fear that there will be a breach of the peace in the Reform Club.

January 1937

THOUGHTS ON
OUR PRESENT DISCONTENTS

J. A. Hobson

IT would be idle to suppose that the experience of the Great War and its prolonged sequel has not had important effects upon the political, economic and moral principles and valuations of all who have endeavoured to understand human conduct. It must be evident to all of us that humanity in its standards and behaviour has been revealed as widely different from what it seemed in 1913. No one could have predicted the possibilities of the collapse of all codes of decent conduct, all standards of justice, truth and honour, not only in international affairs but in the revealed nationalism of the brutalitarian state, the facile acquiescence of whole peoples in the absolute dominion of self-appointed Masters, and perhaps most significant of all, the amazing credulity of the educated classes under the spell of the crudest propaganda.

Such revelations of the irrationality and brutality of 'civilized' peoples cannot fail to affect our ideas of human progress and the values of the social institutions that seemed to express and secure it. Before the war our faith in the alliance of Democracy, Nationalism and Internationalism as permanent and consistent movements for world security and progress remained unbroken, in spite of the economic and political excesses in which Nationalism indulged. Still more remarkable, the interpretation put upon the allied victory by President Wilson and others, as a triumph for Democracy, Self-determination and Internationalism, was accepted as a just and reasonable interpretation. Even when large portions of the territories of the conquered nations were taken from them by force, and their colonies were handed over to the conquerors under the face-saving title 'Mandates', when the right of rearmament and other acts of self-determination were deliberately infringed, when all the liberated nationalities began to set up tariffs and other barriers against amicable relations with neighbouring states, such flagrant violations of the ideals of victory were treated by most 'reasonable' politicians as brief regrettable incidents destined to disappear when the full tide of world progress resumed its sway.

It has taken many years to bring home to political, economic and ethical progressives the scale and nature of the human damage inflicted by the war, and the needed reassessment of the motives of men and, in particular, the psychology of Nationalism and Democracy. The shedding of Monarchy in Germany, Austria, Russia and Spain, the erection of the noble fabric of a League of Nations, helped us for some time to believe that we were entering upon a more reasonable and more secure phase of human evolution. It would take a certain time, perhaps longer than we had hoped, for these forces of freedom and cooperation to win their destined supremacy in human self-government, but the belief in their final efficacy remained unshaken.

Only within the last few years has the course of events brought complete disillusionment and sown the seeds of despair. Democracy and self-determination have virtually disappeared under the rule of accepted dictators, events in Manchuria, Abyssinia and Spain have completely discredited the League of Nations as the instrument of world peace, and the rapid rearmament of all 'Powers' appears as the opening phase of another and a more destructive war. The amiable platitudes by which our statesmen endeavour to allay alarm, the feeble fumbling methods they propose for handling a situation which grows graver every month have led many to the conviction that statecraft does not seriously believe it can do anything effective to stay 'the course of events'.

What is the cause of this despair? Does it mean that man is not sufficiently reasonable to perceive the identity of his interests with those of other men, or that the pride and prestige of personality and nationality are so strong that he prefers a smaller and insecurer advantage for himself, his class, his people, to the general welfare and security of the world at large? If either or both of these suppositions be true, they seem to inhibit any schemes which rely upon rational appeals to identity of interests as methods of attaining the common welfare. For if this common welfare has no emotional or intellectual significance, either for peoples or their rulers, political and economic, the reversion to militant isolationism or limited alliances seems justified as the only method of postponing conflicts.

An observer from Mars might readily accept this interpretation, were it not for one strange new word brought into his ken, the word 'ideology'. It does, indeed, seem strange that at a moment in history when men most boast their 'realism', this reference to ideas, as if they had a potent significance, should have appeared. Yet the talk of rival 'ideologies' has found its way even into the House of Commons and the popular platform, as having some bearing upon events in Russia, Spain, Germany and elsewhere. The reference is to some idea or ideal inspiring the rival claims of Communism and Fascism. Now these terms seem at first sight wholly unrelated to the 'cause' or 'causes' of the Great War, as interpreted by Wilson, Clemenceau, Asquith, George, or other peace-makers. It is only the aftermath of the war that brought these 'ideologies' into the forefront of history, disclosing the fact that behind the 'politics' of the war there was operating obscurely this clash of other forces within each nationality. It would be an excess of economic interpretation to say that Russia and Germany were impelled to war by the policy of their ruling and possessing classes, seeking to avert internal strife by following the familiar device 'stay giddy minds with foreign quarrels'. But the menace of approaching class-war, both in Russia and Germany, was undoubtedly a strong contributory cause of 1914. It is now admitted that the danger of growing Communism and Socialism in Germany could only be met by dictatorship extending from the emergency of war into the emergency of peace, while the establishment of Sovietism in Russia was manifestly the outbreak of a class-struggle which had been growing in intensity since the opening of the century. Though Fascism assumes a political guise, it is in reality a successful endeavour of the ruling possessive classes to repress the assault of the working classes upon the rights and powers of property and profit. Capitalism has, no doubt, to pay for this political defence in costly subservience to the totalitarian state and its political leaders. But it is saved from the aggression of organized labour and is allowed considerable latitude in profitable private enterprise. In Russia where the class-war took a different turn, where profiteering capitalism was eliminated and the bourgeoisie along with the aristocracy was bereft of all economic and political status, the goal of revolution and the steps employed do not present Communism as so different from Fascism in its political-economic aspects. In both cases the form of democracy is retained while its substance of free popular self-government disappears. In both cases the State is endowed with supreme power, economic and political, and exercises an absolute censorship upon freedom of thought and expression. The most marked feature of the last few years has been the convergence of Fascism and Communism in their 'real' operation, both political and economic. The virtual autocracy of a single man, with his cluster of chosen lieutenants, utilizing every form of brutal force for the elimination of possible rivals and opponents, the substitution of wide class divergencies of income for the 'needs' principle of Communism, the extension of the right of private property from consumable goods to productive capital not involving the employment of wage-earners – this evolution of Sovietism signifies a repudiation of economic equality and liberty not widely distinguishable from the Government of Germany and Italy in its essential features. In each case Democracy as known and practised in England, France and Scandinavia has ceased to exist.

What then has become of the opposed 'ideologies'? Are they mere rhetorical pretences by which Hitler, Mussolini and Stalin safeguard their personal supremacy over their peoples? The rival despots of Nationalism are not content to present their rivalry in vulgar terms of political and economic opposition, they must find a loftier terminology of intellectual and spiritual appeal! So long as Sovietism meant the dictatorship of the proletariat and Fascism the self-appointed despot, the 'ideologies' were indeed distinct and intelligible. Even when underneath their political cloak was perceived the substance of the economic conflict between Capitalism and Communism, the reality of a class-war was still retained. But now there seems no reason why Hitler or Mussolini should inflame themselves and their peoples with scares about Soviet propaganda, except the persistent need for an enemy to arm against. Does it not look as if the class-war between Capitalism and Communism had been swallowed up by the maw of dictatorship?

Or is this National Socialism only a passing and precarious settlement kept going by series of frantic appeals to sham conflicts of international interests and ideals? We have seen how false, shortsighted, irrational and costly these conflicts are. But we have also seen to our dismay that the appeal to peace and cooperation on grounds of common interest does not convince. Must we not, therefore, suspect that the appeal to reason carries some snag? Is not the substance of the rival 'ideologies' to be found, not in international relations, but in intra-national or class relations. If it can be shown that a 'capitalism' which is challenged by the body of worker-citizens within each nation as unjust, irrational and wasteful, is the direct generator of the political, economic and 'ideological' conflicts between nations which carry the menace of war and the destruction of civilization, this disclosure of the source of international conflict should give a fresh significance to the demand for each nation to 'set its own house in order'. Those nations to whom Democracy has been a real experience could face the facts of this internal situation, and by their common though separate national policy reduce the strain of international conflict. But this peaceful solution cannot be reached merely by urging the advantages of free trade, sound world money, free access to raw materials and free migration, desirable though these reforms are. For they cannot be achieved without a prior removal of the causes within each national economy which have created them. These causes are to be found in the maldistribution of income or spending power within each nation, the excessive income that goes to the possessive and ruling classes, the defective income of the worker-citizens. Unfortunately the excess of Marxist Socialism and Communism in doctrine and declared policy have roused sentiments and activities of class war which have so strengthened the defences of Capitalism in Western Europe and America as to delay the just reforms which by bringing internal peace within each nation could and would furnish the basis of world peace.

There is, however, ground for believing that Western Democracy is beginning to confront with clearer consciousness than heretofore the nature of this problem and the policies for its solution. I have said that Marxist Socialism has been a chief barrier to a rational economy. This is less true of Britain than of other countries. Here a greater obstacle has been a narrow trade union mentality which thinks that by each industrial group of workers improving its condition by separate pressure upon its employers, and fortified by favourable state regulations, the welfare of the whole community can be secured. The merely or mainly formal Socialism to which the Labour Party is committed has been used to screen this group separatism. In the United States, where private profiteering capitalism has had a freer field, the restrictive selfishness of the stronger, better-paid trade unionists made the attainment of a policy of national equity and welfare even more difficult than in Britain. But in both countries it is evident that the true lines of progress are now more clearly visualized. Political democracy is perceiving that its very life depends upon winning economic democracy, and that this latter demands movement along several related routes. The bargaining advantages hitherto enjoyed by capital in purchasing labour must be cancelled: monopolies must be administered or controlled by government: humane services financed out of the unearned incomes of the rich must be applied to equalize the general lack of economic welfare. These policies are moving from their first state of opportunist empiricism into the stage of related conscious experiment. With the new urgency of the situation they are moving faster and bolder than in the past, and what is even more important, they are winning a less grudging acquiescence from large numbers of the owning and possessive classes. This is partly because the latter are aware that in a democratic country they cannot put up a fascist resistance with any confidence of success, partly, because the appeal of reason and justice had shaken their early confidence in their rights to property.

The belief that liberal democracy is doomed to perish in the world from the conflict of the rival 'ideologies' of Communism and Fascism is without foundation. The nineteenth-century Liberalism which virtually excluded economic life from the sphere of government has already perished. It has been replaced by a new Liberalism which differs from the old in that it incorporates economic equality of opportunities in its full sense as equal access to nature, capital, education and enterprise, as an integral factor of popular self-government, and recognizes that property and income are joint products of individual and social activities. While important practical questions still remain unsettled, regarding the place rightly accorded to private enterprise and profit in the economics of a modern democracy, and the part to be assigned to public ownership and control of monopolies and certain key industries, the general principle of such public rule is accepted and applied with diminishing resistance from the interests affected. The freedom which the term liberalism implies is not only extended into the economic field, but is acquiring a clearer and stronger mental and spiritual significance. The astonishing interference with free thought and expression practised by Fascist and Communist rulers alike has done more than anything else to demonstrate 'the falsehood of extremes'. No political or economic system which demands such personal sacrifices can gain the acceptance of any considerable number of persons in this or any other Western country. This places an effective taboo alike on Communism and Fascism. Those who in this country envisage the possibility or probability of a combination of the city, the army, the landed gentry and the 'capitalists', to oppose the socialism of a labour government and to substitute a Fascist autocracy on German or Italian lines, reckon without regard to history. Where political democracy has had short and shallow roots, as in Germany and Italy, this resistance is feasible, but not in countries where it has enjoyed centuries of traditional acceptance and growth. The 'rival ideologies' cut no ice here: full-blooded Socialism and Fascism are equally impossible. A middle course, irregular and opportunist in its concrete application, will continue to be our path of progress. The very reasonability of such a course consists in a refusal to follow dictatorial ideals. A consideration that takes account of relative advantages and defects, that compromises on short- and long-scale utilities, on slow and rapid movements, will continue to hamper and exasperate idealists and plungers. But just in proportion as our new liberalism becomes enlightened and consciously constructive in character, will the waste of its older empiricism be reduced and the pace of its advance be accelerated. We are often told that 'fair play' is a stronger and more general sentiment among English-speaking people than elsewhere. This may be true, but if so, then the light which a reasonable temper sheds upon the nature of 'fair play', especially in the economic sphere, will enable our people to make the necessary steps in economic democracy which are essential to the avoidance of wasteful revolutions on the one hand and are positive securities for internal and external peace upon the other.

For the equitable distribution of opportunities, income and property within our nation will not only ensure internal peace and progress, but by the diminished pressure on the need for external markets for our goods and capital, by reason of the increased volume of home consumption, will abate the perils of aggressive imperialism and of international conflicts. If I am right in believing that a growing recognition of this policy of increased home consumption is taking place in all democratic countries and that means for its application form a growing part of conscious governmental activity, we have a new and vitally important bond which will bind the democratic countries economically, politically, and in the last resort forcibly, in opposition to the aggressive designs of the Fascist autocracies.

The recent anti-Bolshevist pact between Germany, Italy and Japan is in substance a plain intimation of the conscious opposition between Fascism and Democracy. For though the Soviet system is not a political democracy, it carries, even in its later form, the assertion of an economic democracy, which is the real enemy of Fascism. Though considerable inequalities of income exist, they are based upon differences in the importance and efficiency of production and official activities and not upon profits, rents and other unearned gains. If, therefore, the abolition or curtailment of unearned income is the prime necessity for national unity and international peace, the European democracies of the West must reckon Soviet Russia as their ally against declared Fascist aggressors. But such alliance could not be counted a complete security for peace without America. Here the traditional isolationism, temporarily intensified by the experience of the Great War, is still predominant in public opinion, though men with the far-seeing minds of Roosevelt and

Cordell Hull perceive that the isolationism, political and economic, once possible, is no longer practicable. Though much suspicion of 'entangling alliances' still exists, the fear is being gradually displaced by other fears and dangers. One is distinctively economic in origin, the recognition that economic isolationism on the old lines is dangerous to industry and entails strong class conflicts. The productivity of brains in industry and agriculture has hitherto found lucrative vent in supplying the growing needs of a rapidly increasing population, and, after checks upon immigration, in supplying weaker European and South American nations with capital and money loans. The disastrous collapse of industry and employment since 1929 has made it evident that with a declining immigration and reduced export of capital, a full recovery demands higher wages and more leisure for labour, together with an expansion of public expenditure on works and services calculated to reduce the rate of profits for capital. The resistance of the owning classes to this policy may take shape in an organized attack upon popular government as a legislative and executive instrument. This is now for the first time consciously realized as a danger to political democracy, arising from the assertion of the claims of economic democracy in a country where the earlier realities of economic liberty and equality have disappeared. It is, however, unlikely that any such semi-Fascist movement could succeed in face of the new conscious rally of labour and land workers against city capitalism and finance. The traditional and highly-prized democracy of America is in sentiment definitely hostile to the aggressive policy of Germany, Italy and Japan, and the penetration of Fascism into the politics of American States is perhaps more likely to bring the United States into real cooperation with the democratic countries of Europe than any other recent movement. It may, however, take some time before America can realize that her potential strength is necessary to restrain a policy of aggression which, beginning elsewhere, would almost inevitably extend to the American continent and demand from the United States an active policy of war-prevention. For the central argument for the United States coming into early cooperation with the European democracies, is that, by so doing, she would prevent another world war from occurring, into which she would again be drawn if that world war had already broken out and was bringing disaster upon that common civilization to which America belongs. The political economic isolation of America is a dream incapable of fulfilment, and if she feels no moral obligation towards the civilization of Europe which has contributed so much to her own, she cannot entertain a sense of security in a world exposed to the ambitions and aggressions of Fascist power-politics.

January 1938

SOCIAL CHANGE – PEACEFUL
OR VIOLENT?

The Rt Hon. Herbert Morrison, M.P.

PRECISELY because it is for the most part unwritten and has, in the main, been built up by precedent and practice, the British constitution is among the most fascinating of the world's constitutional studies.

There was a book published after the war surveying the written constitutions of the post-war democratic states of Central Europe. It was inevitably a dull affair. Unhappily many of these constitutions have been blown up, either by Fascist revolutions or Fascist aggression. A number of them were supposed to be modelled on the basis of British parliamentary government, and yet how different they really were.

These constitutions were set out in chapter and verse. Each organ of government, the legislature, the executive and the justiciary had its defined rights and limitations. Pains were taken to prevent any one organ of government having too much power. The checks and balances were defined. Even proportional representation – that mathematical product of the minds of political abstractionists – was featured in order that every element of the community should have its say in parliamentary debates. Political liberty was duly provided for. So anxious were the framers to set out the written details of democratic guarantees that some far bigger things than written detail were forgotten. Among the forgotten things were perhaps history, economics and social development; the necessity for authority in government and the final unity of government; the need for national constitutional authority to be able to defend itself effectively against the incursions of unconstitutional agitation and rebellion. In some cases it was overlooked that the personnel of an aristocratic or absolute monarchist regime is unsuited to the functioning of a democratic regime which overnight has succeeded to an undemocratic order.

Of these new democratic states, Czecho-Slovakia survived with credit until the betrayal of Berchtesgaden, Godesberg and Munich. And now the democracy of Czecho-Slovakia itself is in a state of dissolution. That country, which I hold was the best success of the post-war democracies, appears now to be in a process of being wholly or semi-Nazified. It is a sad story.

Is it that these constitutions were divorced from political reality? Were they elaborated before their time? Or is it that the human material within these states was inadequate to the difficult tasks of the post-war period, of which, it must not be forgotten, economic difficulty was a conspicuous feature? Doubtless, the clumsiness and injustice of Versailles treaty and the foolish selfishness of the victors in the Great War had something to do with the break-up of democracy in central Europe. But I am inclined to think that more important factors were the multiplicity of parties, aided by proportional representation, the weakness of democratic leadership, practical difficulties in working rigid constitutions and, of great importance, economic and financial complications.

Successful democracy cannot be divorced from political ability and economic well-being. Democracy is a thing of the spirit no less than of the written word. A muddled democracy is a threatened democracy.

That great country, the United States of America, has, however, been working a written constitution for a long time and, for practical purposes, with democratic success. But the United States is nearer as a problem of government to the whole of Europe than to that of any single European state. For remember that the term United States is in the plural. There are forty-eight states, and the government at Washington constitutionally takes second place as compared with each of the forty-eight states. The states vary; the population is varied; so that what is appropriate to a single European country would almost certainly be inappropriate to the U.S.A.

After its own fashion the American constitution has worked, and even though we may take the view that it would not do for us, there is much to be said for the American constitution in the practical political conditions of that great country. Even so, the supremacy of law is not so unquestioned in America as it is here. The long

fight with gangsterdom and other flagrant illegalities; the mis-
carriages of justice and the notorious evasions of justice; the extensive (though, I hope, decreasing) corruption – these are not
pleasant features of the United States. Nevertheless, we must not
overestimate them, for the United States has a less long experience
of self-government than we and its population is more mixed; and
let us not forget that it is not so very long ago that corruption and
patronage were widespread in British administration, and that they
have not yet been entirely eradicated.

Under President Roosevelt, America is on the move, and I am
not a pessimist about its political future.

Meantime, the British constitution continues to function and to
adapt itself to changing conditions. Of all the great countries in the
world we are, I think, so far, the most successful in the art of self-
government and the most capable in the day-to-day practice of
public administration. This constitution of ours is still functioning
smoothly in the midst of a dangerous world. A large part of Europe
is governed by dictatorships of one sort or another. The Fascist
dictatorships of Germany and Italy, the semi- or seventy-five per
cent dictatorships of other countries, the Communist dictatorship
of the Soviet Union – these facts, together with the political stresses
being experienced by a number of the European democracies, bid
us 'to keep our eyes skinned' and ask ourselves whether in this
confused world the relatively smooth running of British democracy
can be maintained.

This big query mark stares at us again and again from the pages
of two constitutional studies which have just been published by
George Allen & Unwin. One is *Parliamentary Government in
England*, by Professor Harold J. Laski (12s. 6d.), and the other is
The British Constitution, by H. R. G. Greaves (7s. 6d.). These
books are not identical: they are both worth reading for their own
sakes and each of them covers territory which is not wholly covered
by the other. Both authors are associated with the London School
of Economics and Political Science. Indeed, Mr Greaves dedicates
his book to 'Harold J. Laski; his teacher, colleague and friend'.

Both authors pose the query again and again, 'Will British democracy stand the strain of the transformation from capitalism to

Socialism?' To this issue I propose to devote the remainder of this essay, for I am not reviewing these two excellent studies of the British constitution.

Mr Laski has been putting this query with varying degrees of pessimism over a number of years. Perhaps the volume in which he discusses it with the deepest degree of cheerlessness is *The State in Theory and Practice*. But there can be no mistaking his apprehensions in this new volume, *Parliamentary Government in England*. He is almost certain that the privileged classes will resort to Fascist or other unconstitutional action in order to prevent the final and complete triumph of the Labour Party and its ideas. He appears to be almost hopeless about this being prevented through parliamentary democracy. At the same time he advances no policy whereby what he regards as an almost certain catastrophe can be avoided. Which is rather disappointing.

Unless the reader has strong faith and is in possession of that glorious intelligent optimism without which great changes cannot be made, he will stand a fair chance of being driven to the conclusion that he had better sit back in his chair and be comfortable while he may, or that he had better prepare for the inevitable and make terms with Fascism or some other tyranny, which I am sure is the last thing that Mr Laski would wish him to do.

Let us, however, consider the alternative to parliamentary democracy for utilization by the advocates of fundamental change. So far as I can see it can only be force of some character; and if we come to the conclusion that the privileged classes will, with a good prospect of success, resort to methods of violence and dictatorship in order to prevent the complete triumph of Labour, and that parliamentary institutions and the will of the people cannot prevent it, then it seems to me there are only two consequences. One is that we must acquiesce in the present social order, which is unthinkable for any Socialist. The other is that the Left should resort to violence and dictatorship first, so as forcibly to crush the other side before they begin. But at that point we have to consider the probabilities of success, for the man who starts an unsuccessful revolution will not be kindly thought of by his followers when the reaction comes; nor will he hold a very high place in history.

It is more serious than that: for if we resort to violence and dictatorship and do not succeed, then, in company with millions of innocent people we may become the victims of that very Fascist violence and dictatorship which we shall have precipitated and provided with an excuse for its terror. And if we seriously ask ourselves what are the prospects for the success in Britain of a violent revolution of the Left, surely we must answer that there are no such prospects of success.

The triumph of Bolshevism in Russia gives us little or no assistance as an analogy. Russia was economically undeveloped; it had no great and powerful middle class; and its government was both corrupt and inefficient. Revolution in Russia was child's play compared with what it would be here, where none of these factors obtain. We can learn from our experience of the General Strike in 1926, which was a magnificent demonstration of working-class solidarity and was not without its beneficial effects on the political consciousness of labour. Magnificent as it was as a demonstration, the fact has long since been recognized by responsible trade union leaders that after the General Strike had been called, those responsible for its calling were not clear as to what to do with it; and that when the Government resisted and, with the aid of the great middle class, proceeded to the maintenance of services, the strike was doomed to failure unless it had promptly been converted into general revolution, in which case all the grave risks I have indicated would have had to be considered. As it was, the General Council of the Trades Union Congress decided to find means of calling the strike off, which left the miners with a considerable feeling of bitterness, secured from the Communists a great deal of abuse, and from Mr Baldwin one of his fatherly speeches, followed by the Trades Union and Trades Disputes Act, 1927, and a limited amount of victimization.

It may be argued that the actual or threatened industrial action of Labour's Council of Action soon after the war respecting British intervention against the Soviet Bolshevik revolution was successful, and that that experiment could be repeated on other issues, including those of Spain and China. With respect, I do not agree. The Council of Action effort against intervention in Russia came at the end of a long war in which millions of British families had suffered heavily. The nation was in no mood for starting up another military adventure. Ninety per cent of the people – possibly more – were against Mr Churchill and the Government. Consequently the Council of Action was implementing an overwhelming public opinion, and – who knows? – it may well be that a political campaign in the country would have been quite effective for the purpose without industrial action. I was a party to the work of the Council of Action. I agreed with what it did. I reserve the right to advocate similar action where a government, on big issues, is acting in defiance of overwhelming public opinion, and certainly if a government was proposing to destroy our constitutional liberties; for governments that are unconstitutional have no moral right to constitutional respect.

If the people of Germany or Italy wished by forcible means to overthrow their dictatorships, they have every moral right to do so, for dictatorships provide no constitutional means for the proper functioning of public opinion.

With us and other democratic countries it is different.

Are we, however, bound to accept the view that there is little or no possibility of peaceful fundamental social change? I think not; although I fully agree with Mr Laski and Mr Greaves that there is no certainty that the change will be made peacefully. I agree that our reactionaries and our privileged classes are capable of anything, provided they think there is a good chance of success.

The democrat who trusts in the democracy of our Chamberlains is a fool. There is need for vigilance, for looking ahead, for being, as far as we can, ready for trouble. But in the meantime, if we assume that the great change can only successfully come by violence, because otherwise successful violence will be resorted to by the opponents of change, then the parties of democracy must seriously overhaul their tactics and organization and put the inevitability of violence right in the front of their political propaganda. In that case, however, we shall be asking for trouble: we shall run the risk of making inevitable the violence we all wish to avoid.

It is, I suggest, best, therefore, while remaining alert and receptive as to the significance of events as we proceed, that the parties of the Left should stand firm by the principles of parliamentary democracy and be ready to take all practicable steps to increase the difficulties of reaction in resorting to violence. To this end it is necessary that we should, by our propaganda, maintain a lively, virile democratic public opinion; that we should do everything we can to increase the efficiency and effectiveness of parliamentary institutions and all branches of public administration; that we should cultivate a healthy democratic constitutionalism in the armed forces; that we should put our foot down firmly on jobbery and corruption; that we should develop the political and economic education of the people and intensively educate Labour's rank and file for the tasks of government; that we should seek ability and public spirit in our parliamentary and municipal candidates, rather than put the money consideration first which is too often the case today; that we should welcome, rather than discourage, courageous and decisive political leadership and expect individuals to carry their responsibilities rather than to bury them overmuch in committee; and finally, but by no means least important, is the need for Labour in power to achieve things in harmony with the best aspirations of the public and to earn for itself a reputation for capacity and uprightness in the art of government, nationally and locally.

Policies are not enough; for policies have to be implemented by the brains and work of individual men and women. I think a lot of the British Civil Service and of our municipal officers, but the politician who expects the officers to carry him through is asking for trouble, for the politician has, or ought to have, qualities of public leadership and of interpreting the mass mind which public officials are not paid to possess, and in a large proportion of cases do not possess. And if we earn public respect; if we act like a government as well as merely being a government as a matter of official fact; if we carry public opinion with us; then, if reaction engages in sabotage or in violence, reaction can be crushed with all the power and authority of government and with the support of the general body of citizens. Whether a constitution is written or unwritten, whatever its guarantees, it will not be saved if unlawful violence is not sternly repressed and if government is weak and inefficient.

The power of a government to govern, to maintain order, to

command respect, in the end depends upon public opinion. This is even true in the long run of dictatorship, for if and when German and Italian public opinion becomes sufficiently strong against Herr Hitler and Signor Mussolini, and that public opinion can maintain itself, then those two gentlemen will have to look out for other fields of employment. So it is with us. If we do well, if we are capable, if we do not get demoralized by inferiority complex, we shall stand a good chance of coming through. But if we falter, if we muddle, if we steer the ship of State on to the rocks, then anything may happen.

That is how I feel about these things. Neither I nor anybody else can give a hundred per cent guarantee of success, but I believe that along that line is the best hope of that peaceful social change which will bring untold blessings to mankind.

January 1939

LONDON GOVERNMENT

Mary Stocks

WHEN John Stow, Citizen of London, surveyed our metropolis in 1598, he was conscious of certain encroachments in 'the Suburbs Without the Walls' which suggested undisciplined growth. Things were not quite as they had been in FitzStephen's time, when the scholars and youths of the City walked forth on summer evenings to take the air at Clerkenwell and St Clements in the days when their wells were 'sweet, wholesome and clear'. To the north towards Soers ditch there had grown up 'all along a continual building of small and base tenements, for the most part lately erected'; while to the east the City was exuding another 'continual street, or filthy strait passage, with alleys of small tenements, or cottages, built, inhabited by sailors' victuallers, along by the river of Thames, almost to Radcliff, a good mile from the Tower'. Altogether John Stow observed that there was a lot of building going on, much of it of a decidedly mean order. Indeed it was not easy for him to answer 'the accusation of those men, which charge London with the loss and decay of many of the ancient cities, corporate towns, and markets within this realm, by drawing from them to herself alone both all trade of traffic by sea, and the retailing of wares and exercise of manual arts also'. He had to admit that the Court was a considerable magnet. At any rate, for whatever cause, it was impossible to deny that 'the gentlemen of all shires do fly and flock to this City; the younger sort of them to see and shew vanity, and the elder, to save the cost and charge of hospitality and housekeeping'. It was regrettable – but as John Stow points out, 'the daintiness of men cannot be restrained, which will needs seek those things at London', and it is clear that he was not without a Londoner's pride that it should be so. His City of London was a great city, a rich city, a strong city, and withal a beautiful city; a city to inspire not only praise but prayer. So thus he ends: 'Almighty God, grant that her majesty evermore rightly esteem and rule this City; and be given grace, that the citizens may answer duty, as well towards God and her majesty, as towards this whole realm and country. Amen.'

Two centuries later this City had become, in William Cobbett's eyes, a Wen past praying for. His difficulty was, once in, to get out of it. 'From St George's Fields, which are now covered with houses, we go, towards Croydon, between rows of houses, nearly half the way, and the whole way is nine miles. There are, erected within these few years, two entire miles of stockjobbers' houses on this one road, and the work goes on with accelerated force!' 'And how,' he asks, 'is this Wen to be dispersed? I know not whether it be done by knife or by caustic; but dispersed it must be!'

But it has proved to be no easier since Cobbett's time to restrain 'the daintiness of men'. The Wen has gone on growing. The years which immediately followed his Rural Rides carried it out to the edge of what is now the Administrative County of London. The stupendous economic expansiveness of the late Victorian Age carried it far beyond. In our own time, the slowing down of that expansiveness has not reflected itself in a corresponding slowing down in the growth of the Wen. On the contrary, it is exuding along all the highways of the Home Counties. Croydon is engulfed. The London Passenger Transport Board serves the tidal ebb and flow for some nine and a half million souls and cries hungrily for more. But now at long last modern civilization appears about to provide us with the answer to Cobbett's question: 'how is this Wen to be dispersed?' And the suggested method is one which will doubtless at long last and quite effectively 'restrain the daintiness of men'.

But while the problem of London's growth and its restraint has received on the whole little serious thought, the problem of London's Government has, during the past hundred years or so, received a great deal. In his comparison between the town planning of Moscow and the non-town planning of London,[1] Sir Ernest Simon points out that the effective planning of a city as a whole is only possible when the planners know what the ultimate area and population of that City are to be. Thus the Central Committee of the party and the Council of People's Commissars decided by decree in 1935 that the population of Moscow should be stabilized

[1] *Moscow in the Making*, Chapter 7.

at five and a half million, and that this stabilization should be obtained by the threefold method of direction of factory location, passport control, and judicious eviction for slum clearance. But whether the 'daintiness of men' is less insistent in Moscow, or whether some quality other than 'daintiness' is stronger there than elsewhere, the fact remains that in no other great city of the world has this essential background been provided for good government; and those who are grappling with the problem of London today lack that fundamental element of control: the power rationally to determine the size, shape and density of the area to be governed. The reasons for this deprivation are deeply rooted in the structure of our social system. The nature of our property rights and certain limited conceptions of political liberty, which are closely bound up with them, would doubtless, if examined, provide the explanation. But though they may provide the explanation of London's chaotic and unbridled growth they do not, without a certain amount of historical analysis, provide the explanation of why the machinery of London's Government is so inadequately framed to perform the tasks presented by that growth. For such an analysis we must turn to two books whose publication coincides with a contemporary intensification of interest in London problems. The intensification of interest is due partly to the celebration of the L.C.C.'s fiftieth birthday and a focusing of public attention on its achievements, partly to the current deliberations of the Royal Commission on Geographical Distribution of the Industrial Population. The two books are William Robson's *Government and Misgovernment of London* (George Allen & Unwin, 15s. net) and Gibbon and Bell's *History of the London County Council* (Macmillan, 21s.). Of these two books, the first is the more constructive and thought-provoking work, for it analyses defects and suggests remedies. The second is sufficiently infused with the Jubilee spirit to allow its authors to concentrate with greater gusto upon the excellence of what they describe as 'the splendid edifice of London Government'. But taken together, these two considerable volumes make an effective contribution to our understanding of London.

Sir Gwilyn Gibbon and Mr Reginald Bell concentrate, as the title of their books suggests, on a single organ of London Govern-

ment: the L.C.C. Beginning with an admirable and not wholly
uncritical group of chapters on its origins, they carry us through the
brief but inspiring history of the Metropolitan Board of Works to
the passage of the fateful legislation of 1888. That done, they concentrate upon the machinery and functions of the L.C.C., carrying
each section up to date and thus presenting a comprehensive and
really impressive picture of the ramified workings of a single vast
unit of local government. It is only in the last concluding section,
covering less than 100 of the 663 pages of their text, that they stand
back from the picture and fit this single unit into the structure of
national and local government of which it forms so strangely mal-
adjusted a part. It is not, of course, their business, as the L.C.C.'s
Jubilee celebrants, to be acutely conscious of this maladjustment.
Yet at moments, as in their satisfaction (indicated on p. 306)
with the existing liaison between borough child welfare services and
the L.C.C. school medical service, or in their avoidance of any
reference to awkward demarcation problems of U.A.B. and P.A.C.
in their section on training and employment of the able-bodied, one
is tempted to complain that the Jubilee spirit has got a little out of
hand. That should not, however, blind the student of local government to the value of their labours. They have provided him with an
incomparable textbook: 'a splendid edifice' of descriptive writing.
He will find himself returning to it again and again for information,
and always he will find, with the help of its admirable maps, index,
and appendices, the information that he wants.

But Dr Robson's *Government and Misgovernment of London*
remains the more serious work. Its scope is broadly indicated in his
brief preface: 'I regard the metropolis as a vast and difficult problem in municipal administration, different both quantitatively and
qualitatively from anything we have previously known. In order to
discover how it should be dealt with it is necessary to study the
working of the present machinery with care and in detail. But the
present organization cannot be understood without a knowledge of
the manner and causes of its growth. Hence, the book is divided
into three parts, dealing respectively with the past, the present and
the future.'

It is, of course, the past which conditions the awkward pattern of

London Local Government today. It is a story, dating from the exclusion of London from the great Municipal Reform Act of 1835, which is in its main lines fairly familiar to students of Local Government. But seldom has it been told with deadlier precision than in the first fifteen chapters of Dr Robson's book. Reference has been made to property rights and certain limited conceptions of political liberty which are bound up with them, as the great barriers to any wholehearted attempt to limit the size or control the shape of the great urbanized area which is vaguely described as 'London'. Dr Robson analyses in his opening chapters the manner in which such property rights and conceptions of political liberty have operated, not so much to stultify any rationalized direction of population movement – with that larger aspect of social planning he is not here concerned – as to prevent the pattern of local government from responding to the insistent demands of such undirected movement. They have, in fact, so operated as to prescribe as the administrative area for which the largest single London local governing body is today responsible, an area whose size and shape was conditioned by the convenience of the Registrar-General in respect of the Census of 1851. They have further so operated as to prescribe for that authority a sharing of functions with subsidiary local authorities such as is not required of the County Borough Council of any provincial town. Cabined and confined within its 1851 frontiers and deprived of its golden heart of rateable value, the L.C.C. shares the business of government with twenty-eight Metropolitan Boroughs, and a tangle of *ad hoc* regional authorities representing a succession of makeshift attempts to provide for half a dozen different conceptions of Greater London those vital services which even with the worst will in the world, our legislators could not adapt to the frontiers of an early Victorian registration district. The result of this ill-conceived and stultifying balance of powers is described in the second section of Dr Robson's book. The way out is indicated in his third and last; and it is here in this third and last section that he presents his formidable challenge to contemporary administrators. Let them accept his plan of action or think of a better. His plan is roughly as follows:

Let us, he says, begin by recognizing three categories of services:

those calling for direct regional administration; those suitable for local administration under regional guidance; and those which can be left entirely to local control and administration. The first comprises territorial planning, the larger housing projects, drainage and sewage disposal, main roads and bridges, water, fire brigades, hospitals and specialized medical services, education (with certain reservations), aerodromes, open spaces, preservation of ancient monuments and smoke abatement. This does not exhaust Dr Robson's list, but it will serve to indicate the principle on which he works.

The second category comprises services which could be administered by local authorities acting under regional supervision: i.e. public libraries, child protection, ambulance ferries, inspection of nursing homes, registration, baths and wash-houses, inspection and regulation of various food services, weights and measures, the licensing and inspection of nursing homes. Again the list is not exhaustive, but it will serve. Meanwhile, we have here the *raison d'être* of the directly elected Greater London Council which he proposes as his regional authority. It should, he thinks, consist of not more than 150 members. This would mean, of course, large constituencies – but not larger than those which at present elect M.P.s for Outer London. At any rate, size would indicate importance; importance would in its turn attract able and energetic men and women to its membership.

And what are the alternatives? Either an indirectly elected body representing for specified purposes all or some existing authorities in the region – and as such, reproducing many of the defects of 'secondary responsibility' so sadly illustrated in the history of the old Metropolitan Board of Works between 1855 and 1888 – or a joint committee or board with irresponsible financial powers or no effective financial powers at all. Or, third alternative, a series of *ad hoc* regional authorities.

But in fact, a series of *ad hoc* regional authorities is precisely what we have evolved since 1839 when the Commissioners of Police for the Metropolis were first established. The creation of an *ad hoc* body has always proved the line of least resistance when a new regional service had to be performed – only to prove itself the line of maximum resistance when reform was in the air. And Dr Robson has much to say concerning the lack of coordination which has resulted from the separate administration of a number of regional services ministering to the coordinated needs of a great urban area. He is therefore prepared to transfer most – but not all – of the existing functions of *ad hoc* regional authorities to his Greater London Council. And he believes that in the interests of 'education for citizenship' as well as those of immediately efficient local government such a step is desirable, since it transfers important functions of government to the sphere of such live democratic control as is typified by the L.C.C. as we know it today.

There is no doubt that a regional authority capable of absorbing most if not all of our existing Greater London regional services is going to cover a considerable square mileage, but for this Dr Robson is prepared. His proposed area is no less than the 2,419 square miles of the Metropolitan Traffic Commission. In fact, however, the boundaries of his area have been determined by the 'daintiness of men' operating without restraint through the centuries. The size of the problem is none of his choosing. Nevertheless, it is going to eat up the County Councils of London and Middlesex, and a great part of those of Surrey, Hertfordshire and Kent. And for this absorption he is prepared, since his scheme is based upon a double-deck structure of regional and district authorities to which the addition of an intervening layer – producing a triple-deck structure of region, county, and district – would be a costly, cumbersome and inefficient intrusion. Nevertheless, he is sufficiently conscious of the obstinacy of county conservatism to suggest a mild compromise on this question: an inferior alternative or, as he terms it, 'a feeble palliative . . . suited not to the sickness of the patient but to the weakness of the doctor'.

Meanwhile there remain the minor or 'lower deck' authorities within the region, to whom are entrusted the administration of certain regional functions indicated as Dr Robson's second category, not to mention those of the third category of which no mention has yet been made. Here we have in the inner ring of the Administrative County of London, twenty-eight Metropolitan Boroughs of widely varying rateable value, historical tradition, class composition, shape, size, and density, grouped round the innermost ring of the ancient City. We have also, given our Greater London Regional Council, a heterogenous encirclement of County Boroughs, Boroughs, and Districts. His handling of these areas, and their existing authorities is drastic but not wholly merciless. For the City of London he prescribes a change of electoral system and of rating and valuation in relation to Greater London which would rob it of much existing privilege; and a change of ceremonial which would transform its Lord Mayor into the representative of Greater London. For the Metropolitan Boroughs he prescribes a process of consolidation so designed as to produce a dozen large local authorities within whose areas, classes and rateable values would be judiciously mixed. Thus the respectable affluence of Hampstead would be diluted by the poverty of St Pancras. The 'out-county' authorities would be treated on roughly similar lines, which would, however, in view of their present diversity of status, involve an even more drastic operation. The purpose of the change is, of course, to secure the creation throughout the metropolis of a uniform type of secondary authority capable of administering 'category two' services under the direction of the Greater London Council. In regard to the third category of services, those which the subsidiary authorities would administer at their own unfettered discretion, Dr Robson has less to say. They are relegated to half a paragraph at the end of Part 3, Chapter 8. There are not many of them and they are not exciting. They include the destruction of rats and mice and the provision of public conveniences.

It is impossible, in so bare a summary of Dr Robson's plan, to convey to the reader the force and momentum which his carefully integrated edifice of fact and analysis, built up through 469 closely reasoned and documented pages, lends to it. His destructive case against the present makeshift muddle is irrefutable and will not be generally disputed. His bold scheme for reorganization, though it may not be *generally* disputed, will, of course, raise up an army of separatist defenders on behalf of each function, each frontier, and each tradition that he challenges. And these will make, as they have made heretofore, common cause against the onset of reform. But if ordered government, the preservation of beauty, health and social justice are among 'those things which men seek at London' let us endeavour to believe and act on the belief that, as in the days of John Stow, 'the daintiness of men cannot be restrained'.

July 1939

ULSTER AND EIRE

Tom Wilson

THE English Conservative Party can no longer be regarded as a
major obstacle to Irish unity. There is still, it is true, a strong
Unionist element, which would receive the support of a section of
the English Press, but the proposition, profoundly believed in Irish
Republican circles, that the policy of the English Government is
still the old one of *divide et impera* is scarcely plausible. It would be
more true to say that the English Conservative Party and, *a fortiori*,
the other parties, would be much relieved if the whole dispute were
settled. In time of war a friendly Ireland would be a useful neighbour, but so long as the country is disunited the policy which Eire
would adopt in such circumstances is very problematic. On the
other hand, no English party is prepared to use coercive methods
towards the North, and partition therefore continues. It is true that
England could do more to improve the situation by encouraging
friendship between North and South and by restraining the ruling
class in Northern Ireland from infringing the political liberty of its
subjects. But the complete solution of the problem lies beyond her
powers.

It is necessary however to consider the contention that the
English Government subsidizes partition. Northern Ireland, as a
part of the United Kingdom, is expected to make an annual contribution towards Imperial services. The figure at which this contribution was originally fixed (£7,920,000) proved too high and the
contribution is now determined every year by the Joint Exchequer
Board, whose deliberations are always shrouded with mystery. The
contribution is the amount of the surplus revenue after all social
expenditure has been met on a level similar to the English. In years
of depression Northern Ireland has been able to avoid to a considerable extent an increase in taxation or borrowing or a reduction
of expenditure by the simple expedient of reducing her imperial
contribution. Moreover the English Exchequer makes contribu-

tions to various funds in Northern Ireland, most notably to the Unemployment Insurance Fund. As a result Northern Ireland's net contribution to the imperial exchequer has been negative for several years. The figures for 1936–7 were as follows: £1,139,919 received by Northern Ireland; £900,000 paid by Northern Ireland; balance £239,919. The excess balance received by Northern Ireland has never exceeded £400,000. Over the whole period 1922–37,[1] Northern Ireland has made a net contribution to imperial services of only £7 millions. The arrangement can be criticized because it sets no adequate check on the extravagance of the Northern Government, but can it be regarded as a means of subsidizing partition? It could be more fairly described as the necessary assistance given to a special area. Ulster is not, as the imaginative Unionist propagandists declare, a rich prize sought after by the rapacious Southern

[1] The balance of accounts between England and Northern Ireland is as follows:

Year	Imperial Contribution	Payments to Northern Ireland
1922–23	6,685,600	3,994,200
1923–24	4,517,900	3,321,100
1924–25	3,175,000	1,420,800
1925–26	2,275,000	2,073,700
1926–27	1,350,000	1,012,300
1927–28	1,450,000	421,300
1928–29	1,175,000	667,100
1929–30	855,000	588,200
1930–31	545,000	827,400
1931–32	298,000	474,900
1932–33	75,000	182,800
1933–34	76,000	43,700
1934–35	24,000	500
1935–36	365,000	753,600
1936–37	900,000	1,140,000
	£23,766,500	£16,921,600

A balance in excess of receipts, amounting to £6,844,900, has thus been paid by Northern Ireland. Land annuity payments (£660,000 a year) are also retained by the Province.

(The figures are taken from *Hansard*, 6 May 1937, and from the *Ulster Year Book*, 1938.)

politicians. The province is, rather, a grave liability and Eire would be seriously embarrassed if the anti-partition propaganda were to succeed. A certain amount, it is true, could be saved by abolishing the local legislature and reducing the Civil Service – possibly about £150,000 a year – but that would be inadequate. The improvement in economic conditions would not be a sufficient compensation, for Ireland is not an economic unit artificially divided by the Border. Trade between North and South will always be less important than trade between both parts of the country and the United Kingdom. It is therefore not very plausible to accuse the English Parliament of subsidizing partition because it did not embark on a policy which would have led to serious disorder in Northern Ireland and which would have achieved no very great result. At most the province might have been forced to abandon autonomy and return to Westminster.

The main obstacles to union are in Ireland itself. The Unionist Government, which has been in power since the Parliament was set up, is resolutely opposed to change of any kind. How far, it may be asked, does this Government represent the will of the Ulster people? Its majority is, of course, exaggerated by the system of single-member constituencies and by skilful gerrymandering. The Nationalist minority has been virtually deprived of political representation and the strength of the other parties is negligible. Few measures have caused more ill-feeling in the North than those, such as the abolition of proportional representation, which have been designed to exclude all critics from the House. Nevertheless, when all due allowance has been made, it must be admitted that the majority of the people are opposed to an All-Ireland policy. It is essential to appreciate the intensity of the alarm with which most Protestants regard the prospect of Catholic rule. Contrary to the frequent statements by Southern propagandists the primary difficulty is, I believe, fear of religious persecution. In some measure this fear is the sign of a guilty conscience. The Presbyterians, it is true, should have no guilty conscience. They too suffered under the Ascendancy and some of the greatest leaders in the struggle for independence have been Protestants. But the Ascendancy, at that time the Episcopal landlord class, always alarmed by the prospect

of an attack by united Irishmen, was fully capable of exploiting the
religious bigotry, which was always strong, and dividing the Catholic and Protestant allies. The Loyal Orange Order proved a useful
instrument for this purpose and partly as a result of its activities the
nineteenth-century land reforms were much delayed. Finally the
ranks of the united Irishmen were completely broken and in their
place there are today the united Catholics and united Protestants.
The Presbyterians have long since had their more serious grievances
removed and since the memory of the persecution suffered under
the Ascendancy has been forgotten, they are prepared to unite with
the representatives of the Ascendancy, in its present form, against
the common danger of inclusion in a Catholic State. This sectarian
bigotry and fear would be difficult to overcome by the most enlightened government, but in fact they are fostered and kept alive by the
present governing class, which has taken the place of the old land-
owning Ascendancy. During an election these feelings, which
would be strong enough in any case, are worked up into a kind of
hysteria. Independent parties, which are not primarily interested in
the question of partition but prefer to turn to other problems, such
as unemployment, have small chance of success, however loudly
they proclaim their willingness to accept the territorial *status quo*.
They are condemned because they threaten to divide the Protestant
ranks and by this means the Unionist Government secures two
objects. It frees itself from the embarrassment of independent
criticism of its social and economic policy and it perpetuates the
public hysteria necessary for its survival. Ulstermen are calm and
hard-headed in business matters. If the Irish question could be
shelved temporarily for the first time in history and they could turn
to other problems, the psychological effect would be profound. If
the people could learn to bring to bear on political issues something
of the calm judgement they exercise in business the Irish Question
would, in a large measure, solve itself. There is wisdom in the
official Unionist slogan that 'every vote for an independent Unionist
is a vote against partition', and it may be that Mr De Valera and the
Northern minority are profoundly wrong in constantly repeating
their claims, instead of allowing the political ferment to subside.

This is, in effect, the policy of the Northern Ireland Labour

Party, but one small group is powerless so long as the Nationalists and the Eire Labour Party continue to play into the hands of the official Unionists.

The position of the independent Unionist is made difficult and that of the Protestant Nationalist is often made impossible. It is the latter who suffers most in Northern Ireland, not the Catholic. The belief, frequently held outside Ulster, that the Unionist Government only retains its position by using terrorist methods against the Catholic minority is, indeed, quite false. Occasionally alarming reports have appeared in the English and American Press which describe the ill-treatment of this large minority, usually in rather vague terms or by the method of generalizing from a few particular instances. Northern Ireland has been described as a semi-Fascist state where the fundamental British liberties have been lost and the freedom of Protestants in the South has been contrasted with the misery of Catholics in the North. So far, however, as I have been able to discover there is small ground for many of these accusations, with one exception. By a notorious Special Powers Act the Government possesses the most arbitrary powers of arrest and detention. The excuse put forward, even by Cabinet Ministers, that these powers will never be used against law-abiding citizens is scarcely worthy of repetition. It may, however, be argued that the disordered condition of the country makes the Act necessary and it must be borne in mind that, at times, the executive in the Free State made use of similar measures. Moreover the Constitution of Eire provides for the setting up of military tribunals and adds to the clause providing for the issue of the writ of *habeas corpus* the qualification that this guarantee of the individual's liberty must not be allowed to interfere with the preservation of law and order in a time of general unrest. At the time of writing, Mr De Valera is about to introduce two Bills to empower the executive to deal more effectively with the I.R.A. It is doubtful whether these powers are necessary in either part of the country. It might have been more politic for the Northern Government to combat the 'dangerous elements' by the ordinary methods, rather than to add a further cause of discontent, although the frequent attempts to intimidate witnesses made it difficult to rely upon those methods. Worst of all, the Act has been

made permanent since 1933. It is true, of course, that the vast bulk
of the Catholic minority is unaffected by the Special Powers Act,
but the Act nevertheless indicates a semi-Fascist tendency which is
rightly condemned. Now that the South is adopting similar
measures these complaints from the Catholic side will carry less
weight.

The Catholics complain that they do not receive fair treatment
when appointments to the Civil Service are being made. It is impossible, of course, to get much accurate information but, if one may
judge by the pronouncements of the Unionist leaders, discrimination is to be expected. The Minister for Agriculture declared some
time ago that no Protestant should employ a Catholic and that advice
it not untypical. On the other hand it must be remembered that
some of these remarks were made during Twelfth of July celebra-
tions and although they do illustrate the way in which the members
of the Government encourage, rather than resist, the wild bigotry
of the Orange Order, it must not be assumed that they themselves
are so harsh in their treatment of Catholics as their words suggest.
In fact a considerable number of Catholics do appear to be employed
in the Civil Service, although it is no doubt true that the Protestants
are in a more favourable position even in the lower ranks. In private
business there is unquestionably some discrimination on the part of
employers against employees of a different religion, and since most
of the employers are Protestants it is the Catholics who suffer most.
This discrimination is not altogether the result of bigotry but is
partly due to the belief that Catholics are gradually moving into the
Province from Eire in order ultimately to outvote the Protestants.
There is no evidence in support of these fears and the notion that
the necessary half a million people could migrate secretly for this
purpose is, to say the least of it, absurd. Yet it is seriously believed.

It should be noted that the difficulty of finding employment in
an area where for years some twenty per cent of the insured population has been unemployed, is one of the reasons for continued ill-
feeling. The competition for jobs soon ceases to be a competition
between workman and workman and becomes a struggle, in the
traditional way, between Catholic and Protestant. A Marxian interpretation, based on this fact of the conflict between the two religious

groups would be over-simplified, but it would contain an important truth which must be borne in mind.

Fair treatment has been accorded to the minority by the Unionist Ministry of Education. Whereas the majority of elementary schools formerly under Protestant control have been brought under government management, the Catholics have been permitted to retain their position without sacrificing all official financial support. Together with those Protestant schools which have not yet been transferred, they receive grants for new buildings and extensions, which are, of course, less than the grants given to transferred schools, and half the running and maintenance costs. All teachers are paid by the Government. Irish is taught in the Catholic schools and is included as a voluntary subject in many public examinations. Education, in the narrow sense, compares very favourably with educational policy in the South where a knowledge of Irish is necessary for most public appointments – although the number of true native speakers is extremely small – and an attempt is being made to teach other subjects through the medium of Irish to children, the overwhelmingly majority of whom are obliged to learn Irish like any foreign language.

It would seem, then, that the grievances of the Catholic minority in Northern Ireland are less serious than is sometimes supposed. There is freedom of speech,[1] of worship and of the Press – and the Catholic Press in Belfast is extraordinarily outspoken in its criticism. There is, however, a kind of cultural persecution. Catholics are despised and distrusted by the Protestant majority and are made, in many small ways, to feel their 'inferiority'. Where two classes so distinct as the Protestant Unionists and the Catholic Nationalists exist side by side, it is, perhaps, natural, though none the less deplorable, that this should happen and the Protestant minority might be in a similar position in a United Ireland, with this difference, however, that a part of it would continue to be in the controlling business class.

[1] Since this was written nearly all anti-partition meetings have been prohibited, and a magazine called *Irish Freedom* has been banned. The policy of the Northern government is tending to become more repressive. Under the Civil Authorities (Special Powers) Act, freedom of speech and of the Press may be abolished.

It would, indeed, be impossible to explain the supposed anti-Catholic terror in the North, unless it were entirely the result of bigotry and sadism, for the Unionist Government would have nothing to gain from such a policy. The minority is not likely to abandon its opposition to the Border, but it would be unwise to increase its discontent with the present state of affairs. The minority is too small to change the status of the North and it is deprived of what representation it should have. When that has been done it can be allowed comparative freedom of expression, for Nationalist meetings are only attended by Nationalists and the Nationalist newspapers do not find their way into Protestant homes. So long as there is no defection among the Protestant majority the Unionist position is therefore secure. It is the Protestant Nationalist who is regarded as the greatest danger, for he might succeed in dividing the Protestants and reviving the old ideals of the United Irishmen. He is subjected to pressure in many ways. It will be difficult to find, or to retain, employment. (By these means many liberals have been forced to leave the country.) The Protestant Press will reject his articles, and in many ways he will find that he is being cut off from other Protestants. The study of Irish history is discouraged in the schools. It is never an important subject in public examinations and only those Protestants who are prepared to read on their own account have any understanding of the Irish Question. It would be wrong, and, indeed, absurd, to say that the division of the Irish people is entirely due to the work of an Ascendancy, past or present; but it can be said, with complete justice, that the Belfast Government makes no attempt to improve the situation by an enlightened educational policy and the atmosphere of suspicion and distrust continues to exist largely as a result of its activities.

There is little in the treatment of Protestants in the South to justify the Northern Protestants' fear. The position of some Protestants was made very difficult in the early days of the Free State, which was natural enough after a civil war, but the gloomy predictions made by Unionists everywhere in 1921 have been almost completely falsified by events. At the present time Protestants, who were believed to have been 'surrendered to an evil fate' in 1921, are constantly declaring that they are well treated. To quote from a

Methodist paper: 'We (the Protestants in Eire) enjoy a liberty of action, of speech, and of worship denied to many Europeans.' Two points, however, must be borne in mind: (1) the Protestant minority is very small and it is easy to treat it generously; (2) the minority is often loud-voiced in its praise of the Dublin regime, whereas the larger minority in a united Ireland would take a strong line on matters of policy and would be less sycophantic. On the other hand, it cannot be assumed that the old party divisions would necessarily continue in a United Ireland – the parties in the South have been divided on somewhat different lines since 1922. A new alignment of interests might take place.

Many of the Protestants who advocate unity believe that the vigour and initiative which enables the small Protestant minority in Eire to play an extremely important part in the business world would enable a larger minority to retain an even stronger position in a united country. The Orangeman would predict that, if this were to occur, it would provoke a severe and discriminatory policy on the part of the Government. Moreover, since most Civil Servants in Eire must have some knowledge of the Irish language, the present generation of Protestants would be excluded from administrative positions. He would also point out that the Catholic religion is recognized in the new Constitution to be, in a special sense, the religion of Eire and in this he would discern a sinister threat. He would ignore the fact that other creeds are also recognized in the Constitution and that no church can be State-endowed. (Constitution of Eire, Article 44.) He would not pause to consider that the Establishment of the Anglican Church of England is, on the same grounds, still more unjustifiable. On the other hand he would be little concerned by the influence of Catholic morality on the law of censorship or on laws relating to divorce and birth-control. The Northern Puritan and the Catholic moralist have much in common and it is the liberals, who welcome union on other grounds, who would suffer most in these respects.

Mr De Valera has offered, as a concession to Protestant fears, to allow the North to retain its autonomy as a safeguard against Catholic discrimination. Proportional representation would, however, be introduced for the Belfast as well as the Dublin Parliament.

This would strengthen the position of Catholics at Belfast and of Protestants at Dublin. He demands, moreover, that there shall be adequate safeguards for the Northern minority and this guarantee might give him a right of interference with the Belfast Parliament which would reduce accordingly the value of the concession as a safeguard for Protestants. The importance of the offer is, however, very great and if union is ever achieved it will probably be on these lines. In the past, however, the North has been offered more than its due representation in a Dublin Parliament, but the offer was rejected at once. Even if both areas retained complete internal independence and returned an equal number of representatives to a common Parliament dealing with matters of mutual concern, it is not likely that Unionist fears would be overcome for some time. Moreover if these fears could in some way be satisfied, another difficulty, almost as serious as that created by sectarian bigotry, would have to be faced, namely the attitude of a united Ireland to the British Empire.

There is still strong anti-British feeling in Eire. During the last election, which took place after the Anglo-Eire Agreement had been signed, some candidates stressed the importance of English friendship, but others used more normal language and boasted of the triumph of Irish diplomacy over the traditional foe. In the words of Mr Sean T. O'Kelly, they claimed to have 'whipped John Bull right, left and centre'. These sentiments are not merely the result of the past. So long as partition remains it is difficult for any Dublin Government to establish close relations with England. (It should be noted that Mr De Valera's friendship with Mr Chamberlain provoked critical comment in Dublin.) On the other hand, friendship with England is necessary as a first step towards union with the North and thus the vicious circle is joined. The Agreement may be regarded as an attempt by Mr De Valera to break that circle. The other conditions of friendship have already been fulfilled. England and Eire can meet as sovereign states on a footing of equality. Every sign of imperial domination has gone. England has abandoned the policy, described by Griffith in 1921, 'which threatened war if Ireland declined to join voluntarily a free associa- of free nations'.

> Bond from the toil of hate we may not cease:
> Free we are free to be your friend.
>
> *Tom Kettle*

We are, however, caught once more in a vicious circle. In order to reach the position of independence necessary before an *entente* with England could be made which would not involve a sacrifice of national pride, it was believed to be necessary to remove various symbols and ceremonials and strategic rights which indicated political inferiority. In the North, however, these things are regarded as absolutely essential. The flag, the Oath, and the national anthem are therefore serious obstacles in the way of unity, for Eire cannot retrace her steps. In 1932 Senator Douglas warned the Government that 'the real issue which we have before us is not the merits or otherwise of the Oath in the Constitution. Far more serious issues are involved, and the passing of this Bill not only raises the question of our Treaty obligations but may also affect our position in the British Empire – our trade and commerce and last but not least the ultimate political unity of Ireland.' If a less doctrinaire Republican policy had been followed the situation would have been less difficult today. Both sides respond to all suggestions with a blank *non possumus*. In the words of Mr De Valera, 'a certain treaty of free association with' – not within – 'the British Commonwealth group, as with a partial League of Nations' . . . 'is in my judgement the farthest distance that the majority of the people of Ireland will ever go to meet the sentiment of the majority in the Six Counties'.[1] If some method can be found of satisfying sectarian fears, the most likely solution of the Irish Question would be a close form of Dominion Status for the whole island. For that step, it would seem, Eire is not prepared.

The division in the country is thus very deep and not something entirely due to the activities of the Northern Ascendancy. It has been said that the explanation is racial. The races, however, are no longer distinct – if they ever were! Moreover, why should the same racial problem be surmountable in, say, Leinster, but not in Ulster? It would be more true to say that there are two nations in

[1] *Evening Standard*, 17 October 1938.

Ireland separated in the first place by religion, but possessing different cultural backgrounds and brought up to accept different political beliefs, as well as different theological creeds. The Northern Protestants are Loyalist and the old Protestant Republican tradition is so dead that they have no sympathy with the Irish patriotic movement, which they regard as an evil plot by the Vatican to weaken the Empire. The Southern Catholic would describe in similar language the British nationalism of the North. Educational policy in Eire is, indeed, as anti-British in its bias as is Ulster's educational policy in the other direction. The problem is to find some means of bringing both 'nations' to understand and respect each other's cultural background and to foster the feeble sense of common nationality which still exists. Neither the Dublin nor the Belfast authorities are making any serious attempt to perform that task.

In conclusion, however, I believe that the forces making for unity will ultimately prove the stronger. With the passage of time old and bitter memories of the Civil War will be forgotten and new currents of thought will do much to modify the traditional attitudes of both sections of the people. Increased friendship between England and Eire will be a deciding factor. England for her part might use her influence to modify public opinion in the North and she might well use her financial power over the Unionist Government to check any anti-liberal movement. Both sides in Ireland have much to learn and both must move a long distance, but a solution should not in the long run be impossible in spite of the policies of their respective governments.

A gradual solution of this kind is, I believe, preferable. Mr De Valera, however, will try to force the issue immediately if war breaks out in Europe. He has recently declared that he will make unity a condition of his cooperation with England. If the Northern Loyalists, it has been argued, are really concerned for the safety of the Empire they will surely not deprive it, through their obstinacy, of valuable support. On the other hand, Mr De Valera's position is not as strong as it might appear to be. On 17 October 1938, he conceded that 'it is possible to visualize a critical situation arising in the future in which a United Free Ireland would be willing to cooperate with Britain to resist a common attack', but 'if British forces were in occupation of any part of Ireland, Irish sentiment would definitely be hostile to any cooperation'. But in the circumstances visualized, namely, a common attack, he would be obliged to cooperate whether partition were abolished or not. If only England were attacked he does not promise assistance and Ulster might thus 'surrender' herself for no purpose. His government has 'definitely committed itself to the proposition that this island shall not be used as a base for enemy attacks upon Great Britain' and the pledge holds whether partition remains or not. Indeed her geographical position makes it improbable that she could maintain her neutrality for long. Mr De Valera has recently admitted as much (16 February 1939). Moreover, the defeat of England would mean for her, as for the other small states of Europe, the end of political freedom; for England whatever she may have been in the past, is now the protector of Irish liberty. The North would therefore have some grounds for refusing to yield and the negotiations would only have the effect of widening still further the gap between the two sections of the Irish people. To be part of a state whose support of the Empire was not unconditional would be intolerable to the ardent Northern imperialists. If, on the other hand, the people in the South could be induced to cooperate fully with Great Britain from the outbreak of war, the two sections of the country would be brought close together in the common struggle and many old prejudices would be overcome. A policy of this kind would do much to solve the Irish question. Unfortunately it is unlikely that such a policy would be acceptable to the Southern people. They still have bitter memories of the policy of England, 'the protector of small nations', and the employer of 'the Black and Tans', and they, themselves, it must be remembered, got very little credit for the support given to England in the last war, whereas the North, whose number of ex-servicemen per head of population was about the same, got all the praise and glory. It is not surprising that Mr De Valera would have a difficult task to induce the people to fight at once along with the English. The situation, indeed, might become very serious in the event of war for Mr De Valera would be obliged to control an extreme section which would certainly try to prevent cooperation with England and to act according to the slogan that 'England's extremity is Ireland's opportunity' by seizing the North by force. Such a policy could only have disastrous results, and would be resolutely opposed by Mr De Valera. It is not very likely that he would be forced to yield or to give place to a less statesman-like leader. The recent outrages have at least had this good result, namely, that strong measures have already been taken against the extremists by both English and Irish governments and the danger would, therefore, be less in time of war. It is fairly certain, however, that violent disturbances in both parts of the country could not be prevented and this would increase the friction engendered by Mr De Valera's negotiations with England. It is therefore to be hoped that a crisis will not occur and that the intransigence of North and South will ultimately be worn down by peaceful methods.

July 1939

LABOUR AND
COMPULSORY MILITARY SERVICE

R. H. S. Crossman

A SHAM OPPOSITION

THE country has accepted compulsory military service with an apathetic equanimity impossible a year ago. The campaign, launched by all the forces of organized Labour, has fallen flat; only in Scotland have the trade unions shown any serious desire to use industrial action to prevent its accomplishment. Elsewhere those who preached blank intransigence when the Government first announced its decision, have now accepted the fact of conscription. The T.U.C. has not even withdrawn its support from National Service and is prepared to collaborate on the Tribunals and Hardship Committees; the Parliamentary Labour Party, finding the Government in a conciliatory mood, has introduced many improvements into the Bill, while Labour candidates in the crop of May by-elections soon discovered that an attack on the 'bob a day for militiamen' was more effective than mere protestations against the principle of compulsion.

And yet, when the announcement was first made, Labour decided, with a concord unique in the past four years, to oppose compulsion blankly. The *Daily Herald* and the *Daily Worker*, Mr Bevin and Mr Pritt, united to denounce the Premier's broken pledges, and even Sir Stafford Cripps found himself in momentary agreement with his late colleagues on the Executive. In this babel of unanimity, only the modest voice of the *New Statesmen* and the abstentions of a few Labour M.P.s indicated the doubts which existed, unvoiced but widely felt, throughout the movement. Even if a few courageous individuals had dared to express their doubts publicly, they would have endured three weeks of intense unpopularity; and when their diagnosis had been proved correct, they would have gained no credit for it inside the Party. This was probably the reason why the gap between opinions expressed privately and publicly was more than usually large upon this issue. Many prominent Socialists who held blank opposition to be mistaken considered that the movement must be allowed 'to let off steam'!

But the opposition, though unanimous, was half-hearted. The nation-wide campaign petered out into expressions of pained but harmless protestation, and the Labour Movement got the worst of both worlds. For to the rest of the country, it was only too apparent that Labour was opposing 'on principle'; and the Government was delighted to assume an air of kindly toleration and to say in effect: 'Poor fellows, they have got to make their protest, but they will be quite all right when it is over.' The spectacle of an opposition encouraged to let off steam by their opponents was too humiliating to be funny; and the electorate indicated its judgement by mass abstention from the May by-elections. What is the good of voting when your choice is between a professional government and a professional opposition?

THE CAUSES OF COMPULSORY MILITARY SERVICE

It is the self-induced hallucination of many Socialists that Mr Chamberlain willingly introduced compulsion as a first step to Fascism. To believe this is to misunderstand the whole philosophy of the National Government. The drift towards appeasement, which had already begun when Sir John Simon and Mr Eden were Foreign Secretaries, gathered speed in February 1938, when Mr Chamberlain personally took over the direction of foreign affairs, and became a definite policy of Anglo-German cooperation. This policy received the support not only of the City but of the F.B.I. which envisaged an arrangement with the Nazis on the political side similar to that which exists between Imperial Chemicals and I.G.Farben. The deficiencies in our defences disclosed by the Munich crisis proved conclusively that no one in control had envisaged a war with Germany; and the consultations of representatives of the F.B.I. with Nazi industrial leaders at Dusseldorf during the week of Hitler's occupation of Prague showed that British capitalism was prepared, on the economic side, to support the Nazis in their trade-war, even where this meant the violation of American interests.

Mr Chamberlain's sudden protestations of horror in Birmingham in March 1939 were in marked contrast to the resignation with which two days previously he had discussed the Czech crisis in the House. Almost overnight, apparently, he was converted from implicit confidence in Hitler to a belligerent distrust, and the cautious observer was bound to note a close parallel between the Birmingham speech and Sir Samuel Hoare's Geneva oration in 1935. Once again British statesmanship had connived for years at aggression and then suddenly turned round and condemned the aggressor in tones of injured innocence. But here the parallel ends. In the case of Abyssinia, the National Government was able to combine ineffective sanctions with tacit consent and so to permit Mussolini to defeat the League as well as Abyssinia. But in March 1939 the machinery of the League had been smashed and the only alternatives were an anti-Nazi alliance or an Anglo-German alliance. For now the nations of Europe had learnt that the British Government would slip out of any system of collective security in which it was not explicitly pledged to defend the victim of aggression. If Mr Chamberlain wished to give up appeasement, he must be prepared not only to express indignation and horror but to accept the conditions of alliance which any future allies would demand.

When therefore the Premier and Lord Halifax suddenly agreed with the Opposition that Hitler could not be trusted, and began casting round for countries to guarantee, this was no mere modification, but a complete and absolute reversal of policy, fraught with every possible danger and vitally affecting not only politics but industry and finance. The completeness of the reversal and the extent of the danger was not, however, apparent for the reason that the previous Anglo-German collaboration had been studiously concealed. Thus while the public believed we were merely changing from 'appeasement' to collective security, we were actually cutting adrift from Fascist friends before we had found new ones, far less considered the conditions of their friendship. Once the Rumanian guarantee had been added to that of Poland, there was no possibility of a return to appeasement without a split in the Tory Party. The only choice was between an alliance, including Russia, which would be strong enough to defeat the Nazis and an alliance, excluding Russia, which might well be defeated by them. From now on Mr Chamberlain's personal sympathies were immaterial: though he loathed and detested it, he would be forced into opposition to the men whom he still believes to be the bulwark against Bolshevism.

Moreover, whichever alliance he chose, he would be compelled to contribute his share to the pool of defence, and the more he rebuffed Russia, the greater the share would be. Up till March 1939 the Government had only envisaged the employment of an expeditionary force to defend France and the Empire. But now, if Poland or Rumania were to have a chance of survival in war, a British force on the western front, sufficient to immobilize a large section of the German Army, was an immediate necessity. And that expeditionary force was not in existence. Thus the ultimatum demanding conscription, which Mr Chamberlain received in April from his new allies and from France, was a necessary result of his decision to throw up appeasement. When the Labour Party, in Mr Attlee's absence, had welcomed the new policy of guarantees without asking what the cost in terms of British defence requirements would be, it had delivered itself into the Premier's hands. For having approved the end, it could only deny the means by a supreme piece of self-contradiction. Only by opposing all the Eastern European guarantees until an Anglo-Russian alliance had been signed, could it have found a foreign policy compatible with opposition to conscription, and even then its case would not have been overwhelmingly strong.

The Military Service Bill was not a brilliant coup for Mr Chamberlain or an insidious piece of Fascism. On the contrary, it was an admission that the whole policy of appeasement had failed, that the League must be re-created, and that Britain had at last taken the place which Labour policy assigned her, and become a continental power. At the eleventh hour history had compelled Mr Chamberlain to eat not only his hat but his umbrella as well.

The Government's decision gave Labour a supreme chance. If France demanded conscription as a proof of Britain's good faith, the Opposition could reasonably argue that an even more effective proof would be a government addicted not to 'Runcimanades' but to the League. If compulsory military service was necessary for the fight against aggression, then economic mobilization must be necessary too. By welcoming gladly the principle of compulsion, Labour could have wiped out Mr Greenwood's unfortunate enthusiasm for the Polish guarantee, and extorted from an unhappy government the most stringent conditions for its acceptance of the Bill. Once it had approved the principle, it could have dared Mr Chamberlain to face the country's wrath if he refused the conditions it proposed. But Labour did not take this line: instead it opposed the principle.

ANTI-MILITARISM

The conscription issue exposed once again the divorce between Labour's defence and foreign policies. Since the war Labour has gradually adopted a highly realistic foreign policy, based on the fact that Great Britain can no longer achieve security either by splendid isolation or by manipulation of the balance of power. In advocating collective security, it has thrown off our native insularity, and grasped that we are now a continental nation with the same urgent need of collective defence as France; and it has correctly predicted that the Fascist International would not be softened by appeasement and could only be blocked by an overwhelming combination of force. Unfortunately, however, this policy was hatched in the conceptual heaven of Geneva politics, and was never adequately related to the problems of defence. We have behaved as though Fascism could be stopped by resolutions, protocols, pacts and covenants; and whenever anyone has inquired what force would be required for the job, we airily totted up the populations of the 'good' countries and their mineral wealth. And we have always avoided consideration of these naval and military technicalities by repeating (in words lately borrowed by Mr Chamberlain) that what we wanted was not an alliance to fight a war, but a Peace Front to prevent it. Such an argument may be good enough for an English audience, but it neither consoles the French and Russian General Staffs for the deficiencies of our Territorial training nor does it in the least impress Herr Hitler, who has called the bluff of enough 'collective pacifists' to know their measure.

Any party which advocated League action against aggression should, ever since 1933, have been demanding the formation of a People's Army and Air Force in this country. A democratic policy of collective security could only have been enforced by a people trained in warfare, and denouncing the high treason of its government's 'pacifism' and appeasement. But you cannot put over a realistic foreign policy of mutual democratic defence when your own attitude to defence problems is based on anti-militaristic senti-ment and a suspicion of the fighting services. To put it briefly, the only logical consequence of Labour's attitude to compulsion is appeasement: the only logical consequence of its foreign policy is the demand for the mobilization of the nation's man-power, finance and industry for peace or war.

It may be answered that Labour's Defence Policy, as defined by official statements and programmes, has never been pacifist and since the Bournemouth conference has been positive in its approval of rearmament. To this I would agree. But, unfortunately, to adopt a programme is not to work it; and it became clear last April that Labour's conversion to the use of armed force was only skin deep. Underneath all the trappings of collective security, a pacifist heart still beats. In spite of the talk of a Peace Front and the adulation heaped on the Spanish Republican Army, the ideology of the Party springs from the Utopian Liberalism of Bright which Marx and Engels condemned so fiercely. The opposition to conscription which united the movement last April was not really the result of fears of Fascism or industrial conscription or a dislike of broken pledges, nor did it have anything Socialistic in it: on the contrary it sprang from the peaceful sentiments of an island people, guarded for generations by a strong navy, and governed by an adroit ruling class, which could afford to pay men to do its fighting instead of compelling its subjects to do so. Anti-militarism was the luxury of the Whigs, of the Liberal free-traders and of the nonconformist masses in the days when we possessed a monopoly of naval power. Apparently it still inspires many Labour leaders in 1939.

Nothing shows more clearly the sentimental character of the opposition to compulsion than the sudden enthusiasm for the Terri-torials evinced by many spokesmen of the Party in the last few weeks. Men and women who until last April were refusing to make recruiting speeches have been weeping their eyes out at the demise of the voluntary system. Men and women who, as Socialists, demand equality of opportunity and sacrifice, and are prepared to use compulsion where such equality is not obtainable by voluntary means, now proclaim their fervent belief in a reactionary professional army and a Territorial service which ensures that the majority of the population shall be untrained in arms and both physically and psychologically defenceless against their rulers, or their foreign enemies. And yet these same people demand a Peace Alliance against Fascism. No wonder the Frenchman whispers: 'The English Socialist will fight to the last French conscript.'

THE PARTY AND THE PEOPLE

The peculiar tragedy of the conscription issue is that it occurred at the moment when the man in the street had at last been converted to collective security and the need for a Russian alliance. Ever since the Abyssinian fiasco Labour had been fighting against heavy odds. The Government, by disguising the policy of cooperation with the Nazis under the slogans of peace and conciliation, had been able to accuse Labour of war-mongering and urging the nation to interfere in other people's affairs. The occupation of Prague not only destroyed Mr Chamberlain's pretensions; it suddenly made the British people realize that the 'war-mongers' were right and the 'pacifists' frauds. Labour's stock was rising steadily. There is nothing better in politics than to run an unpopular policy for years and to be proved right.

But simultaneously with the public's conversion to the need of collective defence came a second conversion. If the water-logged trenches throughout last winter served no other purpose, they made the people conscious of their danger. In the six months since Munich millions of people slowly saw that they no longer lived on a happy island in the Atlantic; and the occupation of Prague clinched the argument. With a correctness of judgement which most party-politicians do not share, the non-political voter realized that, if Hitler was to be stopped, he must do something himself about it; and, since he knew that *he* would not do anything till he was forced, he concluded that compulsion would have to come. He did not want to fight nor would he advocate a war, but, if the Government said the word, he would obey unenthusiastically but with resignation.

In my experience the non-political voter was completely baffled by the Labour reaction to compulsion. Once again he found to his dismay that common sense and nonsense were shared equally between Government and Opposition. If Mr Chamberlain was right in resisting Germany now, why was Munich peace with honour? If Labour was right in its foreign policy, why did it suddenly turn round and refuse the means to carry it out? As ignorant as many Socialists of the requirements of military training, he could not be convinced that Labour opposed conscription because it seriously believed that the Territorials were a better form of defence. Without many ideological scruples, he could not see the obstacles to a Russian alliance which weighed with Mr Chamberlain. So condemning both sides as party-politicians who disagree for the sake of disagreement, he gave up politics altogether. In Labour meetings up and down the country, the politically conscious minority made speeches to each other. The people stayed away, their distrust of politicians confirmed.

Blank opposition to compulsion not only contradicted the Party's foreign policy and Socialist principles, but was also unpopular in the country. Moreover it prevented the Party from effectively demanding that 'conscription all round' which should be the Socialist policy in time of war. The admirable scheme for a National Defence Levy could not be pressed, while the democratization of the armed forces could hardly be urged persuasively by a party whose will to fight Fascism seemed weaker than its desire to remain in opposition.

THE FUTURE

Political memories are fortunately short, and it is still possible for Labour to recover the respect of the country and to put forward a positive policy with regard to compulsion both as a part of defence and as a factor in social life. Indeed one of the most important results of the Military Service Bill may well be its effect on Labour policy. Until conscription had actually been introduced, it would have needed real courage for Labour spokesmen to support it. But now it has been accepted not only by Parliament but by the nation, the Party must either discard its negative attitude to the fighting services or lose the support of youth. Conscription will in a very short time expose the deficiencies of our existing military methods, just as in the industrial sphere it is already clear that 'business (and profits) as usual' is a slogan incompatible with genuine defence.

In these circumstances the task of Labour is clear. It is to demonstrate that the great problem of resistance to Fascist aggression can only be solved on Socialist lines and by the extension of compulsion beyond the sphere of man-power. The statement on defence presented to the Southport Conference was both constructive and moderate, and it should be supported by a further programme for the national mobilization of finance and industry. But, above all, Labour must show a real understanding of the needs of the new militiamen. To remove men of twenty from their homes, even for a short six months' period, is to introduce a revolutionary change. If genuine educational opportunities are obtained, and if young men of ideas use their influence while serving, the period in the militia may well be a turning-point for thousands who have taken no interest in social or international problems. One reason for the hold which the social oligarchy has upon this country is the parochial life of the working class. The militia will not only remove something of the immobility from the labour market, it will produce a social ferment among the boys who, coming for the first time from South Wales or Lancashire or Glasgow, return to see their home environment with different eyes. While they are in the army they will have complaints which should be remedied; but even more important, when they return home, they must find ready for them if they wish it, a political organization adapted to their new outlook. The Labour Party would do well to consider the formation of militiamen's clubs as a link between the League of Youth and the constituency party organization.

Lastly, the Party should rid itself of that prejudice against the soldier which still lingers in its rank and file. To desire peace is human, to despise the soldier and his profession is not only undemocratic but downright silly. For years Labour has tried to put forward a sensible policy on defence and foreign affairs and at the same time to retain the pacifist vote. By so doing it has succeeded in alienating forces far more valuable to Socialism. Now is the chance to turn over a new leaf and to say frankly to the pacifists: 'Though we respect you, we cannot for your sake destroy the basis of our foreign policy and of our Socialist faith'; and to concentrate every effort on the exposure of the deficiencies of the class-army and to the demand for a people's army and a planned economy fit to defend democracy.

I do not for a moment underestimate the change I am suggesting. One of the difficulties of a democratically organized party is that it is more conservative of traditions and ideas than a party which, like the Conservative, is merely the electoral machine of its leaders. In one sense Labour's opposition to conscription was one of the most democratic things which it has lately done, since it really reflected the sentiments of the Party members. But a party of the Left cannot survive if it advances only at the pace of its slowest member, or even of its majority. The Labour leadership acted democratically on this issue only in the sense that Earl Baldwin was a democrat when, in deference to the wishes of the electorate, he disguised the need for rearmament; and it is doubtful whether the rank and file are really grateful for an anti-conscription campaign which, like sanctions, was never meant to succeed. What we now need are leaders who will dare to speak not only to the Party members but to the nation, and have the will to win a majority, not at a Party Conference but at a General Election. To do that the Party must be anti-Fascist not by resolution but in action, and must be prepared to say to the people that under its leadership, whether in peace or in war, Fascism will be defeated. Mr Chamberlain has reluctantly introduced a measure which can be used to undermine the class-system and to give the people a new awareness both of their own power and their own subjection. He has reluctantly adopted a foreign policy which must end in defeat without a wholehearted cooperation with Russia. He has in fact brought the country to a plight in which only an anti-Fascist Government of the Left can save the peace or win the war. If Labour can see conscription not as a defeat but as an opportunity, an apathetic public would turn to it as a deliverer from trouble.

July 1939

DE PROFUNDIS

Leonard Woolf

THE rat caught in a trap, once he finds that he cannot get out of it, if he were an intelligent rat, would withdraw into a corner at any rate for a few minutes and try to discover how he got into it. The catastrophe which has been hanging over us for over five years has now fallen; the waters are closing over our heads and, as we go down into the depths, it might be well to follow the example of the intelligent rat; before the fog, fury and fuss of war overwhelm us, we might withdraw from it all for a few moments and try to consider objectively what has really brought down upon our heads for the second time in a generation the worst of all social catastrophes. The question is not purely an academic one. The answer to it on this side of the battle-front is already accepted: the war has been caused by the 'senseless ambition' of one man, Hitler. There is a sense in which the answer is true; the final decision with regard to war or peace lay with Hitler and the motive or objects which led him to choose war can be accurately defined as senseless ambitions. But if there is one certain fact about the determination of historical events in the past, it is that the individuals, who at first sight appear to be the ultimate causes, in reality played a very minor role. A Napoleon and a Hitler, even a Pericles and an Augustus, were the puppets or symbols of deep social forces; their strength and their weakness in action came to them from these forces. If you want to know why things happened or why they did not happen, you must investigate not the individuals, but these forces which jerked their arms and legs and minds in one way rather than another. The terrible results of the jerks and senseless ambition of Herr Hitler must not delude us into thinking that he is the only cause of our calamity.

There is another reason why at the beginning of a war – and indeed all through it – it may be useful to take a wide and objective survey of its causes. War begins where peace ends; the failure of peace and the triumph of war are one and the same thing, but the object of every war is again peace. Those who lived through the years 1914 to 1918 know, however, that very soon a terrible delusion falls upon the combatants. Every effort of the entire nation has to be directed to winning the war and to avoiding defeat. The object is necessarily and rightly victory. Gradually a war psychology establishes itself everywhere on both sides of the trenches; people believe that they have only to win the war in order to win peace. The belief is a dangerous delusion, as the last twenty-five years have shown us. Or rather it is one of those dangerous, superficial half-truths or truisms which so often bring disaster upon human beings. It is true that by winning the war you can probably get peace, just as you can also get it by losing the war. But though it is true that war begins where peace ends, it is not true that peace begins where war ends. The so-called peace which has ended so many wars was not peace at all, but a truce. The war of 1914 ended, as everyone can see today, not in peace, but in a truce; it was a truce which differed from that truce which contemporaries called the Peace of Amiens only by a rather longer duration. The reason why war does not necessarily end in peace, even though our own side or the right side wins, is that war settles so very few things upon which the firm establishment of peace depends. I believe that resistance to the Nazi system and to the 'senseless ambitions' of Hitler was right, for peace in Europe is incompatible with them, and that if the French and British governments had honestly organized that resistance through the system of collective security, while there was still time, there would have been no war. When the Chamberlain policy of appeasement had brought us to the desperate pass in which we found ourselves at the beginning of this year, we were still left with no alternative to a policy of resistance, for the Nazi system and Hitler's ambitions were still incompatible with peace and civilization in Europe. We were already caught in the trap, even if we did not know it, for resistance now meant almost certainly war. Now that we are in the war, the defeat of Hitler and the elimination of the Nazi system are a condition precedent to peace.

This shows clearly the limitations of war and victory as instruments for the establishment of peace. At the best their effects are negative. War may eliminate a cause of war and so lay the basis upon which peace might be built, but whether war is followed by a real peace or only a truce depends upon what is done immediately after the war. The building of peace depends upon eliminating all the fundamental causes of war and giving to international society a structure which will allow the inevitable strains and stresses to be borne or resolved peacefully. That is why at the beginning of the war and all through it a steady concentration upon its causes and upon our 'peace aims' is not academic, but essential. For it is not victory, but the use which we make of victory which can give us peace.

I am concerned in this article with the fundamental causes of our catastrophe, for at this stage, in the first week of war, to consider peace aims particularly or in detail would be academic. From this point of view, the problem of war and peace in Europe is, like most political problems, extraordinarily difficult and complicated and yet at the same time extraordinarily simple. In the last seventy years there have been three serious European wars – 1870, 1914 and 1939. They are interconnected and each is progressively more menacing to the whole existence of civilized life in Europe. The fundamental causes of these three wars are the same, and they are really simple and easy to determine. If the European was rational and civilized, it would even be easy to eliminate them and to build up a peaceful society in Europe; the reason why the problem of war and peace is difficult is that other people besides Hitler have 'senseless ambitions' and are neither rational nor civilized.

The fundamental causes of the modern European war are partly economic and partly political. In the nineteenth century there developed the portentous phenomenon of the modern thickly populated, highly industrialized national state, and the problem which confronted Europeans was to develop simultaneously a system through which the economic and political relations of these communities could be regulated equitably and pacifically, i.e. an international economic and political system of 'justice, law and order'. Such a system failed to develop and the three wars are the inevitable result of that failure. Unless an international system based upon both economic and political justice, law and order is established, there can be no peace in Europe; there can indeed, as we are now seeing, be no civilization. If in this war peace is the object for which we are fighting, then our war aims should be rigidly confined to the establishment of such a system. The elimination of Hitler and the Nazi Government of Germany are necessary only because they are themselves incompatible with such a system.

The system under which Europeans have regulated their international relations during the last one hundred years has been one of both economic and political anarchy. The unit and instrument in that anarchy is the national sovereign independent state. The economic anarchy and the political anarchy are each symptoms of the same disease, for it is a delusion to think that either economic or political causes are primary. What it is convenient to call the industrial revolution opened up for European man immense material possibilities, a great potential increase both in wealth and power. The problem which faced him then was how should that wealth be distributed within communities and between communities and – an equally ominous question – how should the power be distributed or controlled within communities and between communities. There were only two possible answers to these questions. The one was that of socialism and democracy, which the early Social-Democrats rightly recognized as the economic obverse and political reverse of the same coin. Such a system required within the community both economic and political democracy, i.e. control of the means of production by the community in order to ensure equal distribution of wealth among individuals and strict communal control of the enormous potential power which the industrial revolution had placed in the hands of governments. But the corollary of internal social-democracy was international social-democracy. This meant that there must be an equitable control and distribution of wealth between the communities or states just as between individuals and a real international control of the potentially devastating power now in the hands of national states and their governments. In other words this was the obvious, common-sense, rational method of obtaining a system of justice, law, and order both within states and between states under the new conditions imposed upon Europe by the industrial revolution and the age of scientific invention.

The alternative system was to base social organization upon 'free competition' instead of socialism and internationalism and upon strong or authoritarian government instead of upon democracy. This meant within the state great inequalities in the distribution of wealth, and therefore in the economic and political power of classes, and the concentration of uncontrolled power in the hands of 'the government', i.e. of individuals or small groups or classes. Internationally it meant exactly the same, except that the units of competition and anarchy were not individuals or classes, but sovereign independent national states. These states were engaged in embittered, uncontrolled economic and political competition for wealth and power. The enormous power which the competitive and undemocratic system concentrated within the state in the hands of individuals and small groups, miscalled governments, was used externally as an instrument of 'national policy' in the form of war and the threat of war. There was no international control of national power, no international organization for preventing war or settling differences or for establishing even the beginnings of internationa justice, law and order.

Hitler and Nazism are really only the logical result of this latter system. It is an insane system, and the logical result of insanity is a *reductio ad absurdum*. If we are thinking in terms of peace and of socialism and democracy, Hitler and Nazism are 'insane ambitions', but if we are thinking in terms of the other system, they are logical. It follows that if this war is to end in peace, victory and the defeat of Hitler are not enough; peace depends upon the complete eradication of the system of which Hitler was the logical conclusion or the *reductio ad absurdum*.

Here there enters another consideration. It is not only Hitler who is afflicted with insane ambitions. Are we sure that we ourselves and our own rulers have been entirely free from them? The international system of which Nazism is the *reductio ad absurdum* is insane, because it attempts to ignore the logic of facts and events. The large-scale industrialization of production[1] has made the

---

[1] People often overlook the important fact that this includes the large-scale industrialization of the industry of agriculture, so that the effect upon countries which are mainly agricultural has been the same as upon countries which are mainly 'industrial'.

economically autarkic sovereign independent state an anachronism and an impossibility, because it created a society which depends for its existence upon a complicated cooperative, instead of competitive, exchange of commodities throughout the world. Such a society is incompatible with the autarkic sovereign state and therefore it must either be destroyed by or must destroy that form of state. This fact is ignored both by the Nazis and by other people. The freetraders of the middle of the nineteenth century had a glimmer of the economic truth through one eye, though they were stone blind in the other. They saw that modern society required international cooperation in the free exchange of commodities and that this must form the *sine qua non* of peace; they made the fatal mistake, being blind in one economic eye, of confusing free exchange with unregulated competition. What the nineteenth-century Europe really required was a highly organized international economic system in which the social units, the national states, cooperated to promote the maximum exchange of commodities between themselves. Such a system is the opposite of competitive free trade on the one hand and of the protectionist, autarkic or imperialist economy of competitive national states on the other.

But economics can never be separated from politics or vice versa. If the peaceful development of nineteenth-century Europe required a particular kind of international economic system, it also required a particular kind of international political system. In fact each system implied or was a corollary of the other. It is fantastic to believe that peaceful economic cooperation is possible between armed sovereign independent states, as we know them today, and it is fantastic to believe that in a world organized for unregulated international economic competition the power of the armed sovereign independent state will not be used as the instrument of that competition. Looked at from one angle, the anarchic economic system creates the anarchy of armed sovereign states; looked at from the other, the anarchy of sovereign states creates the anarchic economic system. That is because they are the economic and political symptoms of exactly the same disease or the two sides of a single coin. In other words, the peaceful development of Europe required a highly developed international political system, in which the organization and use of national power was controlled internationally and provision made for the regulation of international relations and the settlement of international disputes on a basis of international justice, law and order. This implied the limitation of national sovereignty and the acceptance of some such system of international government as was contemplated in the League of Nations.

Some people may regard these statements in the last paragraphs as truisms and others may think them 'academic'. Yet if they are not understood and if the truth in them fails once more to determine our actions during and after this war, peace will once more elude and delude us as it did in 1919. For during the last fifty or sixty years, though British governments and the British people have sincerely desired and pursued peace in Europe, they have never been willing to pay the price for it. That was the tragedy of the crucial years 1900 to 1914, of the Versailles settlement, of the British attitude towards the League, and of Mr Chamberlain's fatal policy of 'appeasement'. Twice in a generation the Germans have been the chief active agents in bringing war upon Europe, and the British have been passive agents in both catastrophes. For while German governments have carried out a senseless international system to its logical conclusions and can be justly accused of 'senseless ambition', we in our traditional way have attempted an impossible compromise; we have tried to get the best of both worlds, to eat our cake and have it.

A protectionist British Empire in a world of competing national states is not compatible with peace, because it accepts and is part of an international economic system which is incompatible with peace. That is why, though it is itself pacific, sooner or later it will be challenged by a competitor, and the menace of that challenge means war or the eternal threat of war. Or we can put the same thing in another way: the Empire envisaged by Joseph Chamberlain, which has now been brought into existence and is maintained and defended by his son, even if Hitler is defeated, will provoke the senseless ambitions of another Hitler and war, for essentially it is the stuff which such senseless ambition is made of. The British Empire of Chamberlain with its protection, imperial preference, tariffs and quotas is merely the British version of the economically autarkic sovereign independent state. It is an economic unit in an international system organized for economic warfare, and it is folly to believe that warfare between the modern states of Europe can be confined to economics or that, if they are organized to fight one another economically with tariffs and quotas, they will not sooner or later take to other and more lethal weapons. During this war and when the time comes for 'making peace' we shall have to face the fact – which hitherto we have always refused to face – that the British Empire in its present form and a stable peace are incompatible. We must choose either the one or the other; we cannot have both. In other words, if there is to be economic justice, law and order or economic social-democracy in the society of nations and so an economic basis for peace, we shall have to agree to radical changes in the economic organization of empire.

Within the territory of national states the economic organization nowadays is almost always based on cooperation, not hostility, as between one geographical area or group and another. Difficulties and differences of interest of course arise, but they do not prove insuperable or lead to the kind of economic warfare which is considered normal or even inevitable between states. There is nothing in the geographical area of states which would make it impossible or very difficult to extend the cooperative and pacific economic organization of national societies to international societies. It is the senseless ambitions inside our own heads which cause the difficulties. If we want not merely victory but peace, one of our primary peace aims should be the eradication of such ambitions from our own minds and the extension of an economic system of cooperation from national societies to the society of nations.

The problem of ensuring peace in the political sphere is almost exactly the same as in the economic; the two, as was remarked above, cannot in fact be dissociated. The same problem states itself in one case in economic and in the other in political terms. It is almost true to say that in both cases the most important term is power, and that ultimately war and peace depend upon how economic and political power are organized, used and controlled. Internationalists and pacifists, even our rulers and statesmen, have hitherto paid much more attention to the political than to the economic side of the problem. The ordinary man is aware of its existence. The main lines on which it might be solved are known, and an inchoate, half-hearted or dishonest attempt – it depends upon how you look at it – was even made in the League of Nations to do something about it.

The kernel of the problem is the organization, use and control of political and therefore of military power. Are the inter-state relations to be regulated on a basis of law, order and justice or of power concentrated in the hands of the governments of independent, sovereign national states and operative in the last resort through armies, navies, and airforces? Hitler and Nazi Germany have deliberately and openly chosen to adopt the second system and to carry it to its logical conclusion, to its *reductio ad absurdum*, if necessary. That is why they are incompatible with peace and threaten civilization. But when it comes to the peace-making at the end of the war, it will be more important to remember that it is the system itself which is incompatible with peace and threatens civilization, and further that this country has never wholeheartedly forsworn the system or honestly given the opposite system a fair trial.

For at least ten thousand years the human race has been experimenting in its own government. Already 2,500 years ago there were Europeans, highly civilized, living in states with systems of national and international government. The experience of those years has been sufficient to remove all doubt about the main problems of communal government. If we want to substitute peace for war and anarchy in the relations of European states, we know with absolute certainty the preliminary steps which have to be taken. The sovereign, independent national state, as we know it, claims to be above the law; it is the judge of its own interests and 'honour'; it enters into agreements with other states, but it insists upon being the interpreter of their meaning and the arbiter in any dispute which may arise about their fulfilment and it even claims the right to decide at a moment's notice that it is no longer bound by its obligations. The governments of these states are in control of armed forces and armaments infinitely greater and more destructive than the world has ever known in previous ages; unrestrained by any surely established system of law or contract, they jealously maintain the prerogative of the national state in its relations with other states at any moment in any difference or dispute to refuse agreement or compromise or any kind of pacific settlement and to resort to the arbitrament of force.

We know everything that there is to know about this kind of society. Human beings have tried to live in it unsuccessfully for over 3,000 years. The units have sometimes been individuals, sometimes villages, towns, corporations, classes, states or empires. The result is always the same. The society contains in itself the principle of its own destruction; its existence may be long or short, according to the destructiveness of its weapons or the ferocity of its manners, but whether it consists of individuals, villages, towns, states or empires, it is bloody and barbarous.

If the bitter experience of history has taught us everything about social anarchy and its effects, it has also taught us how to get rid of it. We know that if we do not want a society ruled and ultimately destroyed by violence, we must have society ruled and preserved by law. There are certain elements in a pacific society of individuals or groups or communities which are constant and inevitable: a system of ascertained law and organs for making it; machinery for settling disputes between the social units and for common action in matters affecting their common interests; communal control of communal power and machinery for communal action against resort to force by any section of the community.

There is no doubt or mystery of the broad lines upon which this system will have to be applied to the states of Europe if war is to be prevented. There must be international law and a regular method for making it; there must be organs of international government and organs for interpreting the law and settling disputes; there must be the machinery and procedure for common international action and for making changes to meet changed conditions; there must be international control of national power and provision for common action in the face of a resort to war or the threat of war by any nation. All this implies an acceptance of limitation of the sovereignty and independence of states and the acceptance by each state of certain obligations with regard to 'collective security'.

Unless a system of this kind is accepted and established after the war, no stable peace of justice or democracy will follow; the war will again end, not in peace, but in a truce. About this two points may be noticed. The British people and their governments have for many years sincerely desired peace; but they have never honestly and wholeheartedly accepted the obligations of such a pacific international system. In the crucial years 1900 to 1914 the conservative and liberal governments entered the power politics system of continental Europe and played the game of power politics which ended in the war of 1914. After the war the conservative and national governments occasionally paid lip-service to the League, but in fact they played fast and loose with it. They used it as an instrument, not of international law and order and peace, but of purely national policy. In fact they admitted no limitation of the sovereignty and independence of their own state and no obligation to the common security.

The second point is this. The League was a real attempt to lay the foundations of a pacific system, based upon the limitation of sovereignty, international law, the settlement of disputes, political cooperation for common interests, and common action against aggression. If the time comes again for the making of a real peace, the League may not be resuscitated, but in that case something very like the League will have to be created. It may or may not be a full-blown federation of states. The idea of federation has received much support in recent months owing to the publication of Mr Streit's important book. The federal system has proved to be one of the most effective systems of human government wherever it has been able to establish itself. If accepted and applied by the states of Europe, it would probably solve the problem of peace. But it is not the only possible system for limiting the sovereignty of states and inaugurating the rule of international law and justice. It implies a very advanced form of social cooperation and of communal psychology. It is by no means certain that it could be applied successfully on a wholesale basis to the states of Europe at the end of a devastating war. On the other hand, the idea that a League system, even if honestly accepted by governments, has some fatal defect, because it does not impair the sovereignty of states or could not to be used to impair it, is a misunderstanding. While it might be possible to develop the federal system for parts of Europe, it might at the same time be necessary to combine it with some kind of League system for the whole. If we desire peace as well as victory, this is perhaps the most important of all the questions regarding our 'peace aims' which we shall have to decide at the end of the war.

October 1939